Constructing cybersecurity

MANCHESTER
1824

Manchester University Press

Constructing cybersecurity

Power, expertise and the internet
security industry

Andrew Whiting

Manchester University Press

Published by Manchester University Press
Altrincham Street, Manchester M1 7JA
www.manchesteruniversitypress.co.uk

British Library Cataloguing-in-Publication Data
A catalogue record for this book is available from the British Library

ISBN 978 1 5261 2332 9 hardback

First published 2020

Typeset by Sunrise Setting Ltd, Brixham

Contents

Acknowledgements   vi

Introduction   1
1 Cybersecurity knowledge: cohesion, contestation and constructivism   13
2 Security *dispositifs* and security professionals   45
3 Constructing the milieu   70
4 Constructing cyber-threats   99
5 Constructing cybersecurity   126
Conclusion   150

Notes   157
Bibliography   161
Index   197

Acknowledgements

The process of writing this book began when I started my doctoral thesis in Swansea's Politics and Cultural Studies Department in 2011. A lot changes between a completed PhD thesis and a completed manuscript, but nevertheless I am certainly indebted to the support I received from both members of staff and fellow PhD students across both the Politics and Cultural Studies Department and the Criminology Department at Swansea. In particular I would like to thank Lee Jarvis and Stuart Macdonald, who supervised my PhD, Maura Conway and Mike Sheehan, who examined my thesis, and, finally, Lella Nouri for her friendship, solidarity and good humour throughout our time together at Swansea.

The process of developing my ideas and writing this book have taken place since leaving Swansea University and taking up a lectureship at Birmingham City University. Having arrived in Birmingham, I have been lucky to meet and work alongside a host of colleagues who have challenged my thinking, taken the time to discuss my ideas with me when I felt at an impasse and motivated me to keep going in the more brutal moments of the writing process. Harriet Cutler, Gary Hazeldine, Jill Molloy and Sarah Pemberton deserve particular mention in this regard. I am grateful first and foremost for their friendship but am also indebted to them for their advice and guidance, whether this came in the corridors of the Curzon building or around a table in the Hare and Hounds.

I would like to thank Jonathan de Peyer and Rob Byron at Manchester University Press for their patience and professionalism throughout the process of producing the manuscript. I am also grateful for the comments I received from three anonymous reviewers. Each of these gave me something different to consider but all were very valuable, and in responding to their feedback the manuscript is undoubtedly of a higher quality than it would have been without them having taken the time to read and respond to my writing.

I am both very lucky and immensely grateful to have such great friends, and it is probably the case that people like George and Pete do not realise how important they have been in relation to this book. However, the ability to step away from work to relax in good company or share a laugh helped put the project into perspective and, whether consciously or not, often provided some distance that allowed me to return refreshed and ready to go again.

Two final and very important thanks go, firstly, to Annette for her patience, compassion and unwavering support in this and all things. It was not the case that you always *asked* for my streams of consciousness when I was in the midst of putting this book together, but your willingness to listen and your reassurance were something I was always very thankful for. Finally, as with my friends, it is not lost on me how lucky I am to have such a supportive and encouraging family. It would be impossible to express here the full extent of my appreciation for what my brother Chris and my parents Linda and Richard have done for me, so perhaps it is best just to say that getting to this point would not have been possible without their sacrifices and support.

Introduction

When Bill Gates stepped down as the head of Microsoft in 2008, he said that when he and the late Paul Allen had started the company they had dreamt about putting a computer in every home (Beaumont, 2008). Much has changed since the mid-1970s, when this ambitious vision was set out, but, with 83.2 per cent of households in the developed world now containing a computer, it appears self-evident that the late twentieth and the twenty-first centuries have seen a rapid process of computerisation unfold (ITU, 2018). Alongside the proliferation of affordable computers we have also witnessed the emergence and spread of the internet and the World Wide Web, a development that has brought with it huge increases in interconnectivity at the national and international, public and private levels (Harknett, 2003, p. 18). On this issue there are clear discrepancies between the developed and developing world, with estimated internet usage standing at 80.9 per cent and 45.3 per cent respectively (ITU, 2018). However, the global trend remains one of increased digital connectivity and has subsequently produced significant societal change.

The result of these developments has been swathes of the globe in which networked computer technology is a firmly established feature and where little remains untouched by its influence: consumerism, entertainment, communication, business, everything from managing your finances online to logging exercise via wearable technology. There are near constant reminders of the information age's presence, in our pockets, on our wrists, in our homes, at work, and this ever present feature in our daily lives is only part of the story of the 'computer revolution'. The process of computerisation has produced change at all levels – a dizzying proliferation of technology and platforms has sprawled throughout society, empowering actors and institutions, allowing for greater autonomy and independence but also collaboration and cooperation.

The voice of the individual can be louder than ever, the reach of enterprise wider than ever and the functioning of the State similarly amplified.

A question that has frequently been asked about this transformation is whether it should be viewed in a positive light or not. Despite all of the observable benefits of global connectivity, there remains scepticism around issues such as the (often anonymous) unsavoury or illegal behaviour that this connectivity has empowered, the infringements upon the privacy of individuals in the form of big data collection or systems of mass-surveillance and the spread of misinformation. Put another way, issues of (in)security are not far detached from questions around the societal value of computers and computer networks. How we conceptualise security relies on assumptions *about* security, including deciding whom or what requires securing (Jarvis and Holland, 2015).

However, if we focus momentarily on the most commonly cited referent object (the state) we see how national security strategies consistently reproduce this idea that computerisation is a 'double-edged sword' (Quigley *et al.*, 2015, p. 108), where the tremendous societal and economic benefits it offers must be considered alongside the risks and drawbacks. National cybersecurity strategies the world over reveal the commonality of this perceived trade-off:

> The broad application of information technologies and the rise and development of cyberspace has extremely greatly stimulated economic and social flourishing and progress, but at the same time, has also brought new security risks and challenges. (China Copyright and Media, 2016)

> The UK is one of the world's leading digital nations. Much of our prosperity now depends on our ability to secure our technology, data and networks from the many threats we face. Yet cyber attacks are growing more frequent, sophisticated and damaging when they succeed. So we are taking decisive action to protect both our economy and the privacy of UK citizens. (HM Government (UK), 2016)

> An engine of innovation and wonder, today the Internet connects nearly every person on the planet, helps deliver goods and services all over the globe, and brings ideas and knowledge to those who would otherwise lack access. The United States relies on the Internet and the systems and data of cyberspace for a wide range of critical services. This reliance leaves all of us – individuals, militaries, businesses schools, and government – vulnerable in the face of a real and dangerous cyber threat. (Department of Defense Cyber Strategy (US), 2015)

> The emergence of cyberspace, a virtual global domain, is increasingly impacting almost every aspect of our lives. The domain is transforming our economy and security posture more than ever before, creating opportunities for

innovations and the means to improve general welfare of the citizens. It is transforming many countries' growth, dismantling barriers to commerce, and allowing people across the globe to communicate, collaborate and exchange ideas. However, behind this increasing dependence on cyberspace lies new risks that threaten the national economy and security. Sensitive data, networks and systems that we now trust can be compromised or impaired, in a fashion that detection or defence can be hard, thus undermining our confidence in a connected economy. (Nigerian Computer Emergency Response Team, 2014)

The vulnerability and risk referenced across all of these excerpts manifests as a diverse series of threats, including rival foreign powers and sub-State actors who utilise a variety of computer-facilitated techniques with the aim of degrading the defensive ability of the State or enhancing their own strategic advantage. Viewed as acts of aggression and threats to national security by familiar foes, the State has responded by expanding the national security agenda to incorporate the domain of 'cybersecurity'. Indeed, while cybersecurity is considered a 'broad' and 'indistinct' term (Carr, 2016, p. 49) upon which 'no one can agree precisely' (Bambauer, 2012, p. 587), it is often conflated with the broader national security agenda (Mueller, 2017, p. 419). Stevens (2016, p. 11) offers one such broad definition that usefully captures two distinct aspects of the concept when he writes that cybersecurity is 'a means not only of protecting and defending society and its essential information infrastructures but also a way of prosecuting national and international policies through information-technological means'.

Despite the secondary focus of Stevens's definition that includes the pursuit of policy via information technology, cybersecurity is predominantly discussed in relation to a reactive and defensive strategy designed to address vulnerabilities. These vulnerabilities are not abstract, but tangible weaknesses or flaws within the hardware or software of a system that can subsequently be exploited by malicious actors to compromise the integrity, availability or confidentiality of a resource (Dunn Cavelty, 2018, p. 24). Where such vulnerabilities exist, systems can be exploited to allow modification unbeknown to operators, rendered inaccessible to users or accessed without authorisation. Any of these actions compromise the security of the system and can allow for all manner of more specific consequences, from the stealing of sensitive data to the deliberate sabotage of a process (Dunn Cavelty, 2018, p. 24).

Such vulnerabilities are a feature of these systems, the product of their being built, written or operated by fallible humans. They present risks but the potential impact of these risks is compounded and exacerbated when taken alongside the trend discussed above, whereby digital technology and interconnectivity become so seamlessly and completely threaded into society that these societies are *dependent* upon their smooth functioning (Kizza, 2014, p. 76). 'Cyberspace' has therefore become the focus of a successful securitisation, whereby a raft of new security risks have emerged that have seen governments across the world respond in their capacity as guarantors of security.

These vulnerabilities, and this dependency, have coincided with 'cyber-threats'[1] that are growing in scale and complexity to become increasingly 'asymmetric and global' (HM Government, 2015, p. 19). Efforts to defend 'the digital homeland' have thus required responses on a par with more familiar endeavours such as counter-terrorism (Farmer, 2017). A prominent example of a 'new' security challenge, cybersecurity has quickly moved to the top of national security agendas and has been the subject of significant international attention. However, these developments have not come without differences of opinion and controversy, in particular around a perceived trade-off between security online and privacy, the allocation of particular resources and legislative responses.

In 2020, cybersecurity is very much a part of the national security framework. It is a well-established part of our security imaginaries, and the landscape of discussion and practice herein appears set. Stevens, however, reminds us that there is contestation around what is *meant* by cybersecurity and while this is 'regrettable to some … [it] … also offers opportunities for productive engagements with cybersecurity that interrogate and contest an unsettled field of policy and practice' (Stevens, 2018, p. 1). Dominant discourse is premised upon a particular understanding of cybersecurity (as national security), which has helped structure this field in a way that shares many of the engrained assumptions of realism. However, this is ultimately a contingent knowledge that our investigations can help to expose by revealing the power relations in effect.

This book aims to better understand the construction of this 'cyber security imaginary' (Stevens, 2015), as well as its implications, by exploring private-sector industry expert discourse and the relationships that exist with this source and others. To achieve this I will aim to: first, explore the organisation of dominant cybersecurity knowledge. Second, I will demonstrate the importance of expert knowledge contained within the private sector in the aforementioned construction and finally show how relationships between this source and others have powerful constitutive effects that solidify the conditions of possibility for the extension of a strategy of neoliberal governance.

Motivations, aims, questions and assumptions

Given the desire to better understand how cybersecurity has been framed via the process of social construction, the decision to focus on a particular aspect of the internet security industry[2] may appear less intuitive than other more commonly studied 'sources', such as elite political or popular media discourse. It might also be argued that these are more important or influential in shaping collective consciousness and security practices. I contest these assumptions and explore the importance of industry knowledge on the constitutive process in depth in Chapter 3. However, in this Introduction I provide two main motivations for my decision to focus on the following specific areas.

First, I have focused upon private-sector internet security expertise because doing so pays due regard to the trend towards an increasing privatisation/commercialisation of security (Krahmann, 2003; Leander, 2010) and the proliferation of alternative *expert* discourses that goes beyond the traditional public-sector professionals of politics and security. As this trend continues, so too does private industry's increasing influence and stake in constructing security knowledge, including the constitution of referents and threats. Cybersecurity is no exception to this phenomenon and in the internet security industry we have a wide collection of private firms that generate a specific expert discourse as well as a range of products and services linked to the alleviation of the sorts of threats found within this space. The expert status of these companies, in conjunction with the technified nature of the field (Hansen and Nisenbaum, 2009, p. 1157), leaves this site of discourse uniquely placed to speak to the 'reality' of such threats.

The second motivation is that focusing, as I do, on this industry provides a useful means with which to develop existing cybersecurity research. There are two elements to this: first, despite an increased role within security for the private sector and the emergence of a dedicated internet security industry, there remains a dearth of engagement with these sorts of experts. Instead there has been a tendency to focus on more 'visible political figures' without sufficient consideration given to how their discursive practices 'are facilitated or thwarted by preceding and preparatory linguistic and non-linguistic practices of actors that are not as easily visible, also outside of government' (Dunn Cavelty, 2016, p. 371). This is surprising given the unique claims to epistemic authority that those within this industry have and the ability of these actors to mobilise expert/scientific capital in the production of 'objective' and 'politically neutral' forms of knowledge. Second, while a distinct critical (broadly constructivist) research agenda does certainly exist in relation to cybersecurity (see Chapter 1), it is very much overshadowed by an objectivist and largely realist research project (McCarthy, 2018, p. 5). The research conducted in this book eschews the assumptions underpinning much of this research and argues that by analysing the discourse of internet security companies, we can better understand the intricacies of the constitutive process of knowledge formation that has taken place around cybersecurity. In doing so we can, in this instance, shed light on the importance of these security professionals and develop our understanding of the logics and orthodoxies that are a feature therein as well as the security practices that have been enacted as a result.

Having covered my motivations for focusing on this industry, I will achieve my aims by responding to three sets of overarching questions. First, the book aims to establish the landscape of cybersecurity research to date as a means to situate my own study and determine the significance of the constructions found within this section of private-sector internet security discourse. For example, what assumptions underpin cybersecurity research? Are particular ontological, epistemological, methodological and theoretical commitments more commonplace than others? Is there a discernible homogeneity to what has gone before, or is the landscape characterised by divergence and disagreement? What can be learned from the state of cybersecurity research and where are the gaps in this research that could be usefully pursued to further our understanding?

The book's second aim responds to the question, how is cybersecurity constructed within private-sector internet security discourse? Where, for example, do the companies studied and the experts speaking for them place the focus within this domain? How are they understanding and delimiting 'cybersecurity', 'cyberspace' or 'cyber-threats'? What is their assessment with regards to threat: are they reassured, anxious, alarmed? What themes, tropes and tactics are utilised within this site of discourse to communicate the subject matter? What strategies do they have, if any, to respond to the challenges found within cyberspace? Do these companies speak as a homogenous voice or is there heterogeneity in their understandings and assessments?

Finally, the book aims to answer the 'So what?' question and considers the significance and impact of internet security discourse as part of both the broader inter-subjective process of knowledge construction and the enactment of related security practices. How, if at all, does cybersecurity knowledge in this domain differ from that produced in alternative domains? What is the specific importance of this expert knowledge in structuring popular or elite understandings of what (in)security and risk look like in cyberspace? How can we determine this? What are the ethical and normative consequences of the answers to these sub-questions?

These questions do not have straightforward answers and require detailed theoretical work if headway is to be made. I outline my own theoretical commitments in relation to several core concepts in Chapter 2 of the book, but it is worth noting here that the argument I gradually outline over the course of the following chapters operates with particular conceptualisations of power, knowledge and security that, I argue, adds value to the cybersecurity debate. I do, however, accept that these conceptualisations do not always lend themselves to the clear prescription/assessment/diagnosis that is a more familiar feature of the majority of cybersecurity and indeed security literature. However, while I am operating outside the conventions of much of the cybersecurity literature, I am certainly not in uncharted theoretical and methodological territory and I seek to clarify this in the latter part of Chapter 1. Nevertheless, although the questions I am setting out to answer, and the arguments I will develop, over the course of the book are purposively rejecting some of the assumptions made by much of the previous research, they do rest on at least two assumptions of my own.

First, is the understanding that 'cybersecurity' and 'cyber-threats' do not exist as objective, material phenomena that are able to be captured in our labels and risk assessments, but, rather, are constructed and constituted via a network of competing knowledge claims (Epstein, 2013). Our definitions, understandings and assessments of cyber-threats – in academia, news media, politics, law, industry and elsewhere – create that which they purport only to describe. Cyber-threats are produced through attempts to establish their meaning and significance, with each knowledge claim itself embedded in deeper intertextualities that are reliant upon the posting of sameness and difference, and situated within a nexus of power relations. Cyber-threats are 'made' through inter-subjective social and discursive practices rather than existing extra-discursively. Rather than approaching cyber-threats as external and objective, this book recognises their contingent and constructed nature and consequently seeks to explore the process of construction, why certain knowledge claims gain prominence and what the implications of these are.

Second, and related to the previous assumption, I operate with the belief that the value of research is not found exclusively in its instrumental policy relevance but also in its critical value. To use the Coxian distinction, I therefore adopt a critical theory approach to the subject matter rather than a problem-solving approach (Cox, 1981). I delve into the cybersecurity literature in Chapter 1 but to generalise for a moment here, the majority of cybersecurity knowledge tends to demonstrate its value by aiming to produce truer definitions, more accurate threat assessments or more effective responses. However, my own work rejects the notion that these sorts of conclusions are what constitute valuable research and instead sees this as unnecessarily circumscribing cybersecurity scholarship. With these assumptions in mind, my exploration of the questions I lay out above aim to make three main contributions of my own to academic cybersecurity knowledge.

First, I aim to add further theoretical depth into the study of cybersecurity, in the first instance, with regard to Foucault's work around power/knowledge, governmentality, the *dispositif* and security and, in the second instance, in relation to the role 'expertise' plays in the process of knowledge construction. By conducting this theoretical application across these two broad areas, I aim to better explain the capillary flow of power within the network that exists between different sources and the effect this has on the formation of a dominant cybersecurity knowledge.

Second, by focusing on the discourse produced by the internet security industry I aim to usefully expand the critical cybersecurity research project into sites of discourse previously unstudied by researchers. This is not to say that the only contribution here is to research a domain that remains previously unstudied, but rather that through studying the discourse of the internet security industry in this context I draw attention to an important regime of truth with a unique constitutive and delimiting function. In so doing, I also aim to contribute to a body of work that has sought to explore how security meaning is made in often-overlooked alternative discursive spaces (Robinson, 2014; Heath-Kelly and Jarvis, 2017).

Finally, I look to demonstrate the broader significance of the empirical work I have conducted and argue for how the tactics and tropes of this discourse resonate outside of the articles, white papers, threat assessments and blogs that make up some of the material considered. I attempt, therefore, to not only link the linguistic particularities of the material I have analysed to the dominant cybersecurity threat framing that exists, but also to show how the security professionals studied here have begun to form communities of mutual recognition with more established security and political professionals as part of a reorganisation of the security *dispositif*. This reorganisation has seen the strengthening of linkages between these different sources to aid in the sedimentation of a specific cybersecurity knowledge which makes possible security and legislative responses, among other things.

Reflections on method

I elaborate upon methodology and method in more detail prior to the conclusion of Chapter 2, but it is worth reflecting briefly here upon how I have conducted the analysis that in part informs my answers to the questions I have posed thus far. The book concentrates on an analysis of a diverse range of documents published by eighteen internet security companies. These documents are made publicly available via the companies' websites[3] and have been analysed to identify how cybersecurity is understood within this site and what this can tell us about wider cybersecurity knowledge. The companies studied as part of this project are those probably best known for their anti-virus software; notable among these are the likes of Symantec, AVG and McAfee. This, of course, only represents one aspect of a far broader industry, and I have chosen to describe them as internet security companies rather than anti-virus vendors on account of the fact that using the latter term would give a misleading impression of the full range of products and services some of these companies offer; everything from anti-virus to workspace virtualisation (Symantec, 2019).

Other than the fact that they publish regularly on issues of cybersecurity and consist of the sorts of security professionals that I am interested in studying, these particular companies were selected for a range of purposive factors which included: accessibility via the presence of an internal online archive of content; their position in the industry; and language, such that the content was provided in the medium of English. All of the companies included can be considered 'international' insofar as they all make their products available to an international market and often have multiple offices around the globe. There was some considerable diversity when it came to where these companies' main headquarters were based, including: Spain, Germany, the US, Japan, South Korea, the UK, Romania, Russia, India, Canada, Finland, Slovakia, the Czech Republic and the Netherlands.

The material for this study was collected by searching through different archives within each company's website. In certain cases this entailed searching through over a decade of news articles, press releases and blogs; however, the amount of material and the variety of formats differed between companies. No limit was placed on how far backwards in time the search went;

however, the data collected went no further forward than 31 December 2013. Within these parameters the earliest document included in this corpus was published on 29 January 1997 and the latest included was published on 29 December 2013, giving a fifteen-year coverage.

Book organisation

The book begins, in Chapter 1, by providing an in-depth overview of existing cybersecurity knowledge drawn from various disciplines including politics and international relations, law and computer science. The first part of this chapter is structured around the organising themes of definition, threat and response, and provides an important foundation upon which subsequent theoretical and empirical work is based. This chapter identifies a broad homogeneity across this knowledge and demonstrates how it operates within a wider national security framing that reproduces the features, tropes and tactics found therein. However, in the second part of this chapter I also go beyond the 'problem-solving' conventions of cybersecurity knowledge to reveal a smaller body of critical and broadly constructivist research that investigates the same object, but in a manner that eschews the commonplace agenda. By highlighting this work I do two things: first, I situate my own study in a wider academic body of work that sets out to investigate cybersecurity by utilising different ontological, epistemological and methodological assumptions to those typically found in cybersecurity research. Second, by revealing this heterogeneity I project a path forward for my own theoretical and empirical work that recognises the importance of a broader inter-subjective process of knowledge construction which requires engagement with this part of the internet security industry.

Chapter 2 provides the theoretical framework for the book's empirical analysis and clarifies a number of theoretical and conceptual tools that are central to its objectives and contributions. Power and security are two such concepts and the chapter begins by clarifying the conceptualisation of power outlined by Michel Foucault by elaborating upon one of his ideas: power/knowledge. From here the chapter hones in on the 'third modality' of power, that of governmentality, to demonstrate how this functions across society and the role that the security *dispositif* plays in allowing this form of power to function. Prior to embarking on the empirical analysis, this chapter ties together the work on power, governance and security with established work on both 'epistemic communities' and 'security professionals'. I elaborate on these theorisations to link the productive functioning of power with the role played by particular 'privileged' experts within the *dispositif* to give meaning to the phenomenon of security, sediment certain understandings, prioritise particular responses and foreclose alternative thinking. It is in this section that I most explicitly make the argument for the need to conduct constructivist research into private security industry expertise. Finally, the chapter draws to a close with reflections on methodology and method and addresses some questions that present when conducting a Foucauldian-inspired discourse analysis such as this.

Chapters 3 and 4 represent the book's main empirical contribution and illuminate how various discursive tactics have been deployed to sediment a particular cybersecurity knowledge, imbuing the space itself, as well as the phenomenon, within with particular characteristics that accentuate unease and risk. Chapter 3 begins the empirical analysis by conducting an analysis of 'cyberspace', characterised as the milieu within which (in)security plays out. Here, I reveal the vulnerable underpinnings that are an inherent feature of this space as well as how knowns and unknowns produce a threat that is unknowable in terms of timing and form, but inevitable in terms of its arrival. Chapter 4 continues the analysis, but shifts the focus from the 'space' to the 'threats'. In this chapter I consider how danger and destructiveness are constituted as self-evident features of various nefarious acts executed by a diverse range of actors that present salient and credible threats in the present as well as the future.

In both of these chapters the focus is placed primarily on how this specific expert site of discourse produces a particular and largely apprehensive risk knowledge around computers, networks, the internet, devices, etc. However, the message is not a wholly homogenous one and, indeed, in both of these chapters, efforts are made to identify the scepticism and contestation that exist and that lead experts to question the accuracy or focus of fellow experts' claims, in order for me to reveal a less overt counter-hegemonic discourse. These seeds of scepticism – as well as a dearth of examples of cyber-terrorism or cyber-war, despite over a decade of conversation about their imminence or arrival – present alternative (expert) framings and understandings as well as disrupting the cohesiveness of dominant cybersecurity discourse.

Chapter 5 draws together all these previous threads to reflect on the importance of the internet security industry in the construction of cybersecurity knowledge and the role that relationships between private entities and professionals of politics plays in the sedimentation of cybersecurity as analogous with national security. I begin by highlighting the broad homogeneity that exists between the expert discourse that I have studied and the 'dominant threat frame' identified by others such as Dunn Cavelty (2008) before theorising as to why this is and what impact it has on a broader process of knowledge construction. To achieve this, I pay particular attention to the position and *raison d'être* of the companies I have studied as well as the formation of communities of mutual recognition that have provided benefits for both the industry and the state. I conclude that the arrival of the 'technological age' poses challenges to the traditional Weberian model of security governance. Subsequently, there has been an expansion and reorganisation of the security *dispositif* to more fully include private expertise as a means of overcoming a sovereignty gap, allowing for the continuation of a strategy of neoliberal governance. In the book's conclusion I summarise the main contributions of my research and reflect upon how similarly motivated constructivist research in this domain could provide scope for further development.

Chapter 1

Cybersecurity knowledge: cohesion, contestation and constructivism

Assertions about the threat posed by malicious actions in cyberspace has seen cybersecurity become a major focus of national security agendas, especially in the most technically developed and computerised nations. Despite not having the same storied history and decade's worth of extensive analysis that some other objects of security do have, cybersecurity knowledge has emerged quite rapidly, coming to the fore in the 1990s and picking up noticeably after the turn of the millennium. The argument contained within this book responds to the way in which cybersecurity has formed as a stable object of knowledge, the assumptions and foci that underpin this, the *how* of this particular formation and the effects it has. Before addressing this argument, a couple of important preliminaries need to be established. First, we must consider the make-up of cybersecurity knowledge, including both where the dominant homogeneity exists and disruptive counter-hegemonic accounts. Second, we must establish the theoretical tools that will allow for the constructivist analysis contained in subsequent chapters. Chapter 2 deals with the theoretical tools, but it is in this chapter that I will address and problematise established cybersecurity knowledge. With this in mind, Chapter 1 aims to achieve two objectives.

First, I intend to provide an in-depth overview of cybersecurity knowledge to date that spans academic disciplines, including politics, international relations, security studies, law and computer science. When exploring this research, my aim is to draw attention to the broad ontological, epistemological and methodological homogeneity that is evidenced by a thematic trichotomy of definition, assessment and response. Having established how this predominant aspect of the discourse looks and considered its inherent assumptions and logics, this chapter's second objective is to identify and draw out alternative, more radical, accounts of cybersecurity that eschew aspects of this orthodoxy. I reveal in this chapter that this appears both as a form of sceptical realism or more radically via the use of constructivist ontologies and interpretivist epistemologies. Again, rather than simply describing dissident accounts, I include this material to demonstrate the wider heterogeneity that exists within cybersecurity discourse when understood in a broader and more inclusive manner. Moreover, with reference to the constructivist research in particular, I argue for its value in exposing the limits of entrenched realism and elaborate upon the constitutive function such knowledge performs. In so doing, this constructivist knowledge not only provides the useful means with which to extend the cybersecurity research agenda; it also reveals the contestable and contingent nature of that which purports to be reflective of reality.

I situate my own study alongside this smaller body of constructivist research and conclude by arguing that dominant cybersecurity knowledge has rapidly and seemingly non-problematically conflated cybersecurity with national security in a manner that excludes alternative knowledge claims. Given the ramifications that flow from cyber-(national) security being elevated to the status of truth, it also highlights the importance that should be given to locating and revealing the inter-subjective process of cybersecurity knowledge construction. In particular, I emphasise the role that expert knowledge plays within the security *dispositif*.

Defining cybersecurity

The cyber-lexicon is said to be vast and very unclear (Jarvis and Macdonald, 2014), made up of 'fuzzy' concepts (Dunn Cavelty, 2008, p. 14) that are difficult to pin down concretely. Indeed, there exist a number of distinct terms, acts and concepts as well as a penchant for prefixing an established phenomenon with 'cyber', 'information' or 'electronic' to produce something else. I would not disagree with these assessments around clarity, but merely stress the point that this has not come about through a lack of effort but rather disagreement as to how key terminology should be defined. Indeed, one of the most prominent organising themes (and our starting point) concerns the volume of work spent doing definitional work.

Starting at the broader end of the spectrum with (the 'rather vague') 'cyber-threat' (Dunn Cavelty, 2008, p. 1), questions abound as to whether this 'catch-all' should be solely 'cyber' in means and what bearing the objective or actor may have on how it is understood. ICS-CERT defines 'cyber-threats to a control system' as unauthorised attempts to gain 'access to a control system device and/or network using a data communications pathway' (ICS-CERT, 2015). In this regard, ICS-CERT have the cyber means criteria in common with others like Brenner, although she specifies further that cyber-threats must successfully undermine 'a society's ability to maintain internal or external order' (Brenner, 2006a, p. 454). Cyber means as necessary for a cyber-threat? Intuitive perhaps, but not a source of universal agreement.

By drawing on definitions of cyber-war, efforts are made to help clarify 'cyber-attack' (Clarke, 2010, p. 6; Gjelten, 2010), but a tendency to synonymise terms such as 'information warfare', 'cyber warfare' and 'cyber-threats', as well as a laissez-faire approach to their interchangeable usage, often presents definitional headaches. Such an environment may have occurred because scholars rely on 'intuitive definitions' or act under the 'erroneous' assumption that a standardised definition is in existence (Nguyen, 2013, p. 1085).

Nevertheless, a 'superior operational definition' is put forward by Hathaway *et al.* that concisely defines cyber-attack as 'any action taken to undermine the functions of a computer network for political or national security purposes' (Hathaway *et al.*, 2012, p. 826). This pithy definition is expanded upon somewhat, using a five-fold criteria and looks to define cyber-attack by objective rather than by actor, effect or means. Objective-based definitions are in evidence elsewhere – for example, focusing on the *destructive payload* of a particular technique rather than just the mere exploitation of a computer network (Lin, 2010, p. 130). Similarly, Droege writes that attacks must be acts of violence and cannot comprise operations that 'would be tantamount to economic sanctions' and therefore, like Lin, concludes that not all operations that 'interfere with civilian communication systems' should be considered 'attacks' (Droege, 2012, pp. 557–60).

Objective definitions may well be a poor fit from a legal perspective, though, on account of the fact that 'computers and computer networks hold no special legal status relative to other potential targets for destruction' (Nguyen, 2013, p. 1088). Consequently, they create unnecessary confusion because cyber-attack 'intuitively connotes a mode of attack' and yet the definitions are centred on the objectives of the attacker:

> Just as an 'air assault' denotes a military attack using aircraft, or as an 'amphibious assault' denotes an assault by land and sea executed on a hostile shore, a 'cyber attack' can denote an attack executed by means of a

computer or computer network. Here, a cyber attack is an *instrument* or *method* of attack, a *weapon* or *capability* that is used to effectuate a particular objective. (Nguyen, 2013, p. 1088)

The transition from cyber-attack to the more specific and presumably more significant cyber-war or 'armed attack' occurs when 'physical damage or injury to people akin to damage or casualties in traditional war' is sustained (Farwell and Rohozinski, 2011, p. 30). Cyber-war may require a consequential physical impact (McGraw, 2013, p. 112) or possibly a war-like aftermath (Nye, 2011, p. 21). A 'softer' definition considers disruption or damage to 'networks, systems, and web sites' as cyber-war and is thus clearly distinguishable from cyber-espionage (Eun and Aßmann, 2015, pp. 4–5).

More specifically still, cyber-war is said to involve interfering or disabling *government and armed forces* computer systems and 'does not exist outside of traditional war'; rather it is 'a threat of attack both by individual hackers and by terrorist groups and states' (Kapto, 2013, p. 357). Kapto's assertion that cyber-war cannot be distinguished as a separate phenomenon from 'traditional war' here is interesting given the inclusion of 'individual hackers' as being capable of waging war, which appears to put it at odds with orthodox understandings of war. Broadening cyber-war (or war) to this extent is rejected, at least implicitly, elsewhere as being the sole domain of states (Brenner, 2007, p. 402; Khan, 2011, p. 93; RAND 2015).

Thomas Rid returns to the Clausewitzian hallmarks of war to argue that 'cyber-war' would have to be violent, instrumental in nature, a means to an end and political to constitute war (Rid, 2011, pp. 7–8). Rid is not alone in this regard and other contributions fall back on the conceptualisations of war offered by Clausewitz when arriving at their definition (Liff, 2012, p. 408). However, even these widely accepted tenets of warfare are not safe within the definitional debate and *a new definition of war* may be required due to the 'unpredictable nature of damage that cyber-attack can inflict' (Farwell and Rohozinski, 2012, p. 113).

Terrorism provides another rich vein of definitional work, albeit one in which 'the lack of a consistent definition of terrorism' presents a 'significant barrier' (Embar-Seddon, 2002, p. 1034). With no universally agreed-upon definition of terrorism, it is perhaps of little surprise that there is no universal consensus on cyber-terrorism either (Archer, 2014, p. 607). However, a lack of universality in relation to how one should define terrorism is not to say that there does not exist any homogeneity between the existent definitions[1] and it is apparent that many of the commonly cited characteristics of terrorism make their way into definitions of cyber-terrorism. However, the emergence of 'cyber-terrorism' (which is often but not universally viewed as a distinct concept)[2] does present a challenge to existing terrorism knowledge and the choice between 'stretching the concept to the point of vagueness or inventing a new term to cover a wider range of activities' (Weinberg *et al.*, 2004, p. 779). This choice comes on top of the definitional quagmire that cyber-terrorism inherits from its parent concept (Jackson *et al.*, 2011, pp. 99–123) as well as distinct definitional debates.

One of the motivations behind the pursuit of definition is evidenced in Denning's observation that 'cyberterrorism has been used to characterise everything from minor hacks to devastating attacks' (Denning, 2010, p. 198; Embar-Seddon, 2002, p. 1035). Many acts of simple 'hacking' that merely constitute 'unauthorised access to or use of a computer system' (Embar-Seddon, 2002, p. 1037) have been labelled cyberterrorism despite failing to meet the required threshold of acts of terror (p. 1035). Crucial here is the presence of violence (Embar-Seddon, 2002, p. 1037), something Heickerö (2014, p. 555) and Conway also believe must be present for something to constitute cyber-terrorism, with the latter arguing that the act must 'result in death and/or large scale destruction' (Conway, 2002, n.p.). Mimicking its physical counterpart, cyber-terrorism is also argued to distinguish itself given the ability to produce fear in a target audience in furtherance of an ideological goal (Post *et al.*, 2000, p. 101).

Attempts to define cyber-terrorism have tended to be structured along two separate lines: defining the concept by effects and defining the concept by intent (Hua and Bapna, 2012, p. 104; Rollins and Wilson, 2005). As with effects-based definitions of cyber-war, these concentrate on whether or not the attack produces an aftermath comparable to a traditional act of terrorism, while intent-orientated definitions see cyber-terrorism primarily as 'politically motivated computer attacks [that] are done to intimidate or coerce a government or people to further a political objective, or to cause grave harm or severe economic damage' (Hua and Bapna, 2012, p. 104). Such definitions are considered to be either: (1) predicated upon existing definitions of terrorism; (2) predicated upon existing legal statues; or finally (3) combining 'partial elements of the definitional attempts with accounts of specific acts or actions' (Ballard *et al.*, 2002, pp. 992–3).

The most widely cited definition originally surfaced as part of a testimony from Professor Dorothy Denning on 23 May 2000 to the Special Oversight

Panel on Terrorism (Denning, 2000) and has subsequently been used in 'numerous articles and interviews' (Conway, 2004, p. 84).

> Cyberterrorism is the convergence of cyberspace and terrorism. It refers to unlawful attacks and threats of attacks against computers, networks and the information stored therein when done to intimidate or coerce a government or its people in furtherance of political or social objectives. Further, to qualify as cyberterrorism, an attack should result in violence against persons or property, or at least cause enough harm to generate fear. (Denning, 2000)

In her definition Denning does not presuppose that cyberterrorism has to be carried out via a computer but merely that it must be an attack 'against computers, networks, and the information stored therein' (Denning, 2000). The role of objectives within this definition operates contrary to Weimann's definition that puts the onus on the means ('computer network tool') against critical national infrastructures (CNI) (Weimann, 2005, p. 130). Both of these definitions share a commonality in that they define the concept with regard to the effects of the act, be it as 'harm', in Weimann's case, or 'violence against persons or property' for Denning.[3] Such definitions say nothing about the actors involved – for example, whether cyber-terrorism is a sub-state phenomenon or, as more recent research has begun to explore, something carried out by states as well (Heickerö, 2014, p. 556; Macdonald *et al.*, 2015).

Devising a multi-level schema to help identify acts as, or differentiate them from, cyber-terrorism is not uncommon and speaks to the criticism that apparently separate phenomena have overlapped to a problematic degree (Brenner, 2007, pp. 390–8; Nelson *et al.*, 1999, p. 15; Weimann, 2005, p. 141; Denning, 2001a, p. 281). At the broader end of these schema, Angela Clem, Sagar Galwankar and George Buck state that cyber-terrorism can be used to: '(1) help plan other terrorist activities; (2) soften a target prior to a physical attack; or (3) generate more fear and confusion concurrent with other terrorist acts' and therefore could feasibly include altering or destroying health insurance records (Clem *et al.*, 2003, p. 273). These authors implicitly offer a broad definition of cyber-terrorism via their schema, but others aim to distinguish not between cyber-terrorism and other concepts but *within* cyber-terrorism.

Here we see distinctions made between 'cyberterrorism' and 'true' or 'pure' cyber-terrorism (Gordon and Ford, 2003; Malcolm, 2004). In these instances the former tends to refer to computer systems being used for the everyday functions necessary for terrorists to complete their mission or as particular terrorist acts defined in law, while the latter is the potential for destruction brought about by nefarious computer use. Devost *et al.* (1997, p. 78) diverge from this slightly, recognising 'pure information terrorism' as a specific 'computer on computer' form that is set against an alternative form that serves as a facilitator for other terrorist actions. Elsewhere the distinction is between a conventional form (attacks that disrupt information infrastructure) and a unique one – for example, simple communication between terrorists online (Desousza and Hensgen, 2003, pp. 387–8). There is a final three-fold categorisation that sets out the 'three basic types of cyberterrorists': the professionals, the amateurs and the thieves. The professionals 'aim at inflicting physical or cyber damage onto victim's resources', the amateurs 'find pleasure in applying cyber graffiti' and the thieves 'have immediate personal illicit economic benefit from their actions' (Kostopoulos, 2008, p. 165). This final schema would appear to define cyber-terrorism so broadly that practically any misuse of computers could be categorised under this term.[4]

The final part of the cyber-lexicon to consider is *Cyber-crime* and while there is a 'general acceptance' that the concept combines criminal behaviour with cyberspace[5] it will likely come as little surprise that 'there is no single accepted definition of cyber-crime' (Holt, 2012, p. 338). Rob McCusker describes cyber-crime as 'a generic descriptor for any malfeasant online behaviour (whatever the relative differences in complexity and seriousness) ranging from spam emails and denial of service attacks to malware and botnet infiltration' (McCusker, 2006, p. 259).

Nevertheless, regardless of its value in terms of definitional specificity, even the broadest definitions appear to provide some segregation between cyber-crime and cyber-terrorism for instance. Politically and ideologically motivated attacks are argued to be the net result of a distinct process (Carr, 2010, p. 180) that makes them different to more individualistic examples of malicious activity like cyber-crime.[6] Cyber-crime appears to enjoy greater definitional clarity than cyber-terrorism in part due to the absence of such a volatile and value-laden word as 'terrorism'.

Familiar conversations around definition via means or objectives play out again here and are even singled out as the reason for there being no precise definition (Cassim, 2011, p. 124). Causing further problems are whether cyber-crimes should be understood as traditional offences that have been facilitated by computer technology (Grabosky, 2001, pp. 243–9) or whether newer novel and unparalleled acts such as hacking and distributed denial of service (DDoS) should be included or understood as cyber-crime alone (Wall, 1998, pp. 201–18);

a distinction characterised as between 'cyber-enabled crimes' and 'cyber-dependent crimes' (McGuire, 2013).

Of course, for many scholars it is not about either/or, but instead that any definition of cyber-crime should be able to incorporate both new forms of criminal activity 'created' with the arrival of computer technology and those traditional forms of criminality facilitated via this technology. Providing a rationale for this point of view, Brenner uses the example of the DDoS attack that targeted the internet giant Amazon in 2000. In offering her own explanation, Brenner echoes the sort of language we have seen used in relation to cyber-terrorism: '[DDOS]… is not a traditional crime. It is not theft, fraud, extortion, vandalism, burglary, or any crime that was within a pre-twentieth century prosecutor's repertoire. It is an example of a new type of crime: a "pure" cybercrime' (Brenner, 2007, p. 385). For Brenner, DDoS is a crime and one that would not exist without computers and thus it is a 'pure' cyber-crime but one that should be included in any complete definition. Consequently, Brenner defines cyber-crime as 'the use of computer technology to commit crime; to engage in activity that threatens a society's ability to maintain internal order' (Brenner, 2007, p. 385).

Categorisation and typology impact upon definitions of cyber-crime also and early attempts at multi-level categorisation (Parker, 1976, pp. 17–21) are complemented by more recent contributions that have sought to achieve something similar (Downing, 2005, pp. 711–73). However, it is David Wall who produced the widely cited categorisation of cyber-crime in the opening section of his edited volume on the topic (Wall, 2001a). Wall breaks down the concept into acts of cyber-trespass, cyber-deception/theft, cyber-porn/obscenity and cyber-violence (Wall, 2001b, pp. 1–17). Clearly, such a schema indicates the breadth of cyber-crimes; everything from illicitly obtaining passwords, trading child pornography and stalking somebody online can all fit into different sections of this schema.

David Speer takes a more conceptual approach to the categorisation of cyber-crime, looking to distinguish it from other concepts (such as information warfare) by considering the 'nature' of cyber-crime (Speer, 2000, p. 260). This nature, Speer argues, is discernible through the location of the offender, the motivation of the offender and the sorts of victims affected by the crime (Speer, 2000, pp. 260–3). The three-fold categorisations provided by Downing and Speer and the four-fold categorisation offered by Wall is contrasted by a *five-fold* categorisation offered by Yanping Zhang et al. (Zhang et al., 2012, pp. 423–4). Here, Zhang et al. move back towards something closer to that which was offered by Parker and argue that cyber-crime can refer to any of the five points at which computer technology and networks intersect with criminality (Zhang *et al.*, 2012, pp. 423–4). This typology incorporates everything from copyright infringement (under 'computer as tool') through to cyber-terrorism (under 'traditional non-cyber-crimes').[7]

Assessing the threat

Threat assessment is the second point of focus, shifting from the present day to past events (Ford and Spafford, 2007), speculations over the future (O'Brien, 2010, p. 197) and even considering what the past can tell us about the future (Farwell and Rohozinski, 2011). As observed from the previous section on definition, it is generally accepted that there are multiple different kinds of cyber-threat. These differences can manifest in terms of how they are categorised in a technical sense (say between DDoS, malware, social engineering, etc.) or how they are understood conceptually (war, terrorism, attack, activism, etc.) The referent objects vary too and so just as critical infrastructure is said to be at risk, so too are our businesses (Khan, 2011), intellectual property (Finkel, 2010) and privacy (Podesta and Goyle, 2005).

Threat assessment is often apprehensive in tone and has been for a considerable time (Cilluffo and Pattak, 2000, p. 48), with severity increasing as time has passed (Hunton, 2012, p. 225). Over this twelve-year stretch and continuing up to the present day the overall assessment remains fearful and pessimistic; the image of a relentless barrage of attacks remains: 'The digital infrastructure in the United States and other countries around the world is under siege … Every day, computer networks are subject to attacks probing for weaknesses in security systems' (Finkel, 2010, n.p.).

Not only are threats numerous, serious, growing and destabilising (Chourcri and Goldsmith, 2012, p. 71), they are also said to be serious and destructive. Cyber-terrorism threatens a 'Digital Pearl Harbor' (Podesta and Goyle, 2005, p. 516), while cyber-crime has developed from 'a costly nuisance' through to 'sophisticated tools' that present a 'serious security threat for users of the Internet' (Bauer and van Eeten, 2009, p. 706). The threat, it is argued, is so significant that, in fact, now the most credible threat of 'a catastrophic attack on the U.S. homeland' comes not from 'nuclear-armed missiles, but from cyberattacks conducted at the speed of light' (Krepinevich, 2011, p. 80). Things get worse still, for while the 'public face of the cyber threat changes frequently' there exists 'an abiding spectrum of threats that is far broader, and far more dangerous, than is topically appreciated' (Vatis, 2006, p. 56). Such accounts provide an introduction to the general sentiment that exists around the assessment of cyber-threats; however, these assessments also reveal something about the perceived *location* of the threat, the short answer to which may simply be 'everywhere': 'The United States faces threats from peer nations, trading partners, hostile countries, non-state actors, terrorists, organized crime, insiders, and teenage hackers' (Cilluffo and Pattak, 2000, p. 41).

Nevertheless, 'everywhere' is not sufficient to capture all the specificity. *States*, for example, are 'rightly feared' by other states (Farwell and Rohozinski, 2012, p. 109; Khan, 2011, p. 97; Hughes, 2010, p. 523) and as early as 2001, the US Government estimated that over thirty other nations had developed 'aggressive computer-warfare programs', including the likes of Russia, China, Iran and Iraq (Adams, 2001, p. 102). Cyberspace had already become a 'new international battlefield', with operations like Moonlight Maze[8] providing 'just a taste of dangers to come' (Adams, 2001, p. 98). Perhaps the forthcoming dangers referenced here include 'one of the first cyberwars' said to have occurred after the massive DDoS attacks that targeted the Estonian Government in April 2007 (Kapto, 2013, p. 358). Cyberwarfare represents 'a major security concern of political and military leaders around the world' (Liff, 2012, p. 401)[9] and the state is self-evidently a prominent and credible actor in this domain (Akdag, 2019). Notable examples of apparent state-on-state cyber-attack, such as the aforementioned Estonian conflict as well as DDoS attacks in Georgia in 2008, Stuxnet in 2010 and Wannacry in 2017, have bolstered this assessment.

States are understood as both the 'threat actor' and 'referent object' in security equations. Given the financial and human resources available, the threat is often perceived to be (in theory at least) at its sharpest here and likely most pressing in relation to other state rivals. Correspondingly, the possible impact of conflict in cyberspace between multiple states are understood in stark terms: 'cyber disputes in the international system could potentially destroy command and control structures of the military and foreign policy apparatus, wipe out the media communications of a state, destroy financial memory, and wage economic combat' (Valeriano and Maness, 2014, p. 349).

Due to the superior capability states possess, targeting critical infrastructure is a particular concern – for example, knocking out electric power to leave millions of people 'dealing with social disorder' (Clarke, 2009, p. 32). Cyberspace may not afford the strategic possibilities of complete destruction of a rival state that a successful nuclear attack would cause; however, by utilising these 'weapons of mass disruption' states can look to inflict considerable economic impact (Cetron and Davies, 2009, p. 47) and, in circumstances where the US is the target, less capable states could hone in on their 'soft underbelly': the private sector (Adams, 2001, p. 105).

Alongside the nation state as both a threatening actor and a referent, *criminals* also pose a significant threat (Khan, 2011, p. 91). Statistics on the extent of cyber-crime can differ quite significantly – for example, the Ponemon Institute estimated the annual cost to the UK public sector at £1.2 million in 2011 (see Home Office Science Advisory Council, 2018), while an oft-quoted Detica/Cabinet Office report published in 2011 estimated the number at £27 *billion* annually (Detica, 2011).[10] More recent reports, such as the 2019 *Cyber Security Breaches Survey* published by the Department for Digital, Culture, Media and Sport (2019) estimated each cybersecurity breach cost a UK business £4,180 and found that a third of businesses had experienced at least one breach in the twelve months preceding the survey. Shift the focus away from the UK exclusively and we hear how cyber-crime is said to be 'thriving' in Africa (Cassim, 2011, p. 123) and growing in states such as Saudi Arabia (Algani, 2013, p. 498). These global trends presumably offer some explanation for McAfee's global financial cost estimate of $600 billion (Lewis, 2018, p. 4). In contrast to the state being responsible here, we are looking at various different non-state actors; organised criminals, hackers, 'hacktivists' and 'script kiddies' are often prominent actors associated with cyber-crime and all present something different in terms of the severity and referent object.

Cyberspace has afforded a range of different criminals 'endless opportunities for criminal mischief, the boundaries of which extend far beyond the physical scope of a computer itself' (Decker, 2008, p. 964). The diverse range of cyber-criminals operate using an array of means to threaten a range of different referent objects and while monetary motivations are often at the forefront, secure systems housing sensitive data are also a popular target (Finkel, 2010, n.p.). A range of different techniques are utilised by cyber-criminals to threaten users and organisations (Decker, 2008, p. 964), such as malware in the form of viruses, worms and Trojan Horses (Hughes and DeLone, 2007) as well as spyware (Nelson and Simek, 2005). Alternatively, criminals may rely on social engineering (Abraham and Chengalur-Smith, 2010) or phishing attacks (Arachchilage and Love, 2013) to trick the user into giving up usernames, passwords, bank details, etc.

Some hacktivists exist in something of a grey area insofar as when their actions should be considered cyber-enabled legitimate activism or outright criminal activity, but, nevertheless, the authorities have been quick to condemn the actions of particular hacktivists as criminal or even terrorist (Arizona Department of Public Safety, 2011). In line with cyber-criminals more broadly, the hacktivist threat is located at the non-state level and typically manifests itself in the form of web defacement, web sit-ins and DDoS attacks (Denning, 2001b). Such techniques have been disruptive for elements of the private sector and the state (Reynolds, 2011, p. 100). The severity of this threat ranges quite significantly, from the more prankish style of hacktivism often viewed as an embarrassing nuisance through to more serious forms that can allegedly 'disrupt or destroy government operations, banking transactions, city power grids, and even military weapon systems' (Herzog, 2011, p. 49).

We can diversify even further still within the category of cyber-crime and locate this threat at the individual level, particularly in relation to 'the insider'. Given the difficulty in penetrating certain computer networks, attention has shifted onto the threat posed by the 'internal saboteur' or the 'disgruntled employee' who is considered to be perfectly positioned and has knowledge of where sensitive information is stored (Cilluffo and Pattak, 2000, p. 47). Insiders know how their systems work and therefore enjoy relatively trouble-free access to potentially sensitive systems and can easily conduct attacks that may be more damaging than external ones (Esen, 2002, p. 269). The significance of the insider threat was acknowledged specifically in the 2016 UK Cybersecurity Strategy and garnered a far greater level of attention in this strategy than in anything previously outlined by the UK Government (HM Government, 2016, p. 19).

Terrorism is an area upon which much focus is placed when considering threat, although it relies strongly on the hypothetical. Our societies are said to be 'wide-open targets for terrorists' on accounts of two key trends: 'first, the growing technological capacity of small groups and individuals to destroy things and people; and, second, the increasing vulnerability of our economic and technological systems to carefully aimed attacks' (Homer-Dixon, 2002, p. 53). Cyber-terrorists have become 'computer savvy individuals who look for vulnerabilities that can be easily exploited' (Cassim, 2012, p. 381) and, given the number of poorly guarded targets, create a difficult task for the security services (Cassim, 2012, p. 388). Logic such as this creates the conditions for oft-quoted lines such as 'tomorrow's terrorist may be able to do more damage with a keyboard than with a bomb' (National Research Council, 1991, p. 7) and Barry Collin's list of hypothetical nightmare scenarios (Collin, 1997). For those who maintain that these scenarios represent a serious and continuing threat, they stress how terrorist organisations are not reliant on external support (outsourced terrorism) but have actually recruited their own highly capable programmers (Archer, 2014, p. 616). Alongside these accounts experts have also focused on that which is undeniably happening as opposed to just that which might occur. Therefore, the threat from cyber-terrorism is increasingly being understood in terms of cyber-terrorists' disruptive capabilities and their use of cyberspace to further their physical endeavours – for example, the increasing tendency for terrorists online to turn to hacktivism (Cronin, 2002–3, pp. 46–7).

Broader than this, however, are the multiple uses that terrorists make of the internet and the threat these activities present to the security of the state (Goodman *et al.*, 2007, pp. 198–9). While attack is included in this typology, the majority of the focus is on actions that facilitate 'physical terrorism' such as propaganda and communication. Thomas Holt goes so far as to say that, for terrorists, the biggest benefit of the internet is their ability to convey their extremist propaganda effectively and have direct control of how their message is conveyed to the public (Holt, 2012, p. 341). Communication is also vital as a means to train new recruits on weapons and tactics, as well as to plan and fund future attacks (Homer-Dixon, 2002, p. 54).

Having considered the manner in which these threats have been located within cybersecurity knowledge, we can now turn our attention towards *understandings* of how such threats operate. Cyber-threats are considered to differ in certain key ways to physical threats and these differences are ones that serve to raise perceptions of risk. The first and most prominent factor as to the novelty of cyber-threats is their apparent simplicity; the ease with which operations can be conducted in cyberspace is widely believed to be significantly greater – for example, comparing the ease of cyber-war with conventional war (Eun and Aßmann, 2015, p. 12; Sandro, 2012, p. 68). Likewise, cyber-crime 'can be committed with relative ease', requires little in the way of resources and does not require the offender to be present in the jurisdiction of the offence (Cassim, 2009, p. 38). The simplification of criminal activity in this manner and the vast array of different techniques available (Hunton, 2012, p. 225) also create very favourable economies of scale for the cyber-criminal (Brenner, 2006b, p. 194).

Cyber-attacks in general are thought to be 'easy and cheap to carry out', so much so that anyone 'with a modicum of technological sophistication can carry out some form of attack' (Vatis, 2006, p. 58). This includes terrorists who, thanks to 'dual-use applications', can 'easily acquire an inexpensive, yet robust communications intelligence collection capability' (Cilluffo and Pattak, 2000, p. 44) and also cyber-weapons which offer them 'new, low-cost, easily hidden tools to support their cause' (Seabian, 2000). It is the ease of cyber-operations that leads McGraw to the conclusion that cyber-war is 'inevitable', even going so far as to suggest that payloads such as that 'of the Stuxnet variety' are 'easily built' and have levelled the playing field (McGraw, 2013, p. 116).

However, it is not just that so much has been made so easy in cyberspace, but, crucially, that so much has become untraceable or 'plausibly deniable'. The ease of cyber-attack purports to do away with the difficulty of certain malicious activities, but anonymity or maybe even plausible deniability offers the promise of 'getting away with it' and avoiding potentially serious sanctions (Liff, 2012, p. 412). States that would not dare engage in direct confrontation for risk of significant retaliation grow in confidence when operating online, causing them to be 'more reckless when it comes to making decisions regarding attacks or wars' (Eun and Aßmann, 2015, p. 13).

Similarly, terrorists have become more confident in their communication and planning, knowing they are doing so covertly (Grogan, 2009, p. 698), and also more brazen in their operations (such as intercepting sensitive information and running counter-surveillance). Terrorists can operate safe in the knowledge that 'much of this work can be done anonymously, diminishing the risk of reprisal and increasing the likelihood of success' (Cilluffo and Pattak, 2000, p. 44) and posing significant challenges for counter-terrorism (Hua and Bapna, 2012, p. 105). The novelty of online anonymity has also radically changed the way in which certain forms of criminality operate – for example, 'the reliable guarantee of anonymity' provides a 'distinct advantage' for the stalker (Brenner, 2006b, p. 194).

Finally, there is remoteness. Even if attribution can be established and law enforcement or the security services can identify those guilty they will more often than not come up against the issue of physical distance and legal jurisdiction. Cyber-criminals no longer have to be physically present in the act of crime; in fact they no longer have to be present 'entirely within the territory of a single sovereign' (Brenner, 2006b, p. 190). Targeting a system from or through multiple jurisdictions (Finkel, 2010, n.p.) makes attribution more difficult and, if caught, acting upon this information is made significantly more difficult due to the fact that the victim will have to negotiate with another state in order to extradite those they believe are guilty. Moreover, we witness the creation of 'cyber-crime havens' in areas where levels of cyber-security are low and ties with the rest of the international community are fragile (Brenner and Schwerha, 2007, n.p.). As with these other novelties associated with cyber-threats it is not just crime that it affects, states too enjoy plausible deniability while acts of 'pure cyber-terrorism' no longer require the terrorist to physically show up to the location of the attack (Hua and Bapna, 2012, p. 105).

Responding to cyber-threats

With the threats assessed and the conclusion largely fearful, the final organising theme considers how to prevent or at least mitigate against cyber-threats. The first stage in this process is to *identify* the threats before the necessary solutions can be developed. In 2001 Adams said that identifying what was wrong with information security was 'easy', but remedying these problems would be 'much more difficult' (Adams, 2001, p. 107). To a large extent the message has remained the same to the present day. Effective cyber-security is multidimensional (Quigley and Roy, 2012, p. 83), the problems and their solutions reside in all manner of different locations. At the turn of the millennium, Aquilla argued that a preoccupation with Maginot Line-style 'leakproof firewalls and safe areas' was hampering more effective cyber-security (Aquilla, 2000, p. 17), mistakenly conflating cyber-security as 'a purely technical problem' (Brenner, 2013, p. 18; Wulf and Jones, 2009, p. 943). 'Perimeter defence' and hopes to keep the 'good stuff' in and the 'bad guys' out make up part of the conventional knowledge but are increasingly thought to be insufficient on their own (Leuprecht, Skillicorn and Tait, 2016). Even, for example, if impenetrable frontiers could be developed, the 'inside' would still be completely exposed to malicious insiders (Wulf and Jones, 2009, p. 943).

An alternative is a 'depth defence' approach that looks to respond to cyber-threats in a way that complements robust defences against unauthorised external access with numerous counter measures, should these defences be breached, such as strong encryption (Aquilla, 2000, p. 18; Jefferson, 1997, p. 72). It would be a misnomer to suggest that the idea of high walls and strong gates has completely disappeared from the discussion but a more varied offering of defensive strategies has come to the fore, reflected in contributions such as that of Goodman, Kirk and Kirk, who, under the heading 'defending cyberspace', outline two different 'forms of defence' and *sixteen* different 'stages of defence' (Goodman *et al.*, 2007, p. 206)!

The different language around response also alludes to significant differences in the aims and objectives of different strategies. For example, 'resilience' disregards the idea of impenetrable defence and shifts the focus to mitigating against 'the impact of a shock or disturbance and then to recover in its aftermath' (Hardy, 2015, p. 82). Broad conversation about what effective cyber-resilience would look like (Hult and Sivanesan, 2013), the role of risk management (Henrie, 2013) and specific suggestions around techniques such as systems modelling (Chittister and Haimes, 2011) make up some of the knowledge here, as do the challenges posed to such strategies given the level of private-sector CNI ownership (Herrington and Aldrich, 2013). Evron does not use the language of resilience but argues in a similar vein that 'in today's world internet security demands a robust response capability that can utilize defensive measures to ensure cyber, as well as civilian, order' (Evron, 2008, p. 124).

One logic maintains that a technical problem requires a technical solution (Geers, 2012, p. 2), whether it be more anti-virus (Cerf, 2011, p. 62; Nelson and Simek, 2005), new cybersecurity monitoring and management systems (Kotenko and Saenko, 2013) or specific frameworks used to assess vulnerabilities in information systems (Antón, 2003). However, technological solutions are not just understood as implementing more or better technologies, but also scrutinising and increasing the burden on the very companies that produce the hardware and software. These companies have tended to adopt a retroactive policy of patching bugs, but more rigorous beta testing in the development stage is one alternative suggestion to help iron out vulnerabilities that exist in their products (Yang and Hoffstadt, 2006, p. 209). Put another way, 'the software problem', as it is characterised by McGraw, is best confronted by building security into our software (McGraw, 2013, p. 116).

Seemingly more straightforward approaches to cybersecurity are evident in the literature around implementing 'best practices' and applying sound 'cyber-hygiene' that aim to address the 'human vulnerability'. National cyber-defence could be improved markedly if 'every vendor, owner, and operator of information technology systems and networks would put into practice what is actually known about mitigating cyberthreats' (Lin, 2012, p. 78). Here, Lin is referring to aspects such as sound password security (Cerf, 2011, p. 63; Dysart, 2011, p. 45) or rigorously tested systems (Dysart, 2011, p. 45).

Moreover, a lack of knowledge and education around these issues has been noted for decades (Jefferson, 1997, p. 74), but remains a point of emphasis: 'to fight the crime, the root cause must be tackled…many of the people involved in tackling cybercrime are information technology illiterate' (Asokhia, 2010, p. 18). Indeed, speaking to Asokhia's point, research has identified the expertise and care that is required, for example, when compiling digital evidence as part of cyber-crime prosecution (Chaikin, 2006) as well as the number of different roles that need filling to navigate the process properly

(Hunton, 2012). The focus here is on the role of education, awareness and expertise within the criminal justice system, but at a more everyday level the role of cyber-security education in the workplace has also been singled out as having a observable benefit for improving the competency of employees in this regard (Li *et al.*, 2019).

Part of moving away from the aforementioned Maginot mentality is an acceptance that response and defence does not have to be passive or reactive but also possibly pre-emptive and aggressive (Williamson, 2008). What does this mean for cyberspace? It means that military concepts such as 'pre-emptive strikes' that are well established in the physical world can be applied in cyberspace also (Sanger and Shanker, 2013). A number of different nations have developed their cyber-means around these principles (Hughes, 2010, pp. 530–3); however, the plausibility of such a response is hindered by serious practical problems. On the one hand, the frequency with which reliable attribution data is available means that pre-emption would be far riskier online than in physical space as well as likely being less effective given the likelihood of the adversary having suitable back-up facilities. However, such an attack might be able to do enough to 'shake an adversary's confidence in its ability to carry out its attack' (Lin, 2012, p. 81). Perhaps if a pre-emptive strategy could be complemented with strong intelligence analysis and real-time electronic surveillance this approach could be more viable for states (Williams *et al.*, 2010; Pradillo, 2011).

More novel approaches to the issue of response have been suggested, from drawing on mechanisms perhaps more synonymous with public health to the development of an 'e-SOS' facility to aid rapid response (Mulligan and Schneider, 2011; Wible, 2003; Hollis, 2011; Arachcilage and Love, 2013; Huey *et al.*, 2012; Jones, 2007). However, despite these examples there still remains an attachment to the distinctly Cold War-era strategy of deterrence. Geers distinguishes between two forms of deterrence: proactive denial and reactive punishment, but concludes that given the ease with which cyber-means can be acquired, duplicated and concealed, proactive denial is all but impossible (Geers, 2012, p. 5). Reactive punishment provides more promise, but is far from straightforward (Chourcri and Goldsmith, 2012, p. 71; Geers, 2010; Hua and Bapna, 2012, pp. 108–9) where problems of attribution, plausible deniability and rapidity of response exist (Platt, 2012, pp. 161–2). However, these challenges are not necessarily insurmountable and assertions that attribution makes deterrence unworkable online are alleged to be 'too simple' (Nye, 2013, p. 11). Echoing Nye's sentiments, Hua and Bapna propose an entirely new framework for the strategy, which is reliant on enhanced cooperation (see also O'Brien, 2010, p. 204) and interconnectedness at the national and international level as well as from Internet Service Providers, private organisations and among citizens (Hua and Bapna, 2012, p. 110).

Legislative-, *cooperative- and governance-*based responses provide another avenue for confronting the issue, and early efforts to legally define and provide an overview of the legislative framework that exists to confront cyber-crime were provided in 2001 and 2005 (Katyal, 2001; Downing, 2005). These broad overviews consider legal definitions of cyber-crime, through to general principles, appropriate punishments and how these laws can be best tailored to assist law enforcement. Cyber-crime is the main focus here, but the distinct legal dilemma surrounding the legality of a response to cyber-attack also makes up an important question (Peng *et al.*, 2006; Hathaway *et al.*, 2012). Legal debates include the applicability of criminal and international law to phenomenon in cyberspace as well as proposals to reform the current legislative framework in light of developments in cybersecurity such as hacktivism (Kelly, 2012; Kettemann, 2017). The speed with which issues of cybersecurity develop, and the increasing complexity this development entails, has meant that legal mechanisms have struggled to keep up with the latest trends and techniques (Evron, 2008, p. 125) and have subsequently been criticised on these grounds (Glennon, 2012; Hollis, 2011).

The need for a unified, cooperative, often international response is viewed as a necessity of effective cyber-response (Purser, 2011, p. 237; Camp, 2011, p. 103; Solansky and Beck, 2009; Tehrani *et al.*, 2013). Any effective framework for cybersecurity cooperation that allows for enhanced information sharing will help boost resilience, improve best practice and raise awareness of the latest vulnerabilities (Mallinder and Drabwell, 2013; Moore *et al.*, 2009, p. 12). On the point of best practices and standardising security, cooperation is as much about producing an exhaustive knowledge base as it is about ensuring that protection and defence are consistent across sectors (Hirshleifer, 1983; Moore *et al.*, 2009, p. 9). Cooperation aims to drag everybody up to the same level so that there is no weak link, no obvious way for a malicious actor to penetrate the networked environment.

Lack of coordination has seen cybersecurity policy criticised on the grounds that it has been allowed to develop in an *ad hoc* manner, primarily being developed through voluntary partnerships 'that developed in fits and starts because they ultimately rested on a self-interested motivation that was divorced from a cumulative anchor in public good' (Harknett and Stever, 2011, p. 460).[11]

Of course, assuming the development of a more robust, coordinated and genuinely cooperative strategy would be desirable it remains a very difficult proposition. Acknowledging that 'the global nature of the Internet requires international cooperation' is one thing, but it has to be approached with the understanding that 'differences in cultural norms and the difficulty of verification make such treaties hard to negotiate or implement' (Nye, 2013, p. 12). Despite Nye's comments here, the majority of analysis around cooperation tends to be written from a Western perspective or focuses on the West. However, exceptions include national and regional case studies, such as those of New Zealand, India, South Africa or East Asia and BRICS countries (Wanglai, 2018; Kshetri, 2016; Burton, 2013; Cassim, 2011; Thomas, 2009). Institutions (albeit regional ones) such as the EU offer a ready-made framework for international cooperation that may provide an effective means of tackling verification, but questions remain as to the 'coherence' (Carrapico and Barrinha, 2017) of this institution and the hurdles that impede upon its ability to react with haste in a domain that is notorious for developing at pace (Ruohonen *et al.*, 2016, p. 755).

From the more readily available perspective of the US, the question remains whether it 'believes it can adequately protect its infrastructure against interstate cyberattack through its own actions or, instead, finds it needs international cooperation to move toward that goal' (Elliot, 2009, n.p.). Some form of international agreement seems like the most obvious way of achieving the latter but, similarly to Nye Jr, Elliot questions whether a state like the US would be willing to limit itself when it has (and presumably will continue to have) the greatest means in cyberspace (Elliot, 2009, n.p.). Such assessments have left certain commentators pessimistic about the future of a robust international agreement on cybersecurity (Kumar *et al.*, 2014, p. 128).

However, it is hardly the case that there is no precedent for cooperation on the international stage. The European Convention on Cyber Crime, elsewhere referred to as the Budapest Convention, is the most widely cited treaty and it is unprecedented in terms of its multilateral structure and scope. If it holds that 'co-operation among the states at the international, regional or organisational level' remains the 'principle modality' for ensuring security, then the Budapest Convention 'constitutes a modern legal framework' (Ilie *et al.*, 2011, p. 446). Among its strengths, the Convention is said to have real practical application in terms of disrupting cyber-crime havens by ensuring that cyber-criminals can be identified and extradited for prosecution (Brenner and Schwerha, 2007). Outside of this example there are a range of NATO administrative and organisational structures (Yost, 2010), the establishment of the Cooperative Cyber Defence Centre of Excellence at Tallinn, the Computer Emergency Response Team network (CERT) (Chourcri and Goldsmith, 2012) and agreements between particular nations (Kapto, 2013), all of which demonstrate that there already exists a desire and willingness to cooperate on matters of cybersecurity. However, it is not necessarily the case that these institutions and measures go far enough (Chourcri and Goldsmith, 2012, p. 73). For example, Francesco Calderoni identifies reducing friction between national legislation, introducing new investigative powers and facilitating international cooperation as three critical ways in which European criminal justice can seek to improve their combined efforts to respond to cyber-threats (Calderoni, 2010).

Governance may be the biggest hurdle to overcome if this rhetoric is to become a reality: 'Cyber security involves legal issues, human resources practices and policies, operational configurations, and technical expertise. But none of the people overseeing these areas … owns the problem' (Brenner, 2013, p. 19). Calls to establish 'cyber-norms' for the governance of cyberspace are now 'ubiquitous' but the idea of 'who owns' cyberspace and who gets to devise these norms remains complicated (Finnemore and Hollis, 2016, p. 426).

To provide some brief context to the primary issue that presents here, in 1981 the network that ultimately served as the precursor to the internet (ARPANET) was an entirely publicly owned entity that connected around 100 government and university computers almost exclusively contained within the US (Comer, 2007, p. 96). Now, the internet provides access to 4,422,494,622 people (Internet World Stats, 2019) across every continent and, since 1988, has seen increasing privatisation after the National Science Foundation first began working alongside the private sector to build a much higher capacity backbone that could replace ARPANET (Comer, 2007, pp. 75–7). What was at one stage the exception is now very much the rule, and we have witnessed a relatively small group of companies take ownership of the most important aspects of the internet's infrastructure, increasingly working collaboratively with each other to carve out even greater autonomy away from the public sector (Tarnoff, 2016). With such a high degree of private ownership and little interest from these companies in restrictive regulation, the difficulty facing the public sector and NGOs (non-governmental organisations) to provide effective governance becomes apparent.

To date, governance tends to be dichotomised between two competing models – the nation state model and the global model (Van Eeten, 2017, p. 429).

The former of these is characterised by a 'heated debate' as to what part the state in particular should be playing in terms of governance (Shackelford and Craig, 2014, p. 119), while the latter recognises the diverse range of organisations, institutions, departments and individuals that have a stake in this domain (Herrington and Aldrich, 2013, pp. 300–3). An exclusively state-centric approach to cyber-governance may prove very difficult given the multiplicity of actors and interests, as well as problems states have had in protecting their own infrastructure and passing comprehensive cybersecurity legislation (Margulies, 2017, p. 466). A 'polycentric regime', however, that works with the private sector and the general public in a 'multilateral collaboration' could provide the coverage and stakeholder buy-in required (Shackelford and Craig, 2014, p. 184). This latter approach would have more in common with a Western model of multi-stakeholder governance as opposed to the multilateral, state-centric model more commonplace in the likes of Russia or China (Eichenseher, 2015, pp. 346–52) as well as more readily bringing international law to bear on these issues (Kettemann, 2017, p. 289).

Regardless on the model preferred, Van Eeten makes an important distinction between the governance literature and 'actual' governance, namely that the former is not to be conflated with the latter (Van Eeten, 2017, p. 431). He is particularly damning here of the way in which political scientists and international relations scholars have focused on international governance institutions ('an alphabet soup of acronyms') and equated this as governance on account of the standards and norms they devise. To use the author's own words: 'crudely put: anyone can make a standard' (2017, p. 431). Van Eeten highlights a potential shortcoming of the voluminous internet governance literature but on the issue of governance these problems might not insurmountable given that cyberspace is not unprecedented as a multi-stakeholder commons. As Eichenseher usefully reminds us, answers may be found when looking at parallels between cyberspace and governance of the high seas, outer space and Antarctica respectively (Eichenseher, 2015, pp. 336–45).

These sorts of debates quickly reveal the importance of the *private sector* as an integral partner in any multi-stakeholder governance model and the potential for a cooperative relationship with the state.[12] The subject of the private sector and its role in responding to cyber-threat is considered important on account of the critical infrastructure that is in the hands of private industry and which requires securing, just as government operated infrastructure does to avoid the potential for interference. The networked environment is so intertwined that even if it were the case that state-operated networks and infrastructures were able to be protected to the point of invulnerability, it would still leave many developed nations very exposed to hacks and cyber-attacks (Hiller and Russell, 2013, p. 234). To avoid this insecurity, 'industry and government must establish a genuine partnership', or, as Frank Cilluffo and Paul Pattak go on to say, 'in some way, we must introduce the "sandals" to the "wingtips"' (Cilluffo and Pattak, 2000, p. 50).

Lewis argues that the 1990s were a period characterised by an over-optimistic, laissez-faire attitude towards the private sector, whereby a lot of faith was put in the fact that the private sector could be given voluntary responsibility to secure networks and they would do it because it made good business sense (Lewis, 2005a, p. 824). However, 'defense and security are public goods ... the market will not supply them in sufficient quantity to meet a society's needs' (Lewis, 2005a, p. 827). Recent years have seen a much more proactive strategy proposed and adopted towards the private sector that shares many of the characteristics and approaches seen elsewhere in the development of sound cybersecurity, but also novel techniques designed specifically to encourage or enhance security in the private sector.

Preventative measures and critical infrastructure defence still have a significant part to play here, just as they do with military- and government-owned and operated networks. Precautions such as risk analysis (Vande Putte and Verhelst, 2013) isolating control systems from the internet (Brenner, 2013, p. 18) and enhancing training and expertise within businesses (Ionescu et al., 2011, p. 379) are all popular suggestions. In addition to this, the private sector is also afforded a more active role in the promotion of cyber-defence, with experts advocating for government to look *to* them for their innovation as opposed to expecting the solution to come from 'some musty Pentagon basement' (Rothkopf, 2002, p. 56). Jan Messerschmidt even considers the growing (and controversial) trend for private companies to take 'active defence' into their own hands through the practice of 'hackback' (Messerchmidt, 2014).

So, while there are standalone roles for the public and private sectors when it comes to tackling cyber-threats and responding to governance challenges, we should not lose sight of the collaboration. The specific form this collaboration takes is the subject of a significant focus and while 'public–private partnerships' are not unitary in form (Carr, 2016, pp. 54–7), they have been recognised for the positive function they are said to play in relation to aspects such as information sharing (Carr, 2016, p. 58; Christensen and Petersen, 2017, p. 1140) and informing 'best practices', regulations and norms (Clinton, 2015; Rishikof and Lunday, 2011; Sales, 2013). However, barriers continue to exist with these sorts of collaborations, first, with reference to those who argue that interference of any kind is not the answer and things should be left to the market and, second, that genuine collaboration is not what is currently being offered, with governments still adopting a 'compliance and control' mindset that means the private sector is 'reluctant to plan with government' (Quigley and Roy, 2012, pp. 91–2).

However, perhaps this is what it is going to take for businesses to realise the importance of enhancing their cybersecurity. A great many contributions in this discussion focus on cooperative security and sharing both information and the burden of defence, but Yang and Hoffstadt, at least, entertain the possibility of placing the burden of this problem on the private sector itself. They envision a system in which private industry fends for itself, where a 'victim-company would be forced to absorb the losses attributable to any computer intrusion or loss of intellectual property, thereby cutting into its net profitability' (Yang and Hoffstadt, 2006, p. 207). However, such a strategy is risky for government if it perceives defending private networks to be a particular priority. A more proactive strategy may entail incentives; modifying behaviour by government altering the cybersecurity equation to make improving security desirable or failing to secure painful (Bauer and van Eeten, 2009). As part of a comparative analysis between EU and US cybersecurity policies it was revealed that positive incentives have been a feature of EU policy in the form of certifications for voluntary compliance, while in the US a more punitive approach has been adopted that has given the Federal Trade Commission jurisdiction to enforce standards where data breaches have occurred (Hiller and Russell, 2013, p. 239–43).

Counterfactuals, hypotheticals and scepticism

In exploring these three organising themes a lot has been generated, but two primary things stand out. First, that cybersecurity knowledge tends to operate within the confines of a problem-solving national security discourse and, second, that it recognises cyber-threats as credible and is apprehensive of the risks they pose. However, neither of these findings are reflected universally across the entirety of this cybersecurity discourse and, in particular, two notable forms of 'dissident' knowledge are observable. In the first place, there are those accounts that broadly operate from the same ontological and epistemological position as that which we have already seen, but demonstrate a high degree of scepticism around the conclusions typically found here. A second body of dissident knowledge challenges the broadly objectivist ontological position, and the realist assumptions found therein, and adopts a more critical approach often premised on constructivist or post-structuralist positions. I want to consider both of these prior to concluding this chapter and will begin with 'sceptical realism' before moving onto the more radical divergence from conventional positions in the subsequent section.

We have seen that debate has tended to frame cyber-threats as novel, dangerous and credible; however, more sceptical accounts often highlight the reliance placed on counterfactuals and hypothetical scenarios when discussing risk. Consider the following excerpt:

> It's 4 a.m. on a sweltering summer night in July 2003. Across much of the United States, power plants are working full tilt to generate electricity for millions of air conditioners that are keeping a ferocious heat wave at bay. The electricity grid in California has repeatedly buckled under the strain, with rotating black-outs from San Diego to Santa Rosa. In different parts of the state, half a dozen small groups of men and women gather. Each travels in a rented minivan to its prearranged destination-for some, a location outside one of the hundreds of electrical substations dotting the state; for others, a spot upwind from key, high-voltage transmission lines. The groups unload their equipment from the vans. Those outside the substations put together simple mortars made from materials bought at local hardware stores, while those near the transmission lines use helium to inflate weather balloons with long silvery tails. At a precisely coordinated moment, the homemade mortars are fired, sending showers of aluminium chaff over the substations. The balloons are released and drift into transmission lines. (Homer-Dixon, 2002, pp. 52–3)

The level of detail in this scenario is such that one may assume the author is recounting an actual event but it is, in fact, entirely fictional. The threatening aspect of this scenario exists with reference to the hypothetical, potential and counterfactual futures. Homer-Dixon uses this example to stress that such scenarios may have at one point sounded far-fetched but in a post-September 11th world should no longer be viewed as such (Homer-Dixon, 2002, p. 53).

Nightmare scenarios, future predictions, technical possibilities presented as inevitable probabilities; all these elements replace more tangible examples of evidence in some of the accounts contained in the first part of this chapter. Whether it be a massive DDoS bringing down a government, the targeting of supervisory control and data acquisition (SCADA) systems to adversely impact the production of toxic chemicals or the flight paths of aircraft (Goodman *et al.*, 2007, pp. 199–200), the New York Stock Exchange going offline for a few days

(O'Brien, 2010, p. 197), malicious actors compromising or seizing a Chinese nuclear weapon (Grogan, 2009, p. 699), or future cyber-war scenarios (Kelsey, 2008, pp. 1434–46), these sorts of tactics are not uncommon when assessing threat. The rationale for this anxiety is partly premised on risky potential futures: 'ultimately … cyberthreats are dangerous not because of what they have (or have not) done to date, but precisely, because they threaten to generate serious impacts in the future' (Hollis, 2011, p. 382).

Consider how Chad Parks links a real and vivid moment from recent history to the potential for cyber catastrophe, arguing that the absence of something does not mean the threat does not exist: 'It is true that America has never suffered consequences of a true cyber terrorist attack, yet. On September 10, 2001, it was also true that no organized terrorist group had ever hijacked four airplanes, crashed two into the World Trade Center, one into the Pentagon, and one in a field in Pennsylvania, killing over three thousand Americans' (Parks, 2003, p. 11). Similarly, when discussing the lack of substantive examples of cyber-terrorism as a reason to not prioritise this particular threat, Desouza and Hensgen write, '[…] it is likely the Japanese presented the same argument as they prepared, despite forewarning, to meet an expected Allied amphibious invasion in August 1945 while neglecting the defense of facilities located at Hiroshima and Nagasaki' (Desouza and Hensgen, 2003, p. 395).

Risky futures premised on hypothetical assertions have come under scrutiny though, with criticism lamenting the narrative about cyber-risks that has come to be 'dominated by competing expert claims, alongside a media prone to inflate cyber risks' the cumulative effect of which culminates in 'exaggerating claims about the frequency and scale of the attack' (Guinchard, 2011, pp. 76–7; Hughes and DeLone, 2007, p. 82). Talking specifically in relation to cyber-terrorism, there exists 'considerable disagreement' regarding the 'extent to which this phenomenon poses a security threat' (Jarvis et al., 2014, p. 83), with Roland Heickerö dichotomising this distinction between those who view the threats as 'real and considerable' and those who consider there to be 'no threat at all or only a very limited one' (Heickerö, 2014, p. 555). Clearly, 'computer viruses and other types of malware have been widely touted, by the media, the government, and others' (Hughes and DeLone, 2007, p. 92); however, this should not obscure the heterogeneity that does exist and a 'growing chorus of voices criticizes this position for being based on an irrational fear of what often turns out to pose little to no real threat' (Hughes and DeLone, 2007, p. 92).

This knowledge, while contrasting with the typical conclusions of the orthodoxy, rarely goes as far as to question their existence as security threats but instead questions the alarmist nature of commonplace assessments. For example, Evan Kohlman argues that the US Government has mishandled cyber-terrorism, heeding too much of the 'doom-and-gloom predictions that cyberterrorists would wreak havoc on the Internet' provided by 'a host of pundits and supposed experts', while simultaneously leading policymakers 'to overlook the fact that terrorists currently use the Internet as a cheap and efficient way of communicating and organizing' (Kohlmann, 2006, pp. 115–16). Whether or not we consider this kind of thing cyber-terrorism or criminal activity orchestrated by terrorists, it is clearly not the same as 'cyber-attack' targeted at critical infrastructure and it alludes to the character of this critique: that the commonplace assessment has a tendency for the sensational at the expense of the 'reality'.

Cyber-terrorism provides the most contentious example in this regard, with disagreement around terrorists' motivation and capability to launch a devastating attack against CNI. Lewis argues that 'the internet is not a weapon that appeals to terrorists' (Lewis, 2005b, p. 1), something reinforced by cost benefit analysis in 2007 and 2015 (Giacomello, 2007; Al-Garni and Chen, 2015). All of these authors are of the belief that breaking things and killing people remain the most viable and likely to succeed options for terrorists (Giacomello, 2007, p. 388; Denning, 2001b, p. 70). If the lack of clear examples of cyber-terrorism cannot be explained on account of motivation, Michael Stohl concludes that it must be the case that they remain incapable of mounting a sufficiently destructive attack (Stohl, 2006, p. 236). The main takeaway from this commentary is that the potential danger of cyber-terrorism and cybersecurity more generally has been 'overblown and misdirected' (Conway, 2014; Podesta and Goyle, 2005, p. 517; Weimann, 2005, p. 131).

Similar conclusions are drawn in relation to cyber-war (McGraw, 2013, p. 111; Nye, 2013, p. 10). Thomas Rid's conclusions on this point are some of the most explicit in this regard: '[…] cyber war has never happened in the past. Cyber war does not take place in the present. And it is highly unlikely that cyber war will occur in the future' (Rid, 2012, p. 6). Calling events such as those that occurred in Estonia in 2007 'Web War One' are inaccurate, as they 'do not contain the political and violent characterizers of war' (Eun and Aßmann, 2015, p. 12). In fact, according to Rid, the opposite of cyber-war is taking place; violence is becoming less and less in the face of increased, non-violent cyber-attacks (Rid, 2013, p. 142). Related studies that have sought to establish the level of international cyber-conflict have concluded that there is 'little evidence of cyber conflict in the modern era … states will not risk war with their cyber capabilities because there are clear consequences to any use of these technologies' (Valeriano and Maness, 2014, p. 357).

The constructivist turn and constructivist cybersecurity

The second body of dissident cybersecurity knowledge adopts a constructivist approach. The 'constructivist turn' in international relations (IR) (Checkel, 1998) emerged in the 1980s and tends to be associated with the end of the Cold War and the failure of established theories to account for this major event (Theys, 2017, p. 36). Constructivism is concerned with the role that ideas play in IR alongside the material factors and 'physical forces' that tend to take priority in the more established IR approaches. Constructivism, therefore, tends to view the world and what we can know about it as socially constructed (Onuf, 1989) and rejects the notion that the social world can be explained in the same way as the physical world.[13] While constructivism distinguishes itself from post-structuralism insofar as it does not argue that there *is no extra-discursive realm* (Marsh, 2009, p. 680), different constructivist authors differ in terms of their prioritisation of material factors and causal logics (thin constructivism) or ideational factors and constitutive logics (thick constructivism) (Hay, 2002, p. 206). Across this spectrum of thin and thick constructivist IR, both positivist and interpretivist epistemologies are evident (Farrell, 2002, p. 59).

Constructivist IR has provided a powerful critique of core assumptions of 'rationalist' approaches and disputes the 'reality' of organising principles, such as anarchy, as a feature of the international system (Wendt, 1992, 1999). Where realists and neorealists (Morgenthau, 1960; Waltz, 1979; Mearsheimer, 2014) have sought to explain international politics in relation to the agency of rational state actors in the context of an anarchic international structure and thus view states as responding to external forces, constructivism believes that 'International Relations consists primarily of social facts, which are facts only by human agreement' (Adler, 1997, p. 322). The founding logic of constructivism then is *constitutivity*, which 'entails a commitment to theorising the particular, the contingent, the historically situated' (Epstein, 2013, p. 501) and to identify, understand and unpack the construction of international politics through an exploration of social factors, including, but not limited to, norms, culture, identity, time, language and discourse.

Stevens, a prominent proponent of the need to bring greater theoretical and methodological diversity to the study of cybersecurity laments that to date 'the struggle to regulate and govern this complex landscape is mirrored by a lack of diversity in the theory and methods' (Stevens, 2018, p. 1). As indicated in this assessment, and as we have already seen in this chapter, cybersecurity studies remains overwhelmingly problem solving and policy orientated in nature (McCarthy, 2018, p. 5). However, while Steven's assessment is accurate, such critiques also allude to the frustration with this state of affairs and the spaces in which a broadly constructivist impetus has developed that has usefully expanded the narrow confines of the cybersecurity research agenda. Constructivist cybersecurity research represents a second site of dissident knowledge that, contrary to the sceptical realism covered above, adopts a more radical position that eschews the objectivist realist research agenda.

Myriam Dunn Cavelty's seminal text *Cyber-Security and Threat Politics* (2008) provides an early and influential use of the constructivist approach in which the author addresses important overarching questions around the relationship between cybersecurity and national security and the effect of discursive renderings and representations. Continuing in this vein, a later piece by the author captures what I argue remains one of the most important issues within cybersecurity research and a central motivation within the constructivist cybersecurity agenda. Dunn Cavelty writes that 'the link between cyberspace and national security is often presented as an un-questionable and uncontested "truth". However, there is nothing natural or given about this link: it had to be forged, argued, and accepted in the (security) political process' (Dunn Cavelty, 2013, p. 105).

As is correctly pointed out here, the conflation between national security and cybersecurity is not a given but it is one underwritten by a powerful constitutive logic. Moreover, such an understanding leaves cybersecurity 'thin … [and] emptied of substantive content' (McCarthy, 2018, p. 8). The construction of cybersecurity as an extension of national security should therefore be a priority, in particular given what these representations allow. However, alongside particular representations we must also seek to better understand the forging process itself. Both of these are areas that can be usefully addressed by using theoretical and methodological approaches that take us beyond the orthodox problem-solving framework. Consequently, we have seen a body of constructivist research develop that has paid attention to the discursive and non-discursive construction of cyber-threats (Stevens, 2018, p. 2) to add value to existing research by asking alternative research questions informed by alternative ontological, epistemological and methodological assumptions and avoiding some of the common stumbling blocks of realist research (Jarvis *et al.*, 2014).

A popular strand of this alternative agenda concentrates upon how risk and threat in cyberspace have been discursively constructed and the impact these constructions have upon comprehension and/or response (Conway, 2008; Jarvis *et al.*, 2015; Stevens, 2016). In some instances, this is considered alongside the process of securitisation as a means of conveying how particular phenomenon have been taken 'above politics' in such a manner that these representations are at odds with their 'reality' (Dunn Cavelty, 2008, 2013; Hansen and Nissenbaum, 2009). The apprehensive tone of many assessments of risk in cyberspace are often the focus here, especially where they deploy hypothetical 'nightmare scenarios' to communicate this (Weimann, 2006, p. 151). When looking to deconstruct these depictions of threat it is argued that 'the constant drumbeat of cyber-doom scenarios encourages the adoption of counterproductive policies focused on control, militarization, and centralization' (Lawson, 2013, p. 87; see also Lawson, 2012, n.p.) In such a context, other authors have sought to posit alternative frames, such as a global commons, in an effort to reframe (and presumably desecuritise) the space, accentuating its openness over its inherent vulnerability (Hart *et al.*, 2014, p. 2862).

Characteristic in all of this research, where the delimitation of (in)security is the focus and where particular constructions of threat are investigated, is the discursive tactics utilised to achieve particular ends. In this more specific endeavour, a particular focus has been put upon the role of metaphor and analogy in helping to translate the often complex and unfamiliar aspects of information technology and computer networks into a more familiar security context (Betz and Stevens, 2013; Lawson, 2012). While this linguistic trope is sometimes used to liken the threats themselves to other phenomena, this form of reasoning also extends to the environment in a manner that, as has been argued, plays a very important role in policy preference (Osenga, 2013).

In one such example Julie Cohen problematises the popular construction of cyberspace as a separate and distinct space given its failure to recognise the manner in which cyberspace is an extension of 'everyday spatial practice' (Cohen, 2007, p. 213). More than just providing a truer reflection of the spatiality of cyberspace, Cohen asserts that challenging this metaphor will allow for a better understanding of the 'architectural and regulatory challenges' the domain presents (Cohen, 2007, p. 210). Approaches such as these have been used to challenge the assumptions around seemingly fixed, 'intrinsic characteristics of cyberspace' and the impact that their presumed empirical status has on our ability to attain certain strategic outcomes – for example, deterrence in cyberspace (Lupovici, 2016, p. 322). The importance of the sorts of metaphor analysis carried out here by the likes of Cohen and Lupovici is that it reveals how intuitive but often limited or simplified forms of reasoning can have powerful constitute effects and consequently frame how we approach, evaluate and attempt to 'resolve' issues. Whether it is the regulatory challenges Cohen talks about or cyber-deterrence as talked about by Lupovici, constructions of cyberspace have tangible effects.

Sitting alongside the discursive analysis, deconstructions and metaphor analysis covered above, this alternative research agenda also brings to bear theorising around risk and governmentality (Deibert and Rohozinski, 2010; Barnard-Wills and Ashenden, 2012) as well as explorations of the cybersecurity *dispositif* (Aradau, 2010a, 2010b). For example, in a study that eschews policy relevance, Barnard-Wills and Ashenden utilise the Foucauldian notion of governmentality to make sense of, and explain how, cyberspace has been constructed as 'ungovernable, unknowable, a cause of vulnerability, inevitably threatening, and a home to threatening actors' (Barnard-Wills and Ashenden, 2012, p. 110). As we will see in the next chapter, governmentality is an expression of power concerned with the management and organisation of things and people and thus just as pressing here as establishing 'How has this occurred?' is that of 'Whose interest does it serve?' (Vegh, 2002, n.p.).

The path forwards

It is with the constructivist research contained in the previous section that my own research finds common theoretical ground and where I situate this study. However, while this constructivist research is important in and of itself, I argue that it has elevated value given the dominant body of knowledge that it responds to. Indeed, the main focus of this chapter has been to review the overwhelmingly 'problem-solving' literature that has set cybersecurity studies in a familiar realist framework, whereby questions of definition, threat and response are prioritised and where a conflation between cybersecurity and national security has been achieved.

This latter point is of particular note because while dominant cybersecurity knowledge is not entirely homogenous, it does tend to approach the issue in a manner that builds straightforwardly upon a familiar 'national security' discourse (Mueller, 2017, p. 419). Questions of definition, assessment and response dominate, and while novel specificities are evident that reflect cybersecurity's own particularities, the research questions and the agenda broadly emanate from long-standing and widely held positions. Discussion as to how terms should be defined 'best' or how anxious we should be about various different threats implies an understanding that both of these things can be accurately captured within our labels. Cyber-threats are therefore taken as objects of knowledge, the implication being (as Jackson *et al.* write about terrorism) that 'truths' about cyber-threats can be revealed through the 'gradual uncovering of scientific facts through careful observation' (Jackson *et al.*, 2011, p. 103).

The culmination of this approach is one where the cybersecurity produced is one *of* cyberspace, namely, of defending objects against malicious acts and actors. This construction purports to present an apolitical environment where cyberspace is protected against threat in a manner that benefits all. However, as Dunn Cavelty reminds us, while this understanding appears to 'sidestep politics almost completely', it is 'quite obviously very much in its grip' (Dunn Cavelty, 2018, p. 24). Significantly, this contingent construction of cybersecurity frames it as a neutral issue that 'sustains a specific kind of apolitical materiality' and provides the conditions upon which security practices can operate (Dunn Cavelty, 2018, p. 24). Cybersecurity becomes about the straightforward and intuitive process of defending or fixing broken things; however, what this conceals is the manner in which 'the materialisations of objects to be protected also inter-act with materialities of economic and geopolitical structures' (Aradau, 2010a, p. 509). As both Dunn Cavelty and Aradau allude to here, security in this instance is far from politically neutral but, rather, 'security' is instead an effort to 'govern through security' (Lippert *et al.*, 2016, n.p.). Indeed, given the strong attachment that has been formed between cybersecurity and national security, the role of the state as guarantor and 'fixer' is often a natural conclusion which, in turn, informs the sorts of approaches designed to provide security.

It is at this juncture that constructivist approaches demonstrate their primary value: their ability to expose the power relations contained within these seemingly neutral readings. There are fundamental questions of ontology and epistemology at the heart of cybersecurity studies that are not properly addressed, even at the more sceptical end of the orthodoxy. By eschewing the problem-solving orientation of the orthodox agenda, constructivist research is able to highlight alternative considerations and expose the limitations and assumptions of conventional knowledge. Cybersecurity has overwhelmingly been conflated with national security and yet the constructivist research agenda reminds us of the contingent nature of this knowledge as well as revealing what it makes possible and what it precludes. My interests lie with both these aspects and places its focus squarely on expert knowledge in an attempt to answer these questions.

With the express intention of seeking to highlight the manner with which private-sector expert knowledge has contributed to the production of cybersecurity and the construction of particular cyber-threats, my study provides a further contribution to the constructivist research agenda. I endeavour to highlight the assumptions inherent within this entrenched cyber-(national) security, demonstrate how this knowledge serves to support a neoliberal governmentality and explore the communities of mutual recognition that have formed between professionals of security and politics. However, before I can begin with my empirical analysis of private-sector internet security expertise which makes up my focus, I will first consider in greater detail the theoretical tools I use to make this analysis possible. In the next chapter I will outline the specific theoretical positions adopted, elaborate upon a series of important concepts that are vital to the study and explain the specific way in which these are conceptualised and operationalised to achieve my stated objectives.

Chapter 2

Security *dispositifs* and security professionals

In the previous chapter I provided a detailed overview of the characteristics of current cybersecurity knowledge and in doing so identified some of limitations that lay within large sections of the research, while also arguing for the value of the constructivist cybersecurity agenda. What will follow in subsequent chapters is a Foucauldian-inspired constructivist analysis of the expert knowledge produced by private-sector internet security companies and its impact upon the constitution of the sorts of assumptions highlighted in the previous chapter. However, prior to going on to conduct this analysis my study is at a critical juncture whereby the particularities of the approach that will be adopted require further elaboration and exploration. With this in mind, Chapter 2 will outline the theoretical toolkit utilised herein to conduct the analysis and, ultimately, to achieve the stated objectives of the book. Of critical importance to the analysis that follows is further theoretical reflection upon power, the functioning of security, the role of expertise and the significance of epistemic security communities and security professionals.

The chapter will proceed by outlining the Foucauldian model of power, distinguishing between three important modalities before honing in on the modality of most relevance to this study – *governmentality*. Second, the chapter will reflect on security and the role security *dispositifs* play in allowing governmentality to function within society. Third, the chapter will move on to the powerful constitutive and enabling function of expertise and expert knowledge and its ability to elevate particular knowledges to the status of truth or science. Fourth, the chapter will reflect on the industry that makes up the focus of this study by exploring the prevalence of embedded experts within private companies, such as those that make up the focus of my empirical analysis. Finally, the chapter will offer reflections on methodology and method and address some questions that present when conducting a Foucauldian-inspired discourse analysis as I have here.

We begin, then, with power and security, both essentially contested concepts and concepts of importance across the social sciences. Given the centrality of these concepts, a tremendous amount of dedicated theoretical work already exists that my references here will not do justice to (Dahl, 1957; Holsti, 1964; Hay, 1997; Lukes, 2005; Guzzini, 2005; Walt, 1991; Baldwin, 1997; Buzan *et al.*, 1997). It is not the intention of this chapter to try and capture all of this theorisation, but rather to elaborate upon the specific conceptualisation that I will be utilising in this analysis and explain why I feel such an approach can provide another viable avenue for constructivist cybersecurity research that moves it outside of its largely orthodox confines. This book proceeds with a Foucauldian understanding of power and therefore recognises the inextricable relationship between power and knowledge, as well as the functioning and role of the security *dispositifs* within society.

Power/knowledge and governmentality

In Stephen Lukes' (2005) influential study on power, he distinguishes between three 'views' of power. The first view represents the most straightforward account and approaches the concept as something 'negative' that dominates and restricts and that functions in a linear fashion between different but clearly defined actors. Robert Dahl's theory of power, where power is understood as the capacity to which A can get B to do something that B would otherwise not do is a notable and seminal example of such an approach (Dahl, 1957, pp. 202–3). Lukes cites Bachrach and Baratz (1970) to discuss a second view of power that reveals not only the power relations that exist when A makes decisions that directly affect B, but also the ability for A to direct their energy into limiting the scope of B's actions to those that either correspond with A's or are 'comparatively innocuous to A' (p. 7). The final and most complex view Lukes speaks of critiques the behavioural focus of the first and second and hones in on the ability to control the political agenda (not necessarily via a formal decisions) and manage a population's 'perceptions, cognitions and preferences in such a way that they accept their role in the existing order of things' (Lukes, 2005, p. 28).

By means of introduction each of these different views gives some idea of the variance that exists around theorisations of power. Pigeonholing Foucault's theory of power (and its various modalities) into any one of these three would prove difficult but serves at the very least to give some context to the radical position he adopts whereby power is understood not as something that exclusively conceals, represses or censors but is instead *productive*, it 'produces reality; it produces domains of objects and rituals of truth' (Foucault, 1977, p. 194). Most importantly, power produces knowledge; knowledge is always the product of power and power always the function of knowledge, hence the tendency to refer to the joint concept *power/knowledge*. As a consequence of this relationship, multiple different forms of knowledge are 'manufactured and circulated by an institutional matrix, involving the state, politicians, security experts and the media' (Mythen and Walklate, 2006, p. 389).

Moreover, power is not centralised or enacted in a direct and linear manner that is capable of being easily captured in straightforward 'power equations' but instead is diffuse, operating via 'capillary functioning' (Foucault, 1977, 198) whereby power 'circulates throughout the entire social body' (Fraser, 1981, p. 278) across a historically informed societal grid, flowing back and forth between a vast series of elements. One ramification of this model is that power is not something that can be wholly and precisely 'wielded' as such, rather power is a 'machine in which everyone is caught' and given the multiplicity of power relations across society, it is never 'wholly in the hands of one person' (Foucault, 1980a, p. 156). The back and forth capillary action that characterises this understanding of how power operates within society reveals a much more complex and apparently chaotic process. However, the complexity of power relations within society is not chaotic in the sense of being without *any* structure, logic or focal points and to acquire a greater sense of the workings of power and how it operates, one needs to delve deeper into the Foucauldian 'toolbox' in particular with reference to different forms of power (Foucault, 2001, p. 1391).

Power has not operated in the same way throughout history, nor does it operate in a uniform manner within society today. Foucault outlines three modalities of power: sovereign, disciplinary and governmental. Sovereign power (or judicial/legal power) is the most overt manifestation of the three modalities and works in quite a familiar manner by 'laying down a law and fixing a punishment for the person who breaks it' (Foucault, 2007, p. 5). This form of power operates within territorial borders and says to actors 'don't do this, don't do that', controlling those actors through punishment (Foucault, 2007, p. 11). Sovereign power therefore is *prohibitive*. Disciplinary power is less overt and differs from its sovereign counterpart by instead operating within localised spaces and on the bodies of the worker, the culprit or the patient.

Rather than prohibiting in relation to a legal code, disciplinary power is *prescriptive* and controls through instruction as to what you should be doing at all times. Disciplinary power operates through a series of techniques 'which fall within the domain of surveillance, diagnosis, and the possible transformation of individuals' (Foucault, 2007, p. 5). Correspondingly, these techniques sit adjacent to the law and notably manifest themselves in penal, medical and psychological practices.

Finally, there is the 'pre-eminent form of power', that of government (Foucault, 2007, p. 108). The art of government or *governmentality* operates very differently again to these other two modalities. Governmentality is the 'conduct of conduct' and, having the population as its target, seeks to structure 'the field of possible action, to act on our own or others' capacities for action' (Dean, 1994, p. 14) via 'an ensemble formed by institutions, procedures, analyses and reflections, calculations, and tactics' (Foucault, 2007, p. 108). Government does not spell the end for sovereign or disciplinary power, indeed it grants both renewed relevance. However, singling out governmental power as 'a very specific albeit, very complex' form of power (Foucault, 2007, p. 108) and understanding why this modality has been distinguished in this manner is very important to understand its 'pre-eminence' and centrality in this study.

The complexity of governmentality stems from the fact that it does not take as its unit of affection the individual, or a group within a fixed and prescribed space, but instead a *population*, 'a multiplicity of individuals who are and fundamentally and essentially only exist biologically bound to the materiality within which they live' (Foucault, 2007, p. 21). Governmentality looks to manage 'things', rather than exclusively focusing on a geographical demarked space such as the borders of the state or the individual within a proscribed, localised space. Governmental power is tasked with managing a whole nexus of interactions between people and their relationships to a vast and daunting array of phenomena that could include wealth, family, customs and mortality (Foucault, 2007, p. 96). The purpose of governmental power, then, is far broader in scope than the other modalities and begs the question of how such a broad remit can be reasonably affected. The key to appreciating how this is possible is to understand that governing is not a synonym for ruling, commanding or controlling (Foucault, 2007, p. 116), but is more accurately thought of as a form of management or regulation. Rather than command or control, we instead witness the receding of rules in place of a multiplicity of tactics designed to allow for some management of the population (Foucault, 2007, p. 99).

The complexity of this modality of power is evident when one considers the objective of management in a domain fraught with such a wide array of relations and interactions, all with their corresponding variables and uncertainties. Government is tasked with managing 'a space in which a series of uncertain elements unfold … [it must] … plan a *milieu* in terms of events or series of events of possible elements, of series that will have to be regulated within a multivalent and transformable framework' (Foucault, 2007, p. 20, emphasis added). Clearly, the management of the milieu is quite a different remit and thus will require different techniques and apparatus to other modalities but crucially it also looks to achieve very different ends. Governmentality seeks to guarantee circulation (Foucault, 2007, p. 21) as opposed to fix or impose it; to effectively manage the milieu, government in fact intends to 'let things happen' (Foucault, 2007, p. 45) rather than to *control* every aspect.

In this endeavour, governmentality operates from a much more ambitious starting point and aims to manage and regulate the population through the manipulation of seemingly remote factors (Foucault, 2007, p. 72). It achieves this 'either directly through large scale campaigns, or indirectly through techniques that will make possible, without the full awareness of the people' (Foucault 1991, p. 100). Governmentality allows an important eschewing of power relations from modalities that have traditionally said 'no', or that have been prescriptive, to one in which the answer is 'yes' – within established limits of acceptability. This modality of power, therefore, is a central feature of the dominant ideology of modern capital: neoliberalism.

Ambiguity around what is meant by neoliberalism abounds (Flew, 2014), but Harvey, in his seminal contribution, defines it as 'a theory of political economic practices that proposes that human wellbeing can best be advanced by liberating individual entrepreneurial freedoms and skills within an institutional framework characterised by strong property rights, free markets and free trade' (Harvey, 2005, p. 2). Governmentality serves as a principle feature herein that allows for the management of populations insofar as to allow for continued circulation within society that maintains the conditions required for the preservation of neoliberalism. With modern developed society having adopted the network as a central organising principle (Harknett, 2003, p. 18) and globalisation having pushed these networks further and wider, the importance of *computer networks* and, in particular, the internet, in allowing unprecedented circulation and indeed governance to promote and maintain the principles of neoliberalism, cannot be understated.

Allowing for this circulation requires the delimitation of that which is danger-ous or not and rather than this being plucked from thin air, it is instead the product of a politics of knowledge that comes about through the security *disposi-tif* and is subsequently acted upon by it; in so doing, maintaining the very power relations that produced it (Foucault, 1980b p. 194). By defining 'threats to human life as its most basic operation', the security *dispositif* considers the human in *biopolitical* terms (De Larrinaga and Doucet, 2008, p. 528) and aids in the biopo-litical endeavour of management by fabricating, organising and planning the milieu (Foucault, 2007, p. 21), 'not so much establishing limits and frontiers, or fixing locations, as, above all and essentially, making possible, guaranteeing, and ensuring circulations' (Foucault, 2007, p. 29). We have already begun to discuss here the significance of security in understanding the functioning of govern-mentality as well as the role of the security *dispositif*. In the next section I will provide further explanation of both of these things as a means of adequately explaining how the ambition of governmentality is realised.

Security and the security *dispositif*

If governmental power aims to 'let things happen', to allow circulation and ultimately to manage the population to achieve this, then the security *dispositif* is the apparatus by which this can be achieved. Pinning down specifically what it refers to is not straightforward, but in an oft-quoted excerpt from an inter-view entitled 'confessions of the flesh', Foucault clarifies the following about the dispositif:

> What I'm trying to pick out with this term is, firstly, a thoroughly heterogeneous ensemble consisting of discourses, institutions, architectural forms, regulatory decisions, laws, administrative measures, scientific statements, philosophical, moral and philanthropic propositions – in short, the said as much as the unsaid. Such are the elements of the apparatus. The apparatus itself is the system of relations that can be established between these elements. (Foucault, 1980b, p. 194)

So we are talking about a network that operates within and across societies and that brings together a diverse range of elements, some of which are iden-tified above, into a common network (Rabinow and Rose, 2003, p. 10). This common network serves an important productive function and is the matrix through which knowledge and power are co-produced (Silva-Castañeda and Trussart, 2016, p. 492). The *dispositif* generates collective understandings of what constitutes truth, common sense and objectivity (Deleuze, 1988), as well as the techniques for discovering and validating these qualities. The relationship between the modality of government and the security *dispositif* is fundamental, then, as the latter will produce the conditions within which particular knowledge claims and practices can be authenticated.

The interaction between these different elements and the 'direction' of this network provides some explanation as to how the capillary functioning of power operates within society, but as Raffnsøe *et al.* (2014) clarify, 'even though the dispositive is 'something', it is not a 'thing'' (p. 10). By this the authors are alluding to the fact that the *dispositif* exists, plays an integral role in the functioning of power/knowledge and *is* identifiable (albeit not precisely) but is a never a fixed or 'fully formed' unitary phenomenon. For one thing, there are multiple *dispositifs* co-existing alongside one another, some of which have had greater prominence at different points in history and the elements that constitute the network shift and change across space and time. Different lines of power (Deleuze, 1992, p. 165) operate within the *dispositif*, those of sedimentation (that stabilise and bring objects into order) and creativity (that modify and create new formalised knowledge). These two features explain the identification of specific, seemingly homogenous *dispositifs* as well as the latent ability for transformation. Perhaps it was this state of flux and capacity for change that led Foucault to place the emphasis on 'precisely the nature of the connection that can exist between these heterogeneous elements' (Foucault, 1980b, p. 194) and why he was more interested in the arrangement of the elements rather than the specific designated 'sources' within the network (Bussolini, 2010, p. 91). The above covers some generalities of the *dispositif*, but Foucault's specific theorising around security and the operation of the security *dispositif* provides further specific clarification around how this network functions to serve the circulation that characterises governmental power.

Security is a concept that is characterised as getting 'erratic' treatment (Spieker, 2011, p. 190) in Foucault's 1975–76 lectures *Society Must Be Defended* (Foucault, 2004) and in the 1977–78 *Security, Territory, Population* series (Foucault, 2007), where Dider Bigo remarks that Foucault 'did not succeed in thinking out the logics of the functioning and transformation of security' (Bigo, 2011, p. 94). Nevertheless, it is largely from these series of lectures and the secondary literature that surrounds them that we can gain insight into how Foucault conceptualised security and the security *dispositif* and how the latter worked in relation to governmentality.

Contrary to a more orthodox linkage between security and the logic of exception, Foucault considers security to be about normalisation, about establishing statistical distributions across society and defining the actions and behaviours of the majority as the state of security while characterising the margins as abnormal. Using the example of theft, Foucault clarifies how security is 'established' and also alludes to the operation of the security dispositif:

> the apparatus of security inserts the phenomenon in question, namely theft, within a series of probable events. Second, the reactions of power to this phenomenon are inserted in a calculation of cost. Finally, third, instead of a binary division between the permitted and the prohibited, one establishes an average considered as optimal on the one hand, and, on the other, a bandwidth of the acceptable that must not be exceeded. (Foucault, 2007, p. 6)

There are inherent dangers in circulation; the security *dispositif* seeks to soften these sharp edges and bring any 'outliers' in line with that which is normal to sufficiently reduce risk and allow for productive circulation. Security 'starts from cases, from their statistical distribution, from the differential risks posed by each case, from the probabilities of their occurrence and it determines whether they are more or less dangerous, whether they have a greater or lesser chance of occurring in reality' (Bigo, 2011, p. 99).

Security, then, is the practice of the majority, while 'insecurity' is 'defined as that which was deviant, rare, that which was on the margins of classified practices' (Bigo, 2011, p. 103). The security *dispositif* is the assemblage that establishes the normal, defines the abnormal and intervenes upon the latter for upsetting the security of the majority. Governmentality, therefore, is viewed as a feature of liberalism and security is understood as a *result* of the free movement of people and things that is central to the coherence of that broader project:

> if we agree to see in liberalism a new art of governing and governing each other — not a new economic or juridical doctrine — if it really amounts to a technique of governmentality that aims to consume liberties, and by virtue of this, manage and organize them, then the conditions of possibility for acceding to liberty depend on manipulating the interests that engage the security strategies destined to ward off the dangers inherent to the manufacture of liberty, where the constraints, controls, mechanisms or surveillance that play themselves out in disciplinary techniques charged with investing themselves in the behaviour of individuals ... from that point on the idea that living dangerously must be considered as the very currency of liberalism. (Foucault as translated in Bigo, 2008, p. 45)

As a 'strategical effect of specific relations of power, knowledge, and subjectivity' (Wichum, 2013, p. 165), security produces the categories of risk and danger via disassociation with the majority and, subsequently, through the construction of 'risk knowledge', it renders actions and subjects 'pre-emptively governable' (Heath-Kelly, 2013, p. 395). While security applies across the population, it is only actually the margins of this unit that are viewed as risky, dangerous and insecure and only upon these 'abnormalities' that intervention occurs in spaces where circulation is threatened. Achieving this requires that the security *dispositif* projects into the future, making 'a fantasy of homogeneity' (Bigo, 2011, p. 109) and mitigating against the 'uncertain, unpredictable events that might never happen but are always possible' (Wichum, 2013, p. 167).

The fantasy Bigo talks of is one where the insecurity of the margins is rendered obsolete via the deployment of the security *dispositif* – an impossibility because the creation of the category of security necessitates the production of insecurity. The margin is a product of the main. However, insecurity *is* communicated to the population via the complex network of the security *dispositif*, defined in the contemporary era as one of 'precautionary risk' (Aradau and Van Munster, 2007, p. 103) that operates as part of a general governmentality of unease and anxiety (Bigo, 2002; Huysmans and Buonfino, 2008; Skilling, 2014) citing risks 'now associated with a worst-case scenario beyond any calculus of probability' (Bigo 2011, p. 113). These apocalyptic uncertainties see the reintroduction of logics of exception that threaten the way of life and the circulation that is imposed upon the populations, while also providing the justification for sovereign and disciplinary interventions.

We have already discussed the notion of power as a machine in which no one person or group is ever fully in control, and so it is important to stress here that while certain actors operate from positions of greater influence this model does not require us to think in terms of a shadowy puppet master deploying the security *dispositif* instrumentally and precisely as part a campaign of fear designed to realise certain agendas. Rather, it requires us to recognise the role of facilitating conditions (Buzan, Wæver and de Wilde, 1997, pp. 35–42) and the enhanced capital of various actors in different contexts that provide them with a position 'from where to speak with authority' (Bourdieu, 2004, p. 34). In the study that follows over the subsequent chapters, I focus on a specific group of actors – private-sector internet security experts – that, I argue, operate as part of the security dispositif and are imbued with a unique productive function in relation to cyber-threats. Having started broadly with power/ knowledge and drilled down through governmentality and the security *dispositif*, I will now move on to consider the role of epistemic communities within the security *dispositif* and the expert knowledge produced by security professionals as a means of explaining the focus of the empirical research that follows and my rationale for this. As previously mentioned, Foucault himself was more interested in the arrangement of the *dispositif* than he was the specific 'sources' within it (Bussolini, 2010, p. 91), so here I diverge in my desire to focus specifically on one of these very sources.

Security expertise and the internet security industry

Applying the theoretical tools laid out so far in this chapter to the overview of orthodox cybersecurity knowledge provided in Chapter 2 allows for some alternative theorising as to the characteristics and features of this knowledge. Rather than viewing this knowledge as a reflection of the reality of cybersecurity, we begin to see one theoretical path towards a constructivist position whereby cybersecurity knowledge is the product of power relations formed via discursive and non-discursive practices that constitute the objects they purport to reflect. As accentuated in the previous section, the role of the security *dispositif* in the process is particularly important insofar as it categorises (in) security, determines and assesses risk and intervenes upon different spaces in relation to specific cases as a means of regulation.

The heterogeneous ensemble that is the *dispositif* is a network made up of many sources and while power is 'a machine in which everyone is caught' (Foucault, 1980a, p. 156), this is not the same as saying that every source occupies the *same* position vis-à-vis power, indeed: '[…] certain positions, preponderate and permit an effect of supremacy to be produced' (Foucault, 1980a, p. 156). Power and knowledge are inextricably linked; however, the network is not one of symmetrical distribution, and different individuals and groups exist in different arrangements in relation to other sources (these arrangements are themselves subject to lines of sedimentation and creativity). Consequently, not all sources have equal ability to produce knowledge; in other words, we do not have equal access to the machine's controls. To talk of *complete* 'control' or mastery of this process is always a fallacy because there will always be unintended consequences of power and power/knowledge is always connected via the multifarious sources of the *dispositif*. However, those sources with 'enhanced epistemic credibility' around a specific object are able to better employ *tactics* of power, understood as the 'intentional actions carried out in determinate political contexts' (Heller, 1996, p. 87). To take this out of the abstract and place it in a more tangible context, I will return to the subject matter of cybersecurity and talk specifically about the role of security expertise that will be the focus of this study.

Dunn Cavelty writes that there is nothing 'natural or given' about the link between cyberspace and national security and it had to be 'forged, argued, and accepted in the political process' (Dunn Cavelty, 2013, p. 105). I would add to this that the framing of cybersecurity as an extension of the national security discourse has come about via the categorisations of (in)security in this domain that identifies 'security' and 'insecurity' in cyberspace as broadly synonymous with (realist) security in 'physical space'. The link between cyberspace and national security that Dunn-Cavelty refers to is the result of the ebb and flow of the security *dispositif*, but the situation we find ourselves in today (the make-up of orthodox cybersecurity knowledge) has come about, in part, because of the disproportionate influence particular security experts have in the formation of objects. When discussing the emergence of objects of discourse, Foucault identifies three types of rules that are worth bearing in mind here: 'surfaces of emergence', 'authorities of delimitation' and the 'grids of specification' (Foucault, 1972, pp. 41–2). The first of these refers to the set of social relations in which particular practices or symptoms become objects of scientific investigation and concern. The second refers to those authorities that are empowered to decide which objects belong to which particular discursive formation. Finally, objects are constituted by being located on 'grids of specification' that function to classify and relate various sorts of objects by virtue of the properties they possess, or the symptoms they exhibit (Howarth, 2000, pp. 52–3).

Cyber-threats emerged in the context of post-Cold War national security where 'previously stable security imaginaries and assumptions were undergoing dramatic challenges, and rapid, radical, change' (Jarvis *et al.*, 2014, p. 27). The falling away of threats that had dominated the security agenda, the desire to fill this void with new security challenges (Hagmann and Dunn Cavelty, 2012, p. 79) and the rapid proliferation of interconnectivity through the internet allowed cyber-threats to emerge as a security risk. In this sudden and rapid transformation, a number of already established security agencies (both internal and external) found themselves needing to reassert their continued relevance in the post-Cold War setting (Bigo, 2001, p. 93). This moment not only demanded that pre-existing agencies re-applied for their own jobs, but also allowed for new agencies and new *expertise* to enter this domain and assert the pre-eminence of their knowledge claims and their ability to identify risks and assess threats.

These agencies and experts no doubt operated as authorities of delimitation insofar as they were part of a group of people who first identified 'cybersecurity' as an object (Hannah, 2007, p. 100), but perhaps more relevant are the 'enunciative modalities' (Foucault, 1972, pp. 50–5) that hold together particular discursive formations and determine the *who, where* and *how* of the right to speak of a given object of discourse (Clifford, 2001, pp. 54–5). Specifically, their status as 'security experts' demarks these individuals and agencies as 'professionals who gain their legitimacy of and power over defining policy problems from trained skills and knowledge and from continuously using these in their work' (Huysmans, 2006, pp. 8–9).

In the introduction to Berling and Bueger's edited collection on security expertise the authors comment that 'we live in an age of expertise' and that these experts assist in the mediation between different knowledge claims (Berling and Bueger, 2015, p. 1). Expertise is recognisable in the individual as someone 'in possession of specialized knowledge that is accepted by the wider society as legitimate' (Schudson, 2006, p. 499; see also: Lindvall, 2009, p. 705), but theorisation around *expertise* tends to recognise this as a broader property of a social collective, 'preserved and refreshed by the member of that group' (Evans, 2015, p. 19; see also: Schudson, 2006, p. 499), where the individual serves as part of a broader network of actors, institutions, etc. (Eyal and Pok, 2015, p. 38). The importance of these experts is their ability to make 'extravalid' if not *scientific* knowledge claims in a context where such claims, especially in Western societies, stand 'metonymically for credibility, for legitimate knowledge, for reliable and useful predictions, for trustable reality' (Gieryn, 1999, p. 1; see also Green, 1966, p. xiv). Scientific and technical expertise often serve as 'aces' or 'trumps' in securitising moves (Berling, 2011, p. 393), in part due to the tendency to view these forms of knowledge as apolitical (Rychnovska *et al.*, 2017, p. 328) and the speakers themselves as operating from a position of 'apocalyptic objectivity' (Foucault, 1986, p. 152).

This sense of neutrality and objectivity seemingly provides something incontestable, presenting things as they 'really are' and sitting outside of the messy social world where 'everyone feels entitled to have their say' (Bourdieu, 2004, p. 87). However, following this path ascribes too much weight to the ontological and epistemological authority of such statements and to science as a field, ignoring the scientific practices of objectivation that serve to shut down the *controversy* that is a defining feature of this field (Berling, 2011, p. 391). The products or 'facts' of science are so often 'black boxes' (Latour, 1987), as well as frequently being incomprehensible to the layperson. Yet the process by which these various products are arrived at is by no means apolitical, objective or autonomous of the social world. Indeed, as Hagmann and Dunn Cavelty (2012) reveal in their study of national risk registers, expert knowledge often serves to mask non-knowledge (p. 81) and may be the product of 'informed subjective estimations' (p. 85) of a small group of people that come to be understood as truth statements. It is the capital these actors hold as experts and the obfuscation that occurs given the technical/scientific nature of their subject matter that redirects focus onto the impactful statements of truth they make rather than how these have been arrived at.

Such qualities reveal the relationship between power and scientific/expert knowledge; however, our analysis of these individuals and institutions (as well as the knowledge claims they make) can reveal that the objectivity of this knowledge 'is a social accomplishment rather than an inherent quality of scientific knowledge of practice' (Evans, 2015, p. 21; see also: Liberatore, 2007, p. 111). From a constructivist perspective, this salient relationship between the expert speaker, their knowledge claims and the ability to elevate such claims to the status of truth has tremendous resonance for international relations in allowing 'researchers to identify the missing link between political objectives, technical knowledge and the formation of interests' (Faleg, 2012, p. 164). Correspondingly, there has been specific attention paid to expertise within international relations across various different 'generations' of research (Bueger, 2014), two of which I will consider in further detail: epistemic communities and security professionals.

Epistemic communities

The 'epistemic communities' research draws on the original work of Ernst Haas that began in the 1990s but remains a popular focus or 'approach' (see Cross, 2015, p. 90) in which efforts were made to identify how particular specialist expert groups with shared normative and causal beliefs could influence policy coordination by virtue of a 'knowledge consensus' that represents a 'temporally bounded notion of truth' (Haas, 1992, p. 23). Characterised not through the desire for material gain but instead policy influence (Sebenius, 1992, p. 364) the ideas and discourses of these groupings can serve as 'powerful vectors of policy change' (Howorth, 2004, p. 229), especially when conditions are conducive to change or the situation is 'unprecedented', with no similar historical reference points. This consensus Haas talks about is achieved through a networked learning process that can occur within the community during networking events such as conferences or workshops where ideas are exchanged and reinforced, as well as between the community and decision makers where these ideas can be diffused and adopted (Faleg, 2012, p. 166).

Haas defines epistemic communities as:

> a network of professionals from a variety of disciplines and backgrounds. They have (1) a shared set of normative and principled beliefs, which provide a value-based rationale for the social action of community members; (2) shared causal beliefs, which are derived from their analysis of practices leading or contributing to a central set of problems in their domain and which the serve as the basis for elucidating the multiple linkages between possible policy actions and desired outcomes; (3) shared notions of validity – that is, intersubjective, internally defined criteria for weighing and validating knowledge in the domain of their expertise; and (4) a common policy enterprise – that is, a set of common practices associated with a set of problems to which their professional competence is directed, presumably out of the conviction that human welfare will be enhanced as a consequence. (Haas, 1992, p. 3; see also: Sebenius, 1992, p. 351)

On account of these features, uncertainty is the condition within which epistemic communities operate and where their expertise is typically sought (Radaelli, 1999). In an era supposedly fraught with uncertainty (Beck, 1992, 2008, 2009) and a proliferation of issue-areas that are 'characterized by uncertainties', these communities can offer 'plausible claims to technical expertise' (Sebenius, 1992, p. 323; see also: Faleg, 2012, p. 164) without which governments 'risk making choices that not only ignore the interlinkages with other issues, but also highly discount the uncertain future' (Haas, 1992, p. 13). Adler and Haas elaborate as to the 'how' of epistemic communities' operation and specify a process of policy innovation, diffusion, selection and persistence that (if successful) culminates with the aim of stimulating the desired policy evolution (Adler and Haas, 1992). Where this process is successful, epistemic communities are able to gain influence within policy making circles and often have national governments 'exert power on behalf of the values and practices promoted by the epistemic community' (Adler and Haas, 1992, p. 371).

Clearly then, the space for epistemic communities within the diagram of power/knowledge outlined above is evident; however, it is important not to mistake these groups as the new hegemonic force in the diagram of power and recognise that their ability to influence the policy process has limitations (Adler and Haas, 1992, p. 371). Rather than being puppet masters, epistemic communities operate as one influential aspect of the power/knowledge nexus with an important role framing collective debate and fostering 'international co-operation in conditions and policy areas characterised by knowledge deficits and uncertainty' (Dunlop, 2000, p. 139). These groups are typically constrained, however, by the correlation that exists between 'the issue' and their own expert knowledge, as the strength of this correlation allows for more authoritative knowledge claims and recommendations to their target audience (Cross, 2013, p. 52).

Not all groups of experts should be considered epistemic communities, and various different professional/expert groups exist internationally that would not operate in the same way as an epistemic community (Cross, 2015). Similarly, neither should every epistemic community be assumed to be as 'strong' as another. Stronger epistemic communities may 'go beyond their formal professional role as a group' to achieve fundamental policy change and weaker ones only manage incremental change (Cross, 2013, p. 91). Nevertheless, the identification of these networks, and the work that has been done investigating them, reveals something of great interest to this study that potentially bridges the gap between the uncertainty of cybersecurity, the formation of a particular orthodox knowledge and the role of technical expertise in this formation.

Epistemic communities tell us a great deal about the functioning of expertise and the ability of particular networks to influence decision making, and while they were not first conceptualised with security specifically in mind, the application of this work to the domain of security is immediately apparent. However, it is also worth considering more contemporary theorising around the relationship between expertise and security. Dider Bigo's work looking at the role of 'security professionals' and their capacity to be 'managers of unease' has been a major contribution that has helped illuminate the consequences of the everyday workings of security expertise in the production of truths (Berling, 2011, p. 389), and the *making of security* (Berling and Bueger, 2015, p. 1).

Security professionals

Bigo's term 'security professionals' refers to those within society that are in charge of managing fear, risk and unease. Security professionals are held in high esteem and are understood to be able to provide 'more accurate' information and assessments than the layperson. For example, when the head of MI6 remarks that the threat from terrorism is 'severe', this holds more weight than the layperson's remarks because the former is presumably drawing on 'secret' information that only a select few privileged actors are privy to. Security professionals offer something 'above' that of the layperson and speak from a particular position that is closer to the truth and often beyond reproach.

In Bigo's own words, security professionals are '[…] invested with the institutional knowledge about threats and with a range of technologies suitable for responding to these threats. They benefit from the belief that they know what "we" (nonprofessionals, amateurs) do not know and that they have specific modes of action of a technical nature that we are not supposed to know about' (Bigo, 2002, p. 80).

As the continuum of threats and unease grows broader, we witness more and more of these professionals appearing, many outside of the traditional confines of the state (Salter, 2008, p. 324), and subsequently justifying their existence and activities in relation to their expertise in a particular site or sites of the continuum. All claim 'they are only responding to new threats requiring exceptional measures beyond the normal demands of everyday politics' but all further their own immediate interests, be they resources or responsibility (Bigo, 2002, pp. 63–4). These professionals can stake claims of expertise within already established domains of security or, by virtue of their privileged position as experts, contribute to the power struggle that produces new domains of security through the creation of particular knowledges.

As with epistemic communities, security professionals are not irreproachable speakers of an ontologically stable truth but, rather, are able to exercise a particularly authoritative status (Foucault, 1972, pp. 50–5) and even function as authorities of delimitation (Foucault, 1972, p. 41). They demark what is sayable and unsayable, can close off debates (Berling, 2011, p. 390) and are empowered to decide which objects belong to which particular discursive formations.[1] They are part of a reciprocal relationship and may even form part of an epistemic community, acquiring legitimacy within a broader regime of truth through which power permeates, dictating the techniques used for discerning truth, empowering certain actors and legitimising their statements while rejecting others (Foucault, 1984, p. 73). Consequently, in practice, often their assessments quickly ascend to the status of reflecting how things 'actually are' and such assessments are faithfully reproduced across communities of mutual recognition made up of other security professionals (Bigo, 2002, p. 74).

The production of a cybersecurity orthodoxy that closely reflects a pre-existing national security framework is the culmination of vying, competing knowledge claims. Groups, including but not limited to political professionals, the media and the security professionals, engage in a stock exchange of fear and unease (Bigo, 2002, p. 75) where 'everyone's knowledge and technological resources produce a hierarchy of threats' (Bigo, 2002, p. 76). In particular, the influence that technical expertise has upon how insecurity is organised

(Hagmann and Dunn Cavelty, 2012, p. 87) means that these knowledge claims have a powerful *constitutive* effect while purporting to merely reflect an external reality:

> many different actors, as in a stock market, exchange their different fears and determine their hierarchy and the priority of the struggles against these dangers, through a process of competition based on their supposed authority coming from their knowledge reputation, the scale of the information they gather and exchange, their technical know-how and their capacity to claim secrecy when questioned. This process of assemblage escapes the will of a dominant actor of a coalition of actors and is the result of their overall relations of competition, alliance and strategies of distinction, and as such its list of priorities appears as 'natural' to all of them, as a 'reflection' of reality justifying their common beliefs in the rise of a dangerous globalised world. (Bigo, 2004, p. 109, cited in Bigo and Guittet, 2011, p. 487)

Both these bodies of work on the role of security professionals and epistemic communities provide useful theoretical depth to my own project in their recognition of the manner in which security expertise operates as part of the *dispositif* and how the situated knowledge they produce assists in the process of making (in)security. As mentioned above, while Foucault's own studies were more interested in the arrangement within the *dispositif* than of specific 'sources', I diverge from this approach and argue that constructivist theorising into expertise, the likes of which has been covered in this chapter, helps to clarify the importance of these actors and institutions within the *dispositif* and their unique role in the construction of security knowledge.

Theorising on epistemic communities helps in the understanding of how expertise can function within the nexus of power/knowledge. It is apparent that the experts I cover in my empirical analysis and the networks that exist between them exhibit many of the hallmarks of epistemic communities. The diverse range of private internet security companies that operate within the industry, as I will demonstrate, clearly operate in the conditions of uncertainty that are characteristic of an epistemic community, engage in networked learning processes and *are* increasingly developing stronger ties to decision-making bodies. This demonstrates how they increasingly operate as part of a network that is broader than just their competitors (see Chapter 5), but I do not think it is the case that policy influence can be said to be the primary objective for these companies over material gain. There is value to be found, therefore, in the work on epistemic communities and its application to the analysis of the internet security discourse, but a more apt categorisation of this industry would be as a knowledge community or business network rather than primarily as an epistemic community as typically understood.

Bigo's work speaks more closely to the actors I will be studying, first and most straightforwardly because I believe that these companies operate unambiguously as security professionals. They represent prominent actors within the privatised cybersecurity industry and are new emergent expert 'agencies' that have staked their claim within the management of cyber-unease. Each company is made from experts with specialist knowledge who are researching the threat presented from malware and are privy to information that the layperson is not. Assessing and evaluating the nature of the 'threat landscape' is one of the primary roles that these professionals carry out, and thus they are also involved in the management of unease and uncertainty around this international security risk.

Second, the value attributed to the knowledge produced by these professionals is accentuated given the specific technical know-how they possess and the *technified* nature of the field within which they operate. What this means is not only is this industry 'just' made up of experts with access to specialist information, but also specialist information that is largely incomprehensible to those without a specific technical expertise (in this case a particular subdiscipline of computer science). As Hansen and Nissenbaum clarify, cybersecurity is technified because it is 'reliant upon expert, technical knowledge for its resolution and hence as politically neutral or unquestionably normatively desirable' (Hansen and Nisenbaum, 2009, p. 1157). This technification, alongside a process of hypersecuritisation and a relation to the day-to-day lived experience of increasingly computer-reliant people, assists in the production of something that is simultaneously threatening, tangible but also requiring a specialist body of knowledge and skills for its 'solution'. While this status is not completely unique to the aspect of the industry studied here it does afford these speakers a sharper delimiting effect, as these experts are required to identify, categorise, assess and resolve cyber-threats and thus have the 'last word over the truth concerning the evaluation of the future dangers and the construction of categories of danger and desirability' (Bigo, 2012, p. 205).

A consequence of this technification is that the pool of technical expert knowledge is not as deep for cybersecurity as it is for more entrenched and 'better understood' security risks. Alternative actors in the stock exchange of fear and unease, such as the media, will find covering and communicating issues of cybersecurity more difficult, leading to them to often simply reproduce technical expert knowledge from sources such as the internet security industry (Jarvis *et al.*, 2016, p. 616). Various authorities are present, but the influence is concentrated more acutely with those that speak the technical expert knowledge required and the knowledge produced here by these authorities will resonate and be amplified across and throughout a range of other institutions. Our collective knowledge surrounding cybersecurity is predicated to a large degree on the insight of a comparatively small body of experts whose discourse plays an important role in designating how cybersecurity looks, threatens us and should be responded to.

Finally, this being a private industry there is a clear *raison d'être* at work here. Much like other private and corporate security actors (Leander, 2005, p. 806), the internet security industry will only continue to exist so long as the 'life-blood' of risk and insecurity (O'Reilly, 2010, p. 188) remains and their ventures can continue to generate profits through the selling of services, products and security solutions. In this regard they operate in the same way as the 'management gurus' analysed by Quigley *et al.* (2015, p. 108), insofar as they speak to particular pressing and complex issues, persuade audiences of the usefulness of their ideas and profit from selling their solutions.

Methodology and method

The chapters that follow begin the examination of the materials produced by the eighteen internet security companies I am focusing on to establish how cybersecurity is constructed within this part of internet security discourse, as well as to consider the significance of this is as part of both the broader inter-subjective process of knowledge construction and the enactment of related security practices. However, before moving on to this, it is worth first reflecting on my approach and considering questions of methodology; that is, 'the rationale and the philosophical assumptions that underlie any natural, social or human science study' and method understood as the 'techniques and procedures followed to conduct research … determined *by* the methodology' (McGregor and Murnane, 2010, p. 420).

In the early parts of this chapter in particular, I demonstrated my own theoretical leanings towards Foucauldian notions of power and security as well as the relationship that exists between governmental forms of power and the security *dispositif*. Consequently, I have sought to remain consistent in how I approach the analysis contained in Chapters 3 and 4 and have allowed these theoretical and philosophical assumptions to inform the techniques I have used to conduct my research. However, doing so is not without challenge as Foucault leaves us with 'less than a structured methodology' and rather:

> a set of profound philosophical and methodological suspicions toward the objects of knowledge that we confront, a set of suspicions that stretch to our relationships to such objects, and to the uses to which such related knowledges are put. (Hook, 2005, p. 4)

Despite at least two phases to Foucault's work (archaeology and genealogy), one is more likely to come across reference to Foucault's 'genealogical method' than any explicit method being linked to archaeology (Howarth, 2000, p. 67). I am not conducting a genealogy of cybersecurity in this book, but my methodology *is* informed by assumptions and particular conceptualisations drawn from Foucault's work. Following this, the discourse analysis I conduct seeks to identify the effects of power that have come to make possible a particular 'natural' cybersecurity discourse as well as how this has served to support established relations of power. However, despite this important qualification, it is important to address some methodological problems that present when conducting a study such as this to avoid 'the very real danger in one's work being dismissed as un Foucauldian – if one does not get it right' (Graham, 2005, p. 2). A significant problem is that which I refer to above, namely, that Foucault did not spend a tremendous amount of time on the specifics of his method. Indeed, his propensity towards a lack of prescription has even seen his approach characterised as 'anti-method' (Shiner, 1982; Vucetic, 2011, p. 1296).

Two explanations can be put forward for this lack of prescription. First, Foucault took care 'not to dictate how things should be' (Foucault, 1994, p. 288), a principle that is consistent with his desire to disrupt the certitude of the sciences and one that explains why he wished to 'avoid the "positivist trap" of essentialising the research method' (Harwood, 2000, p. 59). Second, Foucault was not concerned about others precisely duplicating his approach and rather than viewing his studies as providing a manual to be followed, instead saw them as a series of separate tools: 'tools of analysis which take their starting point in the political-intellectual conflicts of the present' (Shiner, 1982, p. 386). Foucault went further with this analogy:

> I would like my books to be a kind of toolbox that people can rummage through to find a tool they can use however they wish in their own area [. . .] I don't write for an audience, I write for users, not readers. (Foucault, 2001, p. 1391)

Such an attitude encourages 'users' to adopt particular concepts and approaches and apply them as they see fit, detached from a broader method *per se*. However, as Graham alludes to, an inevitable tension occurs when one wishes to make use of Foucault's approach 'without appearing vague or, for the want of a better word, uncertain of what I am doing?' (Graham, 2005, p. 6). To answer this question we can usefully look to the secondary literature as well as those places where Foucault did more explicitly consider some methodological prescriptions (Foucault, 1981, pp. 97 – 100), even if these may actually serve more to outline what would be '*inappropriate* given the epistemological and ontological assumptions being made by Foucauldian Scholars' (Meadmore *et al.*, 2000, p. 466). For example, in a section entitled 'method' within *The History of Sexuality*, Foucault clarifies the aim of his study in looking to answer how a specific discourse (on sex) developed, what the most immediate power relations at work were that produced this discourse and how these discourses were used to support power relations (Foucault, 1981, p. 97). With these intentions in mind, he then covers a series of rules which are not intended as methodological imperatives but are at most 'cautionary prescriptions' (Foucault, 1981, p. 97). It is worth briefly outlining these, as they provide useful insight and direction.

The rule of immanence is a reminder that there does not exist an object of discourse that would be 'the legitimate concern of free and disinterested scientific inquiry' but that if (in this case) cybersecurity was constituted as an area of investigation, it was 'only because relations of power had established it as a possible object' (Foucault, 1981, p. 97). The *rules of continual variations* instruct not to look for power relations with the aim of seeing who has power and who is deprived of it, but instead to 'seek rather the pattern of the modifications which the relationships of force imply by the very nature of their process' (Foucault, 1981, p. 99). *The rules of double conditioning* refer to Foucault's understanding of discourse as strategic and his belief that a pattern of transformation 'cannot function if, through a series of sequences, it did not eventually enter into an over-all strategy' (Foucault, 1981, pp. 99–100). Finally, *the rules of tactical polyvalence of discourses* explain that the world is not split simply between accepted and excluded discourse, or between dominant and dominated but as discontinuous and unstable: 'a multiplicity of discursive elements that can come into play in various strategies' (Foucault, 1981, p. 100).

These rules do not provide a clear route map for one's research; however, taken alongside the specific conceptualisations I outline across the earlier part of this chapter, they do go some way to clarifying the purpose and direction of a study such as this as well as where the researcher might look for answers. Foucault sought to identify a problem 'expressed in the terms current today' (Foucault, 1988, p. 262) and then, by identifying and analysing the effects of power, to understand why the problem is constituted in a certain way in the present, including how this might support existing relations of power and subjugate/silence alternative knowledges in the process. The role of the 'intellectual', therefore, is to uncover the 'specificity of the mechanisms of power' that produces these ways of thinking (Foucault, 1980c, p. 145). The rules outlined in the *History of Sexuality* ring true with that motivation and further clarify the centrality of power/knowledge and discourse in our investigations.

When looking for a slightly more consistent framework for conducting the sort of research I am undertaking here, the secondary literature proves particularly useful (Meadmore *et al.*, 2000, p. 464). Having identified and defined the problem, the next step is the collection of a large corpus of text for the study (Williams, 1999, p. 258). As I have already clarified in this and previous chapters, I chose to investigate one aspect of private-sector industry expert discourse given that this was a clear and notably understudied site of discourse that related to the problem I was investigating (Williams, 1999, p. 258) rather than, for example, focusing on other factors such as 'the arbitrary use of historical time frames or historical dates' (Meadmore *et al.*, 2000, p. 466; Kendall and Wickham, 2003, p. 22).

My analysis sought to identify themes, tropes and tactics that revealed the effects of power within the discourse that could explain not only how social items became possible but also 'their consequence in the social and political world' (Vucetic, 2011, p. 1296). This endeavour involved considering to what extent it might be possible to think differently about cybersecurity by identifying a particular reality 'that holds us captive' (Foucault, 1986, p. 7; Owen, 2002, p. 224). I searched within the online archives of these eighteen companies, conducting a close reading of the material and on each occasion I asked a series of questions of each piece to decide upon whether it should be included in the corpus. As part of this process I considered a range of factors such as, what the major focus of the piece was, whether specific events were mentioned and how these were covered, the sources that were quoted or mentioned in the piece, the overall tone of the piece, the level of knowledge required to understand the piece, etc. I considered my analysis complete when the addition of new documents failed to produce any new 'theoretical categories' (Milliken, 1999, p. 234). Via this process, I reduced the corpus down to 454 documents that I judged could tell me something about the emergence of a particular cybersecurity knowledge and its consequences. The examples I cite throughout my analysis are some of these 454 documents.

A final question that remains unaddressed is how we can judge such an analysis to be *valid*. Proponents of 'inquiry-guided research', as Elliot Mishler characterises it, 'have long been aware that the standard approach to validity assessment is largely irrelevant to our concerns and problems' (Mishler, 1990, p. 416). However, the validity of the analysis of discourse as research is viewed problematically by certain critics (Cohen and Manion, 2008, p. 391; Flick, 2002, p. 201). One reason for this is elaborated upon by Denscombe (2007, p. 310):

> A disadvantage of using discourse analysis . . . is that it does not lend itself to the kind of audit trail that might be needed to satisfy conventional evaluations of the research. It is not easy to verify its methods and findings. This is because the approach places particularly heavy reliance on the insights and intuition of the researcher for interpreting the data.

Compared to positivistic benchmarks of validity, conducting the sort of discourse analysis I have can leave the researcher in the unenviable 'postmodernist position' where the findings are viewed as nothing more than the researcher's interpretations; no more or less valid than anybody else's (Denscombe, 2007, p. 310). My time spent elaborating upon theoretical positions and conceptual tools earlier in this chapter and methodological questions here are in part a retort to these sorts of charges to help clarify that this is not interpretation conducted on a whim, but instead predicated on particular understandings of power, knowledge, security, expertise, science, truth, etc. This is an interpretation that utilises heavily theorised concepts as analytical tools that provide it with a logic and coherence.

Of course, conversely none of this should be thought to grant this approach status 'superior to other methods in objectivity and comprehensiveness' (Shiner, 1982, p. 386) and we would do well to remember Nietzsche's words when talking about the aims of his genealogical approach as 'replacing the improbable with the more probable and in some circumstances to replace one error with another' (Nietzsche, 1989, p. 18). The litmus test for the quality of Foucauldian discourse analysis, therefore, is not how it holds up against an external validity test but, first, whether or not it can clearly and successfully display an ability 'to foreground how the conventional assumptions about the world have implications for our present-day reasoning and, second, to suggest, directly or indirectly, alternative ways to constitute the aspects of humanity under study' (Vucetic, 2011, p. 1296).

Expertise and the construction of threat

In this chapter I have laid out the theoretical framework that informs the analysis and discussion contained across the remaining chapters as well as providing reflections on methodology and method. At various points in this chapter I have sought to provide the theoretical underpinnings of an explanation as to why cybersecurity knowledge has settled in a particular form, what the significance of this particular form is, as well as highlighting the contingency therein. In short, rather than viewing this orthodox knowledge as a reflection of reality I have outlined specific conceptualisations of power, knowledge and security to present an alternative account of this knowledge as the effect of power that is constituted through a heterogeneous ensemble across society. Within this ensemble I have specifically highlighted the important productive role of expertise that will make up the focus of my empirical research.

The conflation of cybersecurity with national security is not natural, but something that had to be 'forged, argued, and accepted in the political process' (Dunn Cavelty, 2013, p. 105). Notions of risk at the heart of this framing are not ones that can be directly observed, but rather they require construction and communication to an audience (Quigley *et al.*, 2015, p. 109). This process of construction and communication is an inter-subjective one, but, as this chapter has outlined, not one whereby every actor or organisation has equal influence. Security expertise offers something 'extra' within this process premised not only on security experts' familiarity with a technical and specialised subject area but also the epistemic authority that flows from here and elevates their judgement of risks (Shires, 2018, p. 33). By mediating 'between knowledge pools for strategic advantage', experts can operate as 'arbiters' on the forms of knowledge and specific practices that are deemed most important or influential (Seabrooke, 2014, p. 1).

This means that expert assessments and the frames that they produce/ deploy as part of these assessments are particularly significant for collective understanding of what cybersecurity entails, who it threatens as well as what strategies can be implemented to mitigate against the risks found therein. Individuals respond to their *perceptions* of risk, regardless of relationships between these perceptions and how things 'really are'. Given the status of cybersecurity as an 'uncertain risk' (Renn, 2008), the epistemic authority of the industry and the biases that exist in relation to inferences of risk in the face of uncertainty (Quigley *et al.*, 2015, p. 109), the productive power of industry expertise quickly becomes apparent. All of this points towards the need to better understand the form expert knowledge takes, the discursive tactics and techniques utilised and the specificity of the message framing (De Bruijn and Janssen, 2017).

Having sought to justify the significance of these specialised forms of knowledge, I will now aim to achieve this goal and move on to consider the form and role of expert discourse across a number of companies within the internet security industry. Developing the sorts of constructivist cybersecurity research highlighted in Chapter 1, the following chapters provide analysis and discussion of this discourse to reveal the 'microphysics of power' (Foucault, 1977, p. 26) and the operation of these companies within the security *dispositif*. In so doing, I will demonstrate how expert knowledge produced by security professionals within the industry constructs and conflates cybersecurity with national security discourse in a manner that serves the industry as well as extending a neoliberal governmentality.

Chapter 3

Constructing the milieu

In his lectures Foucault conceptualised the milieu as the 'space in which a series of uncertain elements unfold' (Foucault, 2007, p. 20), and in the first of my chapters examining internet security discourse I will be focusing on 'cyberspace' as understood in these very terms. In this chapter, I chart how the private internet security industry operates as a specific aspect of the security *dispositif* and contributes to a broader risk knowledge that, in part, explains the characteristics of the dominant cybersecurity knowledge as well as the enabling conditions of governmental strategies. However, to talk of 'cyberspace' as if it is an unambiguous and well-defined phenomenon is to ignore the very general manner in which it tends to be discussed.

Cyberspace can conjure up images of an ethereal autonomous space that exists outside of the physical when, in reality, talking of cyberspace usually makes reference to a huge network of networks built upon a foundation of extensive and very tangible hardware. I have and will continue to be making reference to 'cyberspace' and 'the internet' throughout this book and indeed this distinction gets to the heart of one of the key definitional issues regarding cyberspace, namely, to what extent are they the same/different? As Mueller notes, while the internet and cyberspace are not the same, 'the internet plays the most critical role in transforming "information technology infrastructures", "telecommunications networks", "computer systems" and "embedded processors and controllers" into a world, a space or a domain in which humans can interact'. The internet, Mueller adds, 'acts as the connective commons that makes cyberspace navigable' (2017, p. 419).

In this chapter I will be focusing on these technologies, networks and hardware as well as the interconnectedness and interdependence that exists between these elements to make up cyberspace. I will be doing so with the express intention of trying to better understand what internet security industry expertise has to say about this domain. I will consider the characteristics of the vulnerability and uncertainty/certainty binary that exists, to explain how they are constructed as inherent features of the milieu and the manner in which industry experts establish (in)security via the demarcation of the deviant to render actions and subjects 'pre-emptively governable' (Heath-Kelly, 2013, p. 395).

Vulnerability

Cyberspace is said to be a space fraught with inherent weaknesses that make security measures and practices a necessity but more often than not *reactive*. Security can be, and is, 'built in', but it must contend with the intrinsic weaknesses that intersperse this space. The networks are man-made entities and correspondingly the weaknesses discussed here are not abstract, but instead are manifest as errors, oversights, 'bugs' as well as carelessness, poor practice, ignorance or naivety on the part of the user. In a general sense there is no distinction between who these sorts of weaknesses can impact; a fraudulent link taking a user to a malware-laden webpage could be accessed by you browsing online at home or the Director of the FBI. Where there is weakness, there is vulnerability; exploitable access points that allow for unauthorised entry are a primary concern and are unknowingly built into the various different components that make up the architecture of networks (Kaspersky Labs, 2002b).

Take one example already touched upon in chapter one: SCADA systems. These systems are identified as a source of major vulnerability on account of their critical function and their lack of built-in security (Business Wire, 2010). In fact, despite the criticality of their function, 'most protocols used for the exchange of information used in SCADA and PLC (programmable logic controller)[1] don't require any user identification or authorization', meaning that any device that can get onto these networks can send and receive commands to any other device on the network (Kaspersky Labs' Global Research & Analysis Team, 2012b). Given the attention now given to cybersecurity, one might assume that these critical systems could be 'fixed', updated or retro-fitted with the necessary security to close off these vulnerabilities. However, a significant hurdle to doing this presents itself as engineers have to deal with 'massively connected, intricate systems' (McAfee, 2009) and the likely cost and disruption that modifying them would entail. Set up at a time where security was more about 'guards, gates and guns' than external cyber-attack (Business Wire, 2010), there remains a reluctance to interfere with them on account of their ability to oversee and manage very important processes reliably and effectively (Kaspersky Labs' Global Research & Analysis Team, 2012b). There is a tendency not to patch vulnerabilities or take other measures such as introducing intrusion detection systems to the network out of a fear of 'glitchy updates disrupting the operation of the very same critical systems they're meant to protect' (Erlanger, 2012).

These sorts of problems suggest that systems, SCADA or otherwise, are vulnerable to being 'broken into, infected, made to work incorrectly or completely malfunction' (Kaspersky Labs' Global Research & Analysis Team, 2012b). The dragging of feet or outright denial of the need to secure these systems brings with it risk and the use of networked computers and the internet to run 'the financial, transportation, energy, and healthcare sectors ... also provides criminals and terrorists opportunities to strike countries where they will feel it most' (Trend Micro, 2013). Critical sites such as those within the energy, finance, telecommunication and government cyber-network infrastructures are deemed particularly open to attack (Kaspersky Labs, 2012c; Hawes, 2013d), with the targeting of Saudi Aramco, the world's biggest oil producer, providing one prominent example of this (Emm and Raiu, 2012). If targeted, PLCs within critical infrastructure systems could be made to 'run amuck', so that 'chemical level sensors, temperature sensors, robotic equipment, large hydroelectric control mechanisms and the like can behave strangely, possibly causing substantial damage'. More worryingly, if hackers could launch a 'widespread simultaneous attack on some such vulnerability, the impact can rise exponentially' (Camp, 2011b). Such realities make it 'easy for just about anyone' to recognise the 'potentially devastating effects' of a future attack on these critical systems (Kaspersky Labs' Global Research & Analysis Team, 2012b).

While not enjoying universal consensus, the conventional wisdom purports that attacks on national industrial or institutional systems is likely (AhnLab, 2011a), which leaves critical infrastructures 'extremely vulnerable' (Kaspersky Labs, 2013b). Electricity generation and distribution, the energy sector as well as financial exchanges are potential targets for adversaries as diverse as 'terrorists, activists and corporate snoops' (Hawes, 2013a, 2013b, 2013c). Other critical or sensitive networks, such as military, government and industrial systems, are not without their own weaknesses. Carnegie Mellon University research that is cited by Kaspersky Labs reveals that 'military and industrial software contains between five and ten defects for every thousand lines of code' (Kaspersky Labs' Global Research & Analysis Team, 2012b). For the sake of comparisons, they point out that the kernel of a Windows OS has over five million lines of code and thus it is 'not difficult to calculate the number of theoretically possible vulnerabilities that could be exploited for carrying out a cyber-attack' (Kaspersky Labs' Global Research & Analysis Team, 2012b).

The size and scale of these critical networks and the inherent vulnerabilities that underpin them illustrate the sheer extent of the uncertainty and complexity that industry expertise purports to feature in this space. In these early reflections we can begin to see how cyberspace provides something akin to the *milieu*, especially when we consider its centrality to contemporary societal circulation. The theme of vulnerability that has been characterised above imbues the space with a degree of potentially harmful and inherent unpredictability that will require management. These vulnerabilities identified in some of the most critical and important computer systems have laid down an apprehensive foundation to the milieu and fortify a logic of pre-emption in the face of future catastrophic cascading attacks. The portrayal of this vulnerability implies thick margins of insecurity, but this position is not completely consistent throughout the industry and we witness contestation in particular with reference to the *likelihood* of such disruption taking place and the *ease* with which it could be carried out.

For example, one form that scepticism takes is with reference to the sheer level of protection given to these critical systems: 'These systems are established and protected by the richest governments in the world, institutions with the industry's finest technical brains at their disposal, pumping billions into ensuring that such essential utilities run smoothly and ceaselessly' (Beckham, 2012). Therefore, while theoretically possible, accessing and compromising such systems to produce a security breach would not be 'humanly achievable' (Beckham, 2012). Of course, Beckham's argument does stand at odds with high-profile examples of unauthorised access and exploitation such as that brought about by Stuxnet and more recent high-profile events such as WannaCry.

Falling within the period of time studied for this book, Stuxnet represents the highest profile piece of malware that garnered significant attention and fuelled the argument that such a discovery has subsequently confirmed the ability for complex malware to cause destruction to vulnerable critical infrastructure. Continuing with the observable scepticism, however, such assessments were not universal and, in fact, some of the 'hype' that surrounded Stuxnet and the claims made in relation to it singled it out for specific attention. David Harley reminds his readers that this exceptional piece of malware was designed to target one very specific system, as well as being the beneficiary of copious resources and research and development time. Such factors must be taken into consideration before extrapolating to render all global critical infrastructure insecure in such a manner. Quoting Will Gilpin, an 'IT security consultant to the UK government', Harley responds to the idea that the discovery of Stuxnet and it falling into the wrong hands could see malicious actors disrupt several major elements of national infrastructure. Responding to the idea that malicious actors could successfully 'shut down the police 999 system', he says: 'Really? The emergency services switchboard is pump-driven?' (Harley, 2010).

And that hospital systems and equipment could be shut down:

> At a (biiiiiiig) stretch, perhaps. *Some* systems, maybe. In the unlikely event that they use equipment supplied from Tehran or Finland in certain therapeutic contexts. (Harley, 2010)

After a close reading it becomes apparent that a dissenting position is in evidence that, similarly to the sceptical realism identified in Chapter 1, focuses on the accuracy of the claims being made rather than more fundamental critiques.

When considering vulnerability, it is certainly not the case that all discussion is focused on vital critical infrastructure; on the contrary, discussion is pitched across levels of analysis, from those issues perhaps more relevant to states down to the home user via businesses large and small. This should not come as a surprise, given that these companies focus on providing endpoint security solutions for the public as one of their main products. Consequently, a considerable proportion of the knowledge in this space is concerned with the home user's experience.

The breadth of referents covered by these companies is in part due to the fact that the risks that present themselves in this space do not belong in clear and well-defined groups of 'threats to governments/infrastructure/companies' and 'threats to the user', etc. Malware could very well pose a threat to both the home user and the government official, either through design or as an unintended consequence of its release into 'the wild' and its subsequent proliferation. The grey area exists because, ultimately, malicious actors and malware just look to exploit vulnerabilities, be they human or otherwise; they need an exploitable weakness. Occasionally, this weakness is very specific and targeted but often it is a common and prevalent one to assist in the malware's spread. Phishing attacks, for example, have targeted government officials (Kaspersky Labs' Global Research & Analysis Team, 2014) and major corporations (Cluley, 2011b; Zetter, 2011), as well as millions of home users.

So while these companies do pitch their content to a specific audience (user, business, IT professionals, government), with the exception of very technical, data-heavy reports, they tend not to do so in a manner that closes off the topic to a certain demographic. From the industry's perspective, all of these threats are of relevance to everybody who relies on computers and the internet; cybersecurity is a collective, all-encompassing problem. Even the presence of terms like 'cyber-war', 'cyber-terrorism' and 'cyber-crime' should not be read as synonyms for 'only of interest to government officials' or 'only of interest to home users'. In fact, the industry appears keen to stress that cybersecurity is everyone's responsibility; we all have a stake in it, from banal spam emails right up to Advanced Persistent Threats (APT):

> From a controller for a critical piece of infrastructure, to data shared on smart phones, to the new intelligence systems running in our next generation vehicles, security has become everyone's responsibility and has to be considered at every juncture. From the manufacturing floor, to the website, to the data center, security must be a priority across an organization. Implementing a host lock-down policy is a critical step for hardening against malware infiltration. But that is only one step in a connected world that shows no signs of slowing down. (Parker, 2011a)

A critical vulnerability in a popular web browser could affect the home user, just as it would a national government if both were using unpatched versions of that software. While the sources of vulnerability can be quite different depending on the specificity of the attack and the target, the message from the industry remains consistent: the discovery of these vulnerabilities will 'remain the major cause of epidemics' (Kaspersky Labs, 2009b). Users of all kinds need to be protected from 'unforeseen threats to system data' and still remain vulnerable, even if they 'diligently backup their systems', due to the threat of 'today's most prevalent and potentially system crippling threats' (Symantec, 2009b). Vulnerabilities and their associated threats may be pitched differently within the discourse, but their significance is of relevant to us all and thus all users must be cybersecurity savvy. To provide further empirical evidence of the coming together between risks and common vulnerabilities, let us consider three different subjects in turn: unpatched software, digital signatures and users themselves.

Older versions of the popular web browser Internet Explorer[2] are open to 'countless exploits' from malicious websites (Raiu, 2009) and industry research 'paints an alarming picture' of the extent of this problem with over 25 per cent of users failing to update old browsers, leaving 'millions of potentially vulnerable machines, constantly attacked using new and well known web-born threats' (Efremoy, 2012). Reinforcing these statistics is a study carried out by AV-TEST, that showed how the popular programs Acrobat Reader, Adobe Flash and Java made up 66 per cent of exploited vulnerabilities in Windows systems (Comodo, 2013). The continuing exploitation of popular software is a cause for concern, as is the increased prevalence of zero-day vulnerabilities,[3] which a 'couple of years ago was something to write home about' but now represents a common occurrence (Gostev, 2011). It is worth noting here how zero-day exploits (the most sought after exploits for malicious actors online) have tended to be a feature of the most complex malware, but are nevertheless included within these discussions as something that affects 'us all'. This serves to reinforce the earlier point that no particular kind of user is said to be exempt from the relevance of any vulnerability and highlights the interconnectedness and interplay across both levels of analysis and the 'threat spectrum'.

Digital signatures are 'one of the pillars upon which confidence and assurance in the computer world are based' (Gostev, 2010). These signatures are files signed by a trusted manufacturer that let the system know that a piece of software is 'clean' (Gostev, 2010). Such files are a very important topic for the internet security industry because these signatures provide an easy means of allowing trusted software to operate on the system and avoid their own antivirus software producing numerous false positives. If acquired by malicious actors, they can allow malware to pass into a system without suspicion. Acquisition by malicious actors can come either by 'cutting' digital signatures from legitimate software or it can be legally acquired by an 'inventive' interpretation of the purposes for which such a signature is required (Namestnikov, 2010a). As a result these signatures are frequently becoming a feature of malware, allowing it to pass into a system without suspicion. This revelation has 'seriously discredited' the principle of software certification and undermined a critical security protocol (Gostev, 2010).

Users themselves are also often viewed as a major weakness by the industry. Such weakness could come in the form of poor security practice – for example, choosing weak passwords such as 'password' or '123456' that provide little challenge for hackers (Bitdefender, 2013). However, the threat of social engineering that specifically targets people and that strives to make something threatening appear innocuous with the aim of enticing them into clicking or providing secure information is also particularly prevalent. Regular updates, intrusion detection and internet security can often be circumnavigated when the user decides to open an attachment or download a malicious plugin on a website, and often it is 'people [who] are the weakest link, not technology' (Granger, 2010). By extension, the decision of many businesses to implement all manner of security initiatives but not extend these rigorously to the various mobile devices used by employees is the digital equivalent of locking the doors at home and leaving the windows wide open (Hear4U, 2009a).

As these sorts of examples highlight, weakness is not only an inherent feature but also ubiquitous; a diverse range of threats target a dizzying array of weak points. The high profile and potentially catastrophic sits alongside the everyday, but all serve to highlight the danger and uncertainty present. Importantly, the material that is written primarily for the home user is not viewed as distinct from other actors and systems and vice versa. Melih Abdulhayoğlu, the CEO of Comodo Group, talks to this overlap by alluding to the way in which home users invite the threat of cyber-terrorism when they fail to keep their own computers secure:

> I bet you, you don't think you have a weapon at home … that's what you would think but you have a PC at home and those PCs those internet connections combined becomes a weapon that is used by cyber criminals, cyber terrorists. That then creates a real threat of cyber terrorism and cyber criminals. Now you are in control of that weapon, you at home who has a computer an internet connection is a weapon, you are a weapon. It's your responsibility no make sure that weapon is locked away and not utilised, not abused by cyber criminals. (Abdulhayoğlu, 2009)

Abdulhayoğlu likens a vulnerable PC to a weapon that can be utilised by cyber-terrorists, making it clear that it is the user's responsibility to ensure that this weapon is secure from these malicious actors. He is not alone in this assessment either and elsewhere we see it echoed: 'it's increasingly evident that each unprotected individual makes us all vulnerable, so it's vital that as a global society we find ways to address this trend and ensure that we are protected together' (AVG, 2011a). Just as SCADA systems and the critical systems that help run our most vital areas of infrastructure are vulnerable to exploitation, so too are the numerous different devices used at home or in the workplace. Systems are inherently weak and while the security can differ from system to system, a stark reality remains: failure to strengthen these weaknesses at any level can expose everyone to greater risk from the likes of sabotage, crime, terrorism and war.

It is one thing to have a system in which actors are vulnerable and weakness is often a feature, but something entirely more alarming if those same actors are *dependent* upon those same systems: 'our dependence on computers and the Internet grows with each passing day, and so, too, does our vulnerability' (Comodo, n.d.). Technology, it is argued, has been turned against us in the past ('it's a sad example how simple planes caused 9/11') and it is computers and the internet that are the 'next big vulnerable technology that can be turned against us that we are nurturing, that we are depending more on every day' (Abdulhayoğlu, 2008a). This dependence has an effect at all levels, accentuating vulnerabilities due to the 'massive dependence' on computer systems meaning that cyber-attacks targeted at critical infrastructure exhibit 'crippling potential' (McAfee, 2011b). The traditional military/security hierarchy is turned on its head here, and 'unlike with conventional weapons, the more developed countries are actually the most vulnerable to cyber-warfare and cyber-terrorism' due to these states' greater computerisation both within government institutions and across civil society (Kaspersky Labs, 2012c).

As information technology has become such an integral part of our lives and our dependency on it has increased, the benefits have been tempered by 'risks coming from a wide spectrum of external and internal threats' (Kaspersky Labs, 2002b) – in particular, the threat of hackers and their ability to launch attacks via the internet, 'the sheer volume and diversity of which can simply paralyze unprotected computers' (Kaspersky Labs, 2002b). We are dependent on computers and the internet, but these things are inherently vulnerable; this obviously produces a dilemma that exposes us to a major security problem. As this dependency progresses towards its 'ultimate' form: the 'Internet of Things',[4] and a state where connectivity is fully engrained in the lives of those citizens who occupy the world's most developed nations, the possibility of a major cyber-attack threatens to become an even greater concern. To provide one such example, Trend Micro reported that they had exposed serious vulnerabilities in the automatic identification system (AIS) vessel tracking system that could allow attackers to 'hijack communications of existing vessels, create fake vessels, trigger false SOS or collision alerts and even permanently disable AIS tracking on any vessel'. Their research concluded that this critical system is 'comprehensively vulnerable to a wide range of attacks that could be easily carried out by pirates, terrorists or other attackers' (Wilhoit and Balduzzi, 2013).

Vulnerability and dependency come together against the backdrop of a body of threats as numerous as they are diverse and that are increasing at an 'exponential' rate. Not only are they 'growing rapidly' but the effects are being felt, with 46 per cent of US enterprises in 2009 feeling that cyber-threats had somewhat/significantly increased over the previous two years. Furthermore, when these same companies were asked to rank a series of different risks to their organisation by significance, 'those ranking cyber attacks as No. 1 or No. 2 outpaced all other risks by a wide margin (twice as many as natural disasters and traditional crime and four times as many as terrorism)' (Symantec, 2009a). While the focus here is specific, the identification of an increased sophistication of hacker attacks and the 'rapid exploitation of new vulnerabilities' (Check Point, 2006) is not uncommon elsewhere, nor is subsequent increased risk threatening to overwhelm our defences under an 'avalanche of malware' (Corrons, 2009).

The use of statistics is notable when charting malware prevalence and Kaspersky Labs, who regularly conduct such analysis, have reported on striking figures such as 15 million new malicious programs coming in 2009 (Aseev *et al.*, 2010) and 327,598,028 separate attempts to infect users' computers globally in the first quarter of 2010 – 26.8 per cent more than the last quarter of 2009 (Namestnikov, 2010b). The reporting of such figures is consistent with the assessment of Comodo Security, when they say that we are experiencing an 'onslaught of modern cyber-attacks', notably on 'high profile and high value targets' (Judge, 2013a). High-profile targets could include those critical systems in the UK that house the tax and welfare databases and are not only 'liable to attack', but have been experiencing an 'exponential rise in the number of incidents' (AVG, 2011d). Other possible targets include the financial organisations that have been experiencing an exponential rise in the number of crimeware attacks (Mashevsky, 2010), attacks that are said to be running 'rampant' (BullGuard, 2013d). There has been an 'explosive increase' in all manner of different kinds of attacks – in particular mobile malware, for which BullGuard identified a 'six thousand per cent a year' growth rate in 2013 (BullGuard, 2013a). Elsewhere, the 'soaring levels of Android malware [are] marking an increased professionalism in the structure and operations of the organized criminals behind them' and, subsequently, attacks targeting Facebook increased three-fold in 2010 (AVG, 2011c).

Having explored the more overt references made by these security professionals to the inherent weakness and ever-present vulnerability of cyberspace, I conclude this section on vulnerability by shifting my focus onto the usage of two particular metaphors used to communicate vulnerability within cyberspace. First, I look at the appearance of biological/medical metaphors and in particular the attention given to depictions of infection, vaccination and evolution will be considered. Second, there will be an examination of the construction of cyberspace as 'the wild' or the Western Frontier, alongside references to predators and prey. At the close of this chapter, I will explain how these metaphors serve as tactics of power that are deliberately intended to produce particular understandings of this space. However, for now, I will demonstrate how these themes of vulnerability and weakness are woven deeper into the discourse though the prominent use of particular metaphorical references and reasoning.

Biological/medical metaphors

The intertextualities between the internet security discourse and the fields of biology and medicine are apparent, with frequent references to the toxic or poisonous nature of malware and of malware's ability to 'infect' computers and computer systems. This 'rich metaphor' pervades the discourse and has given rise to a standardised language of 'infection', 'viral attack', 'disinfectant' and 'viral damage' that 'lack any precise meaning in relation to computers' but that provides an approximate, comparative understanding of the kind of phenomena that are being referenced when these topics are the focus (Thimbeleby *et al.*, 1998, p. 444). The appearance of this metaphor is by no means distinct to this space, as Julie Barnes notes: 'when malicious, self-replicating computer code began to circulate through the world, the metaphor of a "computer virus" was quickly adopted and terms such as "virus infection" became commonplace' (Barnes, 2009, p. 8). However, its specific use by these particular security professionals is worthy of further investigation.

The amount of unique malware that exists in cyberspace is reported to be astronomically high and subsequently cyberspace is presented as a space that is fraught with risks that could 'potentially infect millions of vulnerable computers' (Bell, 2013a). These security risks make use of a range of different 'infection vectors', be it the browser, email or malicious websites, and 'at the current penetration rate' notable phenomena, including cyber-crime, have 'become pervasive, *pandemic* and increasingly connected with other parts of the criminal ecosystem' (emphasis added) (Debrosse, 2009). Taking the pandemic metaphor further, Melih Abdulhayoğlu, CEO of Comodo Group, likens the spread of malware to the global AIDS crisis: 'If humans were files on PCs then these viruses (malware) would be the worst AIDS virus that is airborne!' (Abdulhayoğlu, 2008b).

The metaphor continues through to propagation, with Faarschi writing about the computer worm Slammer: '[…] the speed at which this worm *propagated* was extremely novel – scary in fact. The worm was released and within ten minutes it had compromised 90% of all vulnerable systems worldwide (emphasis added) (Faarshchi, 2003). On the point of propagation, it is not uncommon to read within the discourse reports similar to those produced by humanitarian organisations that look to raise awareness into the spread of infectious diseases and their infection rates (ESET Research, 2012; Namestnikov, 2010b). These statistic heavy reports outline what the 'threat landscape' looks like as well as the infection rates for particular computer viruses. A key difference in the instance of the internet security industry is that not only do these companies inform the public but they also offer the means of *treatment* (Kaspersky Labs, 2009c), *vaccination* (AhnLab, 2008a, 2008b) and *disinfection* (Namestnikov, 2010a) to nullify the different *strains* (Bell, 2013a) and to prevent a further *outbreak* (Kaspersky Labs, 1999a).

Away from viruses and infection, another example of metaphor that is enacted in this space that makes use of a biological or medically threatening concept is that of toxicity. For example, the 'threat landscape' within cyberspace is described as becoming 'increasingly toxic' (deSouza, 2012), a metaphor also used to describe malware such as the Nuclear Pack exploit kit (Kalnai, 2013). Stuxnet is a worm with 'a particularly venomous, damaging payload' (Mody, 2011), which has heralded a move towards more 'targeted and toxic' attacks (Parker, 2011a). The theme of toxicology is also present when describing the process of 'poisoning' search engines or online advertisements, so that when users click on seemingly harmless links or advertisements they are instead taken to websites housed by a malicious server that can distribute malware to the victim's computer (Naraine, 2009; Sejtko, 2010; Namestnikov, 2010a; AVG Web Threats Research, 2012).

Evolution and the belief that threats in cyberspace undergo a process of natural and rapid improvement represents another prevalent aspect of this closely related body of metaphors (AVG Web Threats Research, 2012; Mustaca, 2010b; BullGuard, 2013b). This comes despite the fact that the process of malware 'evolution' seems to have little in common with the process of biological evolution given that malware is the product of an author and does not inherit useful characteristics or traits as part of the propagation process. However, the use of this metaphor helps to construct threats in cyberspace as constantly shifting, improving and becoming more dangerous. Likewise, it creates an expectation that the internet security industry will also have to adapt or 'evolve' to respond to these threats with new initiatives and defences required to keep out new and innovative attacks.

The wild and the Wild West

The inherent vulnerability of cyberspace is also communicated with recourse to various different depictions of the 'wild', both as an untamed and dangerous wilderness and as a revisionist interpretation of the 'Old West'.[5] The former sees cyberspace constructed as a feral and unruly cyber-state of nature; a domain where malware writers and hackers rule. Malicious actors put their viruses 'into the wild' and cast a wide net to ensure that they snare as many victims as possible (Judge, 2013a). Despite the fact that 'the wild' ultimately refers to the World Wide Web itself, it is often talked of as if it is a separate space entirely, a place deemed to be particularly dangerous for the general user (Raiu, 2009). The metaphor extends into the portrayal of malicious actors as predators and their victims as prey. The result of this development has meant the internet has become 'a dangerous place' (Raiu, 2009), reminiscent of a sort of online jungle where 'predators' (both foreign and domestic), operating in cyberspace are said to threaten a number of different referents (McLean, 2009).

The enactment of hunting metaphors demonstrates a notable overlap with the discourse of the 'War on Terror'. Brigitte Mral argues that George W. Bush's use of the hunting metaphor ('Make no mistake: The United States will hunt down and punish those responsible for these cowardly acts') (Gilmore, 2001) helped to define the opponent as 'cowardly, unmanly and fair game' (Mral, 2006, pp. 58–9). While 'fair game' still holds true to a certain extent, albeit in relation to the 'victim' not the adversary, the hunting/hunter/prey metaphor instead of dehumanising an enemy (linking Al-Qaeda to animals) is utilised here to accentuate the vulnerability of the user if they are foolish enough to step into this wilderness unprotected.

The wild web is full of skilled hunters (malicious actors with computer expertise) and an inability to adequately protect yourself in this largely ungoverned and dangerous space will likely result in your exploitation. Following this logic, computerised businesses and organisations that do not possess adequate anti-virus solutions are depicted as 'easy prey for hackers and virus creators' (Kaspersky Labs, 2002a) and a range of other online users are 'preyed on' by such prevalent threats as drive-by downloads,[6] fake anti-virus software and ransomware (Redfield, 2012). The unpredictability and the speed at which threats can develop, and the uncertainty of how quickly official fixes will become available, has left internet security companies keen to try to be more proactive in combating threats in the wild (Kaspersky Labs, 2003b). However, much like the wild in physical space the cyber-wilderness is unpredictable and very difficult to 'tame'.

The second wilderness metaphor apparent is that of a revisionist Wild West; revisionist in so much as it stands at odds with Fredrick Jackson Turner's 'Frontier Thesis' (Turner, 1940), which characterised early optimistic depictions of cyberspace (Carveth and Metz, 1996, p. 90). Turner argued the formation of modern American democracy was formed by brave, hardworking virtuous individuals who, unburdened by European structures and traditions, were able to establish liberty across the country.[7] The internet security industry eschews Turner's thesis and sits more closely with Alfred Yen's revisionist interpretation that views Turner's as a romanticisation (Yen, 2002, p. 1228). Yen argues that this thesis obscures the reality of the Old West, where 'genocide, racism, and personal exploitation in the name of progress' were widespread (Yen, 2002, p. 1230) and in turn ignores how the absence of the state actually makes cyberspace a dangerous wilderness characterised by 'free pornography, "spam," identity theft, rampant copyright infringement, gambling, and hacking' (Yen, 2002, p. 1223). In summary, it is a place, Yen argues, where only the 'computer savvy Settlers really know how to survive' (Yen, 2002, p. 1224).

The lawlessness and lack of regulation associated with the internet that allows malicious actors to act and malicious software to propagate leads Yuval Ben-Itzhak of AVG to the conclusion that the World Wide Web should 'be re-branded as the World Wild Web', adding: 'Our research indicates that hundreds of live servers operating around the world are active 24/7 to steal users' credentials for online banking and other private assets' (AVG, 2011b). Steve Bell at BullGuard acknowledges that 'there are parts of the internet that are like the Wild West' (Bell, 2013b), while Phil Harris of Symantec, in a piece looking at cyber- defence and cyber-vigilantism, perhaps provides the starkest example of this comparison: 'I've always maintained that the internet is pretty much the Wild West in electronic form where you have good law abiding folks and folks that tend to teeter one way or the other and then folks that are out to do whatever they want even to the wanton destruction of others' (Harris, 2013). The pervasiveness of the Wild West metaphor is further evidenced by the adoption of the terminology 'white hat' and 'black hat' (and sometimes even 'grey hat') that signifies the righteous or nefarious motivations of the hacker in a way that reflects the manner in which cowboys in Westerns were recognisable as 'good guys' or 'bad guys' by the colour of their hats. This is terminology that is present in one of the highest-profile internet security events of the year, the Black Hat conference.

The construction of cyberspace as a wild and unruly space where malicious actors are an ever-present threat and prey on their victims has an impact on how both cyberspace and cyber-threats are understood. The manner in which malicious actors are depicted as masters of this domain, the hunters, familiar in the surroundings of the cyber-wilderness, tormenting less clued-up victims, enhances a broad sense of vulnerability in this space. The discourse entrenches the notion that 'we' are not as safe as we think in cyberspace; we are vulnerable and at risk from those who operate in this lawlessness – from hackers, criminals, terrorists and states.

Uncertainty

There is a palpable and observable anxiety within this expert discourse which develops from the uncertainty that surrounds the risks present in this space. For all the expertise and analysis that is on display there is the unavoidable sense that, despite all that is known, there is still a great deal that is unknown and, more to the point, *cannot be known*. Cyberspace and cyber-threats hardly have the monopoly on stealth; however, there is a consensus within the industry on the sheer extent of these unknowns when dealing with threats online.

Stealth allows malware to hide in plain sight – for example, embedding itself unseen in everyday applications such as web pages (BullGuard, 2013d) after finding its way into vulnerable systems through 'misconfiguration, human error or social engineering' (Cosoi, 2011b). Stealthier forms of infection have resulted in greater success for malicious actors in cyberspace and so has given rise to an influx of new techniques such as 'drive-by malware' or 'drive-by downloads' that make use of 'the browser as the mechanism to connect computer users to servers rigged with malicious exploits' (Naraine, 2009). This is compounded by the ability of these attacks to exploit even the most legitimate looking of sources after they have become compromised by secretly embedded exploit scripts or URL redirection[8] that 'silently launches attacks via the browser' (Kaspersky Labs, 2009a). Alternatively, users could discover (or, more worryingly – not discover) that they have malware running on their PC without any knowledge of this intrusion. These 'insidious, sophisticated and silent methods' used to 'wreak havoc' (Symantec, 2011b) are 'designed to sit silently on users' computers' (Panda, 2011b) until given a command to execute.

Stealth is a feature of all manner of different cyber-threats and all manner of different malicious actors in cyberspace. APTs often make use of the aforementioned 'zero-day' exploits/vulnerabilities and are described as being stealthy to the point of being 'almost invisible'; finding one 'in the wild' is akin to a 'zoologist finding Bigfoot alive' and being attacked by one is likened to being attacked by 'stealth fighters' (Waugh, 2013e). Such attacks are on the rise and are being written and executed by 'well-funded and organized groups' (Haley, 2012b). APTs can be used for destruction, disruption or even theft of sensitive information such as individual's personal data, meaning that the threat of identity lurks 'like ticking time bombs' (Ferguson, 2013) with the malicious actors behind such attacks ready 'to play havoc with our lives' (AVG, 2011e).

These kinds of attacks are known to have hit 'mil, gov and large corporates' in the past and are 'very hard to defend against…and hard to notice' (Thompson, 2010). The use of zero-days to target military and government websites in this instance is thought to be with the express aim of inserting backdoors[9] into the various different computer systems. Thompson warns that 'if these backdoors could be planted in a great many government departments without being noticed, then the enemy has the capability of instructing them all to simultaneously download and execute a brand new, fast infecting virus' (Thompson, 2010).

'In this digital warzone the battle is not always conducted using well-known vulnerabilities in code' (ZoneAlarm, 2013) and, correspondingly, the possibility and ramifications of a major cyber-attack become more plausible when considered in relation to aspects like APTs and zero-day exploits. In a piece that is largely sceptical, Lisa Vaas makes a concession when responding to the question of whether hackers could cause significant damage and death through a cyber-attack to SCADA systems:

> Heaven only knows. Maybe they can. The lack of security around Supervisory Control and Data Acquisition (SCADA) systems is scary. And unsecured SCADA systems are everywhere. They control nuclear and chemical plants, gas pipelines, dams, railroad switches, water treatment plants, air traffic control, metropolitan transportation networks, and the cash flow via financial transaction systems. (Vass, 2012)

MacAfee go a bit further still to argue that while recent history suggests that these systems are vulnerable and future attacks do appear likely, the more pertinent question is: 'How do we know they are not already compromised and actively under attack now?' (McAfee, 2011a). The short answer is that we cannot know for certain that we are not currently 'under attack' or that criminals, rival states or terrorists have not already gained remote access to critical systems undetected. Stephen Cobb refers to the 'hidden 90% of the infrastructure attack iceberg', a series of unpublicised or unknown attacks, including 'espionage, backdoor monitoring of the state of essential utilities with a view to future malicious action, should it become advantageous'. Echoing the hypothetical question posed by McAfee above, Cobb also speculates on the possibility of pre-installed 'currently latent malware' and clarifies that with 'the SCADA scene being what it is, we may not become aware of such breaches until direct malicious action is identified locally or there's some crossover with non-SCADA sites' (Cobb, 2013). We should be doubly nervous of this uncertainty because not only are there attacks that remain completely undetected, there are also those that are known within certain circles but remain unreported in the public domain: 'Indeed, for every attack that is reported and documented in the public domain, there may well be several others which are kept very firmly under wraps' (Mody, 2011).

Cobb concedes that his observations are 'essentially hypothetical, given the increasing awareness of SCADA/ICS vulnerabilities' (Cobb, 2013); however, such scenarios should not simply be dismissed as sensationalism. Accounts of attacks operated by 'unidentified Chinese hackers' are mentioned within the discourse (Cosoi, 2011b), as is specific reference to historic and high-profile operations such as GhostNet, which displayed the existence of, and potential for, extensive unauthorised access going undetected for long periods of time (TheSecDev Group, 2009).[10]

Just as the unknown element covered here creates anxieties within the industry, the inability to accurately assess all threats has opened up this area to a large degree of speculation, conjecture and the framing of cyber-threats in terms of worst-case scenarios. Despite the uncertainty and speculation, there appears to be little impact on the credibility of the security risks within cyberspace. Of course, uncertainty and credibility are by no means oxymoronic but the credibility of the threat is something that the industry is quick to assert (see Chapter 4) and, given the amount of uncertainty that surrounds them, one could perhaps expect more contestation here. However, instead, we witness how the characteristic of stealth, combined with the vulnerability covered in the opening section of this chapter, allows for a plausible explanation as to the lack of an abundant and clearly observable threat and a re-framing of the discussion as one of '*What if?*'

Risky futures

These sorts of 'What if?' assessments operate on the premise that cyber-threats are real and credible, but the uncertainty that is a feature of them means that the presence of a threat is an unknown and therefore the potential for destruction is also an unknown (although, theoretically at least, very high). In such assessments the industry does not take the absence of observable danger as a reassurance but rather as a cause for alarm. Industry experts who are deemed appropriate to make estimations, calculations and to engage in *informed* speculation (or in some cases are called upon or expected to do so) take the uncertainty as unknown but presumably threatening (after all, what security company takes 'unknown' as an invitation to relax?), arriving at a fearful conclusion. This is a conclusion that rationalises the need for consumers to invest in technologies of security (Symantec, 1997).

There is a tendency to focus on specific 'What if?' scenarios or hypothetical nightmare scenarios but, crucially, to relate such scenarios to the memories of past *actual* destructive events. The 11 September 2001 attacks, alongside other less prominent but more timely examples such as Hurricane Sandy, were used as comparative points within the discourse, albeit not always strictly to convey a sense of concern. The manner in which these actual memories combine with imagined nightmare scenarios helps to frame the threat of cyber-attack in a manner that disguises the imagined element behind the perceived destructiveness.

Researchers at F-Secure frame the potential for an attack on critical infrastructure and the subsequent destruction in the context of the 9/11 attacks, explaining how there '[…] is no consensus on what constitutes a significant attack'; does taking down one power grid control station or a town's internet access constitute such an attack? Or in other words as one of the company's analysts put it: 'what would *really* constitute a digital 9/11?' (Alia, 2009a). Symantec makes comparisons to the period of time preceding the 9/11 attacks, citing Cofer Black[11] and his message at the 2011 Black Hat conference that the last time he presented in front of an audience and warned them of a coming threat it was August 2001, but this time it is a warning of a major cyber-attack on the US (Parker, 2011b). Not only does this kind of message reinforce the potential destructiveness of such an attack, it also reinforces the sense of imminence and urgency relating to cyber-threat; the idea that it is just around the corner and requires immediate action.

Other such examples that utilise comparisons to destructive past memories include material published by some of these companies in the aftermath of 'super storm' Sandy, a natural disaster that caused widespread destruction to the US Eastern Seaboard in 2012 and which further demonstrates how the industry operationalises these events to convey the potential catastrophe. After this natural disaster, Department of Homeland Security Director Janet Napolitano warned of the similar effects that could be achieved as a result of a 'systems attack' (Martinez, 2012) and although her comments were met with some scepticism, this did not stop hypothesising within the industry over the possibility of a 'Cyber Sandy'. Leon Erlanger concedes that while it may be difficult to imagine any cyber-attack causing damage comparable to Sandy, it 'doesn't take anything away from the real dangers posed by cyberattacks on the systems that control critical infrastructure'. Erlanger goes on to compare the effects of the 2003 north-eastern power blackout that was caused 'after a few trees hit some transmission lines in Ohio' to the kind of thing a 'knowledgeable hacker might be able to accomplish'. Although the initial conclusion appears to be that such an attack would be difficult, the final evaluation is that 'a sophisticated, widespread, devastating attack is certainly not inconceivable' (Erlanger, 2012).

It is not the case that all these examples of targeted malware attacks on particular systems occur in relation to the memory of past catastrophic events, other examples of more generic imagined nightmare scenarios causing widespread destruction through cascade damage to critical networked infrastructure are also referenced within this discourse. In one such scenario it is explained how we should expect these kinds of attacks to start out by denying popular websites and interrupting email services before moving on to obtaining unauthorised access to government services, communications, transport and finance companies, which would have the result of 'destabilising the functioning of the social system as a whole' (Gostev, 2007).

Such comparisons, however, have not been unquestionably accepted by all corners of the industry. John Hawes describes comments to this effect by ex-FBI Director Louis Freeh as 'tasteless', a point of view that is premised on the fact that there appear to have been no human casualties and no physical effects that have come as a result of cyber-terrorism (Hawes, 2013e). Hawes questions the 'destructiveness' as an essence of cyber-threats – at least in the same way in which 9/11 was destructive. Others, however, merely view the kinds of comparisons included above as an embellishment that misrepresents how the vast majority of nefarious cyber-activity looks. Roger Thompson, writing for AVG, argues that most attacks are low-level and, consequently, 'the world is not going to end' just because we cannot access Whitehouse.gov for a few days (Thompson, 2009). In specific reference to the threat hacker collective 'N4m3le55 Cr3w', made to wipe the US 'off the cyber map' by targeting a series of US based websites, Sorin Mustaca of AVIRA comments that in reality such threats are largely hollow and the results are far from the catastrophic scenes that came as a result of the 9/11 attacks (Mustaca, 2013).

Indeed, this hypothetical juncture remains one of the more notable examples of some fairly stark disagreements within the discourse, even when the speculation is not linked to particular events. For example, Oliver Bilodeau explains how 'most of us in the industry' consider the term APT to be an 'overblown marketing term' that in some cases has been revealed to represent mere 'simplistic B-list attacks', lacking in destructive complexity and presenting minimal risk (Waugh, 2013e).

Urban Schrott makes his frustrations clear with regard to the manner in which speculation is rife surrounding cyber-threats. Talking specifically in relation to Stuxnet, he writes:

> For months now the general public has been bombarded with views from various angles of the Stuxnet worm. What does it really do? Who started it? Why? Was it the Americans and the Israelis? Was it the Chinese? Was it SPECTRE? Oh and there's nuclear facilities. And fundamentalist regimes. And cyber-warfare. And state terrorism. And all kinds of other doomsday buzzwords which we simply cannot ignore, because as we all know, we're always living on the edge of being blown up. (ESET Global Threat Report, 2011)

Stuxnet is singled out elsewhere on account of apparently dubious coverage (Harley, 2010), with one group of authors writing in an ESET white paper: 'Sky News, tired of mere factual reporting and even half-informed speculation, took off for planet Fantasy, where it discovered that the Sky really is falling, claiming that the "super virus" is being traded on the black market and "could be used by terrorists"' (Matrosov *et al.*, 2010). Nevertheless, these examples do provide examples (albeit, quite extreme ones) of the kind of speculative dots that were being joined when so many unknowns surrounded a new ground-breaking piece of malware.

Perhaps Paul Ducklin summarises this sceptical perspective most succinctly in his piece on the Nimda virus, which he wrote ten years after its original discovery on 18 September 2001. The virus was subject to discussion within the industry about whether it was an example of cyber-terrorism, mainly due to its close proximity to the 9/11 attacks. Ducklin elaborates on some of the supposed clues as to the virus's authors that were hidden in the code to establish whether, with hindsight, we can conclude as to who originally launched it:

> The virus code includes the text: Concept Virus (CV) V.5, Copyright(C)2001 R.P. China. Since adjectives go before the noun in English, the country of China is known as PRC, not RPC. Does this tell us something? Is the error the sign of a mistake by a Chinese who knows only a bit of English? Are we looking at a Frenchman pretending to be a Chinese who knows a bit of English? Are we looking at a Russian pretending to be a Frenchman pretending to be a Chinese who knows a bit of English? (Ducklin, 2011)

As the conclusions get more and more convoluted, Ducklin says, 'the answer is, as so often with malware and cybercriminals, that we just can't say. We couldn't know ten years ago when Nimda came out; and we often can't tell today' (Ducklin, 2011). The ability to anonymise and cloak activity in cyberspace often means that the unknown factor will remain unknown and while this does not necessarily negate any kind of informed speculation, it does likely mean that it will remain just that: speculation. The industry has a preoccupation with prediction, threat assessment and worst-case scenarios; the fear of the unknown in cyberspace has left these threats as foreboding and threatening possibilities that *could* wreak havoc. Other experts, however, are critical of this assessment and argue that unknowns are simply unknowns and while this is not an invitation for complacency, it is equally not the precursor for an imminent catastrophe.

With so many unknowns surrounding a range of cybersecurity issues, the scope to speculate on who could be attacking 'us' and to what ends becomes quite broad. However, a less prevalent body of knowledge asserts that 'a real discussion about the actual threats and how best to deal with them' will be very difficult to achieve 'as long as the current frenzied circus of fear, uncertainty and doubt continues' (Urquhart, 2012). A dominant discourse gravitates towards a point where not only are 'known threats' a cause for concern, but those we have not discovered (and, indeed, may be non-existent) are also a serious cause for concern. The appearance of such knowledge results in a construction of cyber-threats as something we can never be wholly 'on top of' and thus requires serious consideration and constant vigilance. The fear of the unknown that surrounds cyber-threats has contributed to a construction that accentuates uncertainty and produces a 'What if?' logic, enhancing their perceived danger.

Inevitable uncertainty

I do want to qualify what exactly is uncertain here though. There is undoubtedly a large degree of uncertainty, unease and anxiety in representations of cyber-threats within this discourse as to the form that impending threats will take and when exactly they will strike. These are quite explicit features of the discourse, as covered in the above section; however, what is perhaps lost in these often evocative and striking accounts is the almost implicit certainty that surrounds their existence and inevitability. Amidst the uncertainty of the *who*, *when* and *where* comes a high degree of confidence in the continued development of cyber-threats and the inevitability of the *will*. While this may on the face of it sound contradictory, the effect is rather to accentuate the anxiety and to continue to assert the credibility of cyber-threats even in seemingly 'quiet' periods. Stealth and obfuscation as features of the threat mean that uncertainty is ever-present, and risky potential is latent in every assessment.

Predicting the future always involves 'a bit of speculation' (Haley, 2012c), but assessments typically conclude as to the inevitability of 'new tricks' (Cosoi, 2011a) that will require a pre-emptive posture online (Dunlaevy, 2013a). The logic underpinning such assessments relates to a combination of factors, including the rapidity with which computer hardware improves, the proliferation of computer technology across new platforms as well as new software design and increasing computer literacy. The rapid pace of change has meant that internet security companies have spent a significant amount of time considering threats of the future, relying on a mixture of both informed speculation and conjecture but consistently arriving at a conclusion that asserts the certainty of the enhanced threat that can be expected in the future.

A 2011 AVG article considers the consequences of ubiquitous computing and stresses how the 'increasingly intuitive interfaces' we enjoy as a result must be considered alongside the creation of a 'new breed' of malicious actor, 'lurking to play havoc with our lives' (AVG, 2011e). As we become more dependent on computer technology and progress closer to a fully realised 'Internet of Things', 'new methods of digital warfare and espionage could include car hacking … cyber-saboteurs may turn their focus to attack our healthcare system … criminals [may] attempt to reprogram our home security from afar' and even nations threatening attacks on 'infrastructure and national grids' could well become a concern (AVG, 2011e). As this computerisation of society continues to spread, and more and more sensitive data is stored on computers, we can expect to lose more 'data, money, and ideas through cyber intrusion' (Hawes, 2013b). The threat is thought to be sufficiently serious and developing at such a rapid pace that Sophos anticipate resources dedicated to tackling cyber-threats to 'equal or even eclipse the resources devoted to non-cyber based terrorist threats' (Hawes, 2013b). Cyber-threats will be promoted over traditional physical threats in the future because of the 'bigger and badder' threats that are on their way, including cyber-terrorism (Symantec, 2010; Kaspersky Labs, 2004b).

Eugene Kaspersky, has spoken about his fear of a future with cyber-terrorism in no uncertain terms, making his case in 2010 that the fight against cyber-threats has escalated from the 1990s, an era characterised by 'cyber-vandals', through the 2000s and 'cyber-criminals', to the present day and the 'age of cyber warfare and cyber terrorism' (Kaspersky Labs, 2010c). He and his company have also been very nervous of what the future may hold in relation to cyber-terrorism, with threats like Helkern putting the internet in 'jeopardy' and warning that without adequate defensive measures, they may 'even cause us to question the Internet's existence' (Kaspersky Labs, 2003a). Interestingly, Kaspersky struck a similar tone in both this 2003 article, where he referred to Helkern as 'the beginning of the end' and a later interview given in 2012 after his company discovered Flame, stating that what we are seeing is '[…] cyber terrorism, and I'm afraid the game is just beginning. Very soon, many countries around the world will know it beyond a shadow of a doubt … I'm afraid it will be the end of the world as we know it … I'm scared, believe me' (Reuters, 2012).

This more threatening future is premised in no small part on the quality of the malicious software being produced. In recent years companies have warned of 'a whole new generation of more organized and more malevolent malware writers' in their predictions for the coming years (Gostev, 2010). As malware writing competence improves we witness a shift, characterised as being from 'malware' to 'Malware 2.0' or similarly from 'spyware' to 'Spyware 2.0'. This new malware will 'leave no stone unturned, examining every document and every photo stored on an infected computer that it can', gathering a whole range of different information from the user's location to their salary and even their hair and eye colour (Gostev, 2010). ESET refer to a similar phenomenon they call 'the industrialization of malware' (the process of 'accelerated malware development'), in which 'more innovation in all aspects of malware' is

observable, including distribution, infection, exploitation and illicit monetisa-
tion (Cobb, 2013). This warning also comes with a disclaimer that these new
threats will 'add to, not replace' old ones, 'so, even as we work to defeat new
threats, we will not be able to let down our guard in other areas' (Cobb, 2013).
It will be a future, then, of familiar and unfamiliar threats where industry
experts and the public will be required to be constantly vigilant.

'Defining' and 'unprecedented' moments represent the 'Rubicon of our
future' (Parker, 2011b) and subsequently the future is something that needs to
be approached with 'trepidation' (Kamluk, 2008). In an 'end of year' piece
that perhaps sums this attitude up best, Deborah Salmi at Avast remarks that
'in a few days, the world will ring in the New Year with renewed hope for a
bright future. Predictions are being made about what 2012 will bring, and
unfortunately, instead of focusing on the positive, many of them are bleak'
(Salmi, 2011). These companies do, of course, stress the analysis they are doing
to stay on top of threats as well as the products and services they provide to
'proactively protect against current and future threats' (Business Wire, 2006).
However, anything other than a defensive and reactive posture is made difficult given the threat landscape and the characteristics of the threat.

The severity of the future threat differs between experts; not all share the
belief that the future will bring inevitable destructive cyber-attacks, but this
is one theme where genuine sustained disagreement is far more difficult to
find. This is slightly surprising, as literature outside of this industry does
point towards more optimistic perspectives surrounding the future of cybersecurity and the manner in which technologies and systems will improve to
face the threats in cyberspace. For example, Hansen and Nissenbaum refer
to the 'techno-utopian' solutions presented to the challenges of cybersecurity in
the 2003 US National Strategy to Secure Cyberspace (The White House,
2003). These authors cite the Strategy to highlight how the document 'couples
a series of securitizations with an exuberant faith in the development' (Hansen
and Nissenbaum, 2009, p. 1167) of 'highly secure, trust-worthy, and resilient
computer systems' that will mean 'in the future, working with a computer, the
Internet, or any other cyber system may become as dependable as turning on
the lights or the water' (The White House, 2003, p. 35). While this article
acknowledges the strategy's shortcoming that 'for the majority of the world's
poor … turning on the light or water may not be entirely dependable', this
perspective nevertheless reflects a 'technological utopianism' that 'sidesteps
the systemic, inherent ontological insecurity that computer scientists consistently emphasize' (Hansen and Nissenbaum, 2009, p. 1167).

When it comes to the future, such a coupling of securitisations with techno-logical utopianisms is not apparent within industry discourse. If different perspectives were more apparent, or even if there was less certitude within the discourse, perhaps a less convincing case could be made for the credibility of cyber-threats going forward. However, while this space is not universally apocalyptic about the future, it is characterised by a feeling of nervousness and apprehension based on the certainty that cyber-threats will become more dangerous and that they will continue to pose a credible (if not more cred-ible) threat in the future.

Constructing the conditions of unease

Having considered how the themes of vulnerability and uncertainty manifest within industry expert discourse I will bring this chapter to a close by consid-ering how what has been covered here speaks to the operation of the security *dispositif* and the significance of this 'source'. In this chapter I have honed in on two features of expert discourse that purport to reflect the reality of cyber-space; namely, that it is inherently weak (rendering us vulnerable) and that it is particularly unknowable in novel ways (rendering the timing and nature of the threats uncertain, if not their existence). These characteristics are not totally unique to this phenomenon or industry and indeed are reproduced elsewhere in other security discourses, including the dominant national cyber-security discourse as covered in Chapter 1. However, given the efforts being made here to establish how such an orthodoxy has rapidly settled, the identi-fication of similar features requires attention given the power/knowledge relationship and the epistemic authority imbued in security professionals such as these. Rather than considering this discourse as separate from the object it purports to reflect, I assume here that it is constitutive of it. The particularities found herein represent discursive tactics of a productive power set against a broader strategy designed to delimit (in)security and render actions and sub-jects governable (Heath-Kelly, 2013, p. 395).

In this chapter we see the clearest examples of the industry determining the foundations of cyberspace as unstable and inherently insecure. The dual themes of vulnerability and uncertainty combine in a familiar manner but one that has unique qualities given the architecture of the internet to produce 'What if?' and indeed 'Not if but when?' mentalities that, to paraphrase Joseba Zulaika and William Douglass (1996), leave us always waiting for cyber-threats.

What has been uncovered within this industry expert discourse appears to offer another example of an aspect of contemporary politics that is being 'defined at the horizon of unknown, yet catastrophic future events' (Aradau and Van Munster, 2012, p. 98). In particular, in the aftermath of the events of 11 September 2001, this mode of thinking has become more commonplace as 'organizations, bureaucracies and intelligence services are required to expect the unexpected and replace the improbable with the mere possible and imaginable' (Aradau, 2010b, p. 3). A consequence of these attacks was not only to enable more space and opportunity for security professionals and security planners, but also to establish for them that 'domestic security threats exist on a scale that was previously imagined only in warfare' and that their potential manifestation was 'wildly unpredictable' (Boyle and Haggerty, 2009, p. 260).

Just as Aradau suggests that institutions and experts are required to expect the unexpected, Boyle and Haggerty note that there is a 'continuous reiteration in official circles that security planners must "think outside the box"'; an approach that is 'meant to signify the need to contemplate a host of exceptionally unlikely but potentially catastrophic events' (Boyle and Haggerty, 2009, p. 260). Correspondingly, the state of exception, one of constant emergency, is established as a prudent and necessary condition through the security *dispositif* just as it is acted upon by the same ensemble. In so doing the various sources, such as these security professionals, justify their own position and work to delimit the categories of security and insecurity as a means of identifying what is normal and intervening upon that which is not, governing in these places to prevent and pre-empt that which threatens a particular circulation.

The appearance of worst-case scenario thinking/assessments and a focus on 'What if?' questions within the industry is of particular interest not only because cybersecurity typically struggles to evidence claims to effects comparable to even fairly low-tech, sub-state attacks (e.g. suicide bombings) or typical military action (e.g. air strikes) but also because similar approaches have been adopted elsewhere as successful tactics of power (Clarke, 2006). Politicians and security experts 'have routinely warned the public about all manner of potential threats, including radiological dispersal devices, biological and chemical attack and airstrikes against nuclear facilities' (Mythen and Walklate, 2008, p. 225). As with Anderson's characterisation of 'the event', the future here is a risky one; not a clearly delimited thing but instead an 'open future that cannot be secured' (Anderson, 2010, p. 228). Perhaps it is inevitable, therefore, that 'the end point is invariably worst-case-scenario thinking' (Mythen and Walklate, 2008, p. 235), with the industry referring to the appearance of certain malware as 'the beginning of the end' or 'the end of the world as we know it'.

This is not to imply that the entire discussion is played out along hypothetical lines, but rather that it is elevated to that of the potentially catastrophic. As Michael Dillon writes, 'in the digital age of virtual security, nothing and nowhere is strategically marginal. Everything and everywhere becomes potentially critical' (Dillon, 2003, p. 541). Statistical-heavy threat reports produced regularly throughout the year provide one means by which the industry aims to empirically concretise the existence and development of threats in cyberspace. We will see more of these sorts of reports in the subsequent chapters, but their presence here demonstrates the industry's efforts to produce statistical distributions and observable trends that indicate their position on the chance of further disruption and possible destruction occurring (Bigo, 2011, p. 99).

If statistics serve as one means by which the threat can be concretised and given greater validity, metaphor presents a prevalent linguistic device that performs a tactical function in making tangible vulnerability in cyberspace. The metaphorical and analogous reasoning identified in this chapter aids in the communication and constitution of vulnerability and does far more than offer a colourful turn of phrase. As Erin Steuter and Deborah Wills write in the opening pages of their book *At War with Metaphor*:

> Metaphors matter. We choose our words from within a dominant system or frame of metaphor that offers us a specific lexicon of language, that defines words in certain specific ways, and shapes both the 'what' and the 'how' of our communication. In this way, figuratively and often literally, through metaphor we make meaning. Our most common metaphors help us to understand problems and conflicts in certain ways, offering us certain available responses, and negating or obscuring others. Metaphor operates in the realm of thought, but its workings reverberate in concrete, active, tangible ways. (Steuter and Wills, 2009, p. 3)

Metaphors assist in the development of collective understandings around an issue or concept (Lakoff and Johnson, 2003) and help to 'distil complex political challenges into more readily graspable concepts' (Cohen, 2011, p. 200) that in turn suggest particular modes of thought, help prioritise certain actions and reject certain responses. As 'complex bundles of meaning' (Chilton, 2004, p. 52), the effect of metaphor cannot be guaranteed as there is no guaranteeing how 'readers' will interpret 'authors' (Barthes, 1983) on account of the unintended effects of power and of resistance. 'Individual motivation', Cohn writes, 'cannot necessarily be read directly from imagery; the imagery itself does not originate in these particular individuals but in a broader cultural context' (Cohn, 1987, p. 693). Nevertheless, discourse serves as 'an instrument and an effect of power' (Foucault, 1981, p. 101) and metaphor is a key linguistic device used within discursive strategies 'to conform with, circumvent, or contest existing power/knowledge relations' (Motion and Leitch, 2007, p. 265).[12]

We shall see even more extensive examples of metaphor in the next chapter, but what has been identified here in relation to metaphors of vulnerability demonstrates how the industry relies on evocative and intuitive metaphors to help translate a complex field, and particularly technical issues, more effectively. Such devices should not be considered innocent or apolitical, but part of a broad array of different tactics designed to produce a particular understanding and knowledge of cybersecurity that likens this area to others that are more graspable to a wider, non-specialist audience. Such tactics help to communicate (in)security and ultimately manage the unease that culminates from this.

Given the novelty of cybersecurity and the characteristics of cyber-threats, this particular security domain is possibly an even more appropriate one for the Rumsfeldian trifecta of known knowns, unknown knowns and unknown unknowns (Rumsfeld, 2002). These qualities breed an uncertainty of who, where and how insecurity will present while recognising the inevitability that they will continue to manifest. This coming together of broad certainty but specific uncertainty compounds apprehensive perceptions of threat and effectively creates 'a particular space for technical expert discourse' to assess and speculate upon the threat of cyber-attack from their unique and seemingly best-placed position of technical expertise (Hansen and Nissenbaum, 2009, p. 1166).

When the threat scenario is unknown but potentially very significant, with referents including CNI being targeted, technical experts such as those studied here are perhaps the most intuitive and credible speculators on account of the fact that they are privy to specialist information and possess technical training and expertise that is not held by the layperson. Individuals without the specialism and background of these professionals will be in a position where 'much is withheld or simply not known' to them and thus 'estimates of damage … [are] … either wildly exaggerated or understated' (Nissenbaum, 2005, p. 72). Such conditions highlight the importance of status in producing and maintaining this discursive formation and in its resonance across the security *dispositif*. The technical know-how allows for a great deal of autonomy when assessing cyber-threats and the conclusions and predictions made are imbued with all the hallmarks of scientific and bureaucratic validity.

The production and management of unease that is a characteristic of these security professionals is not confined to one aspect of this discourse; indeed, the next chapter identifies further means by which anxiety and unease are produced. However, in this chapter I have sought to frame cyberspace as the milieu and sketch out how the industry has constructed it as a domain with inherent weaknesses and risks that 'threats' can exploit. Establishing, as the industry does here, the unsteady foundations upon which cyberspace is built, and the novel features that define actions within this space, premises the opportunity for malicious actors with nefarious intent to threaten the circulation we have come to enjoy, expect and rely upon. These conditions are one aspect of a broader effort to define what (in)security looks like and make clear how industry expert knowledge and services can effectively manage this divide to avoid the encroachment of the margins upon the main.

Chapter 4

Constructing cyber-threats

Cyber-threats are said to be an increasing risk and now represent an 'everyday' reality for users (Symantec, 2002). Indeed, 'hardly a day goes by where we don't learn about a new exploit to a major system that hackers use to wreak havoc on web users' (Comodo, 2013). Prevalence is one thing, but destructiveness is another and several attacks have been observed 'in which the only goal was to cause as much damage as possible'. This worrying trend is to 'grow exponentially … [and] … if attackers can install destructive malware on a large number of machines, the result can be devastating' (McAfee, 2012). The threat posed by cyber-crime is characterised as being more of a risk to the UK than a nuclear strike (BullGuard, 2013c) and even some more conservative assessments still rank similar threats very highly, with only terrorism and nuclear proliferation usurping them (ESET Research, 2010b).

Elsewhere, cyberterrorism is said to be 'the number one national security threat to the U.S.', with terrorist organisations increasingly developing 'digital specialists' with particular interest in exploiting smartphone platforms 'for the theft of sensitive data' (McDermott, 2012). This assessment finds common ground with Mody who argues that, given the level of anxiety that this kind of exploitation could achieve, there is a 'possibility, nay probability, that attempts will be made to cause the targeted destruction of systems in the future, via the mass deployment of malware, in addition to data theft' (Mody, 2011). In considering terrorist organisations as a legitimate destructive force in cyberspace, industry experts share a viewpoint with many Western officials who have heeded such warnings about terrorist organisations and cyber-attack and have subsequently been on 'high alert' to such possibilities (Trend Micro, 2011b).

In the previous chapter, I focused on constructions of the environment in which cybersecurity plays out and identified how tropes of vulnerability and an uncertainty/certainty binary have generated instability and the conditions for a latent insecurity. In this chapter, I shift the focus to that which threatens to expose this insecurity, cyber-threats and the threatening actors themselves. Assertions such as those above give an indication of the destructive and credible threat posed by nefarious activity online. Chapter 3 spoke to this indirectly, for example when covering the manner in which hypothetical nightmare scenarios were deployed as tactics, and clearly there is overlap between these nightmare scenarios and what they say about the qualities of cyber-threats. More specifically, however, we also see overlaps in terms of the way in which discursive tactics are deployed to communicate the danger posed by cyber-threats, their credibility and the manner in which they will be able to exploit inherent weaknesses to cause destruction.

To illustrate this I will consider the continuation of metaphorical reasoning and how, in particular, metaphors of war and militarism materialise as powerful productive tactics that help frame cyber-threats as the bombs and bullets we are more familiar with. The emergence of a complexity/simplicity binary will also make up part of my analysis, as will the notable efforts made within the industry to assert and re-assert the credibility of the threats these security professionals dedicate so much time and energy to identifying, explaining and assessing.

Metaphors of war and militarism

Within the internet security industry a succession of military concepts and phenomena that have physically destructive characteristics or associations are presented interchangeably with various aspects of cyberspace and cyber-threats. Some of these metaphors are very apparent – for example the widespread reference to terms such as 'cyber-war' and 'cyber-weapons' – and yet notwithstanding the importance of these, after a close reading of this discourse it is apparent just how deeply embedded military metaphors are within this space. It is often the case that such tropes are used and presented to the reader as 'a given'.

To try and highlight more clearly the contingency that surrounds framing cyber-threats in a militaristic manner, it is useful to consider the multitude of ways in which such things can be understood. Malware, for example, is defined by Mohamad Fadli Zolkipil and Aman Jantan as: 'Software that has malicious intent to create harm to the computer or network operation' (Zolkipil and Jantan, 2011, p. 209). I am not arguing that this is a universally accepted definition, but for means of illustration it provides a useful and seemingly straightforward starting point to consider divergence within the internet security industry.[1] If we accept this definition, we might similarly consider anti-virus software, firewalls and intrusion detection systems to be software designed to prevent unauthorised access and deny malware from executing to create harm to a computer or network operation.

However, what we witness within industry discourse is the implication or explicit characterisation of cyberspace as a battlefield where malware and internet security software act as 'weapons' of a 'war' between (depending on the specifics) criminals, states, terrorists, users and internet security companies. In fact, wars are being waged against a surprisingly diverse number of adversaries (Namestnikov, 2010b) in a space where one must 'dodge' 'cyber-bullets' (Harley, 2009b) and where cyber-weapons mimic weapons in the physical world with 'warheads' (Kaspersky Labs, 2012d) that deliver their 'payload' (Kaspersky Labs, 2001b; Kaspersky Labs, 2004a; Namestnikov, 2010b; Kaspersky Labs' Global Research & Analysis Team 2012a) with 'surgical precision' (Kaspersky Labs' Global Research & Analysis Team, 2013). In the face of such an onslaught, cyber-strategy in the US has shifted from the 'cyber-defensive' into a 'fully operational Internet-era fighting force', a move that shows how the 'US administration takes cyber warfare seriously' (Waugh, 2013d).

The roots of this trope go far deeper than the use of war metaphors and in fact the industry borrows heavily from a wider military vernacular. Added to this, there are also myriad definitional issues that surround these cyber-threats, both inherited by their parent concepts and distinct to their cyber incarnations. The result of this has been that it is possible for experts to refer to one act as a range of different phenomena. For example, Stuxnet was included under the heading of cyber-sabotage and cyber-espionage at certain junctures (Kaspersky Labs, 2012a) and yet for the target of the attack, Iran, the experience is one of 'cyber-war' or even 'cyber-terrorism' (Penn, 2012).

The proliferation of a broad militaristic language, and the aforementioned definitional issues, has meant that while a distinction is observable between different sorts of acts and means in cyberspace, it remains difficult to discern exactly what experts are referring to when they say that we are now in the time of 'cyber-terrorism, cyber-weapons, and cyber-wars' (Kaspersky Labs, 2010a). While the edges may be blurry and complete clarity may be hard to establish, war and weapons do have commonly held characteristics. For example, referring to a piece of malware as 'a working – and fearsome – prototype of a cyber-weapon that will lead to a new arms race in the world' allows for parallels to conventional weapons as well as Cold War undertones (Kaspersky Labs, 2010a).

Despite the breadth of military vocabulary going further than simply war metaphors, it is certainly not the case that the widespread use of such language implies flippancy or casualness. In fact, sections of the industry stress that there is a war, or wars, ongoing in cyberspace, with the 'grim reality' being that the 'war arsenals of several countries now include cyber-weapons' (Kaspersky Labs' Global Research & Analysis Team, 2012b). To help fight these wars there has been an influx of cyber-warriors, cyber-mercenaries (Kaspersky Labs' Global Research & Analysis Team, 2013) and cyber-commandos (Panda, 2012) on all sides trying to gain the advantage. Anti-virus companies, for one, 'battle' viruses, Trojans and hacking attacks written and delivered by cyber-criminals (Abrams, 2010). These companies do battle by developing their own 'cyber-weapons', the most important of which is their anti-virus software, which picks up threats 'like a laser-guided missile homing in on its target' (Bell, 2013b). However, this software only makes up one piece of the necessary 'comprehensive antivirus arsenal' required to offer full protection (Hear4U, 2009b). Comodo, a company 'dedicated to winning the battle against a plague of viruses, worms, Trojans and other malware' (Scheuer, 2012), highlights spam messaging as the 'key battle field' in the 'war against internet cyber-criminals' (Comodo, 2005). Likewise, Kaspersky Labs recognise the 'serious war' that is being waged against fake anti-virus programs (Namestnikov, 2010b).

Just as these companies help protect users, 'information security warriors' embedded within all manner of organisations also help to shore up defences through the timely application of security fixes and patches (Walter, 2010). Moving further up the hierarchy of information security within organisations, Symantec liken the role of the Chief Information Security Officer (CISO) to that of a battlefield general and, as with military generals, accurate and up-to-date intelligence is integral to success in war. Symantec offer today's CISOs the 'clearest, most up-to-date intelligence' so that the 'general on the cyber-battlefield … will have the tools they need to win the war' (Bernick, 2013).

'Cyber warrior', once a term from science fiction, has become a job classification essential to internet security (Judge, 2013b) and 'governments around the world are recruiting these cyber warriors to fight against the growing threat of both cybercrime and state-sponsored attacks' (Waugh, 2013b). This has culminated in a scenario where, by 2011, almost all of the world's major nations had showed how they were prepared to develop and use their cyber-arsenals (Kaspersky Labs, 2012a). Rich, technologically developed states develop high-tech and destructive weapons like Duqu that show a remarkable similarity with a 'real-life missile', displaying both an 'overclocking module (a worm itself) and a warhead (PLC module)' (Aleks, 2011). While these weapons have intended targets, just as in physical war, Clausewitzian concepts of 'friction' and the 'fog of war' (von Clausewitz, 1989) still apply and thus they sometimes have unintended consequences that threaten us all; the 'collateral damage' of the cyber-war (Haley, 2012a). Meanwhile, much weaker states that fear for their own security, such as North Korea, expand their 'cyber-warrior savvy' by sending the best young programmers abroad to develop their skills and allow their country to 'hold their own in cyber-warfare' (Camp, 2011a). As governments continue to create cyber-commandos for both defensive and offensive purposes in this manner, 'the cyber arms race' will continue to escalate (Panda, 2012).

This cyber-war shares much with conventional physical warfare and the build-up of arms is one such parallel that demonstrates how the old adage *si vis pacem, para bellum* (if you want peace, prepare for war) still prevails in this alternative space (Popp, 2010). As leading world powers openly discuss the need to defend against enemy activity in cyberspace and their correlating need to develop their cyberwarfare capabilities, it 'in turn forces other states to follow suit and have their own highly qualified teams of programmers and hackers to develop specialized cyber-resources' (Kaspersky Labs' Global Research & Analysis Team, 2012b). The 'game changing' malware Stuxnet, Flame and Gauss led us towards the 'very first steps of a new cyber arms race' (F-Secure, 2012a) that has since got 'well under way' (F-Secure, 2012b):

> The game is on, and I don't think there's anything we could do to stop it any more. International espionage has already gone digital. Any future real-world crisis will have cyberelements in play as well. So will any future war. The cyber-arms race has now officially started. And nobody seems to know where it will take us. (Hyppönen, 2012a)

Although talk of a cyber-arms race is largely targeted at the actions of the technologically developed states and their competitors, this metaphor is used with some flexibility. For example, it is used to describe the relationship between cyber-criminals and IT security companies in which the anti-virus industry has had to rapidly develop 'new technologies for detection and disinfection in order to balance the threat' (Namestnikov, 2010a).

Despite the assertion that we are witnessing an arms race between the most powerful and technologically developed states in the world, there is an acceptance that this particular arms race differs to examples of traditional arms races. For example, Mikko Hyppönen concedes that:

> the main point of any arms race is to let your adversaries know about your capabilities so they don't even think about starting a fight. We're not at this stage in the cyber arms race. Almost all of the development in this area is secret and classified. (Hyppönen, 2012b)

This raises the question of whether an arms race is an appropriate metaphor at all. Nevertheless, it has gained traction to the extent that it has sparked discussions surrounding the need for greater arms control within cyberspace, much like that which already exists surrounding nuclear weapons (Kaspersky Labs, 2012b). The comparison between the need for an arms control treaty similar to that which already exists for nuclear weapons may be a coincidence. However, nuclear weapons and in particular the Cold War are frequently compared to the emerging threat of cyber-weaponry alongside a succession of other relevant military historical metaphors and analogies.

With the emergence of Stuxnet as the 'first of its kind' example of destructive malware drawing comparisons within the industry to the 1945 Trinity Tests (ESET Research, 2010d), the need for arms control and the comparisons with nuclear weaponry have brought about Cold War analogies or talk of a 'new Cold War'. Cybersecurity is said to be the 'front line in a new Cold War … a front that stretches from the Pentagon, to the corporate board room and to the living room' (Kaspersky Labs, 2011a). Granted, it is a Cold War with differences where weapons are now measured in megaping as opposed to mega tonnage (ESET Research, 2010c), but one where old principles of mutually assured destruction could still have value so long as 'the most solid hope for protection becomes the fear of retaliation'. In this new Cold War, states may well be restrained from serious aggression knowing that taking down one state's power grid, for example, will be met with their own going down 'in seconds' (Popp, 2010). The Cold War was a period of superpower tension in which the very real possibility of nuclear Armageddon loomed. The comparison made here implies that we face something similar with cyberwar, where logics of deterrence still hold value and where the potential for catastrophic destruction is very real.

Alongside the Cold War, cyber-threats are linked to a series of other noncyber military historical events and threats. Second World War comparisons are evident within this discourse, with Bitdefender citing ex-senior UK politician and current member of the House of Lords William Hague and his likening of the cybersecurity challenge to the Second World War-era code breakers. Hague deemed the former 'every bit as serious as some of those confronted in the Second World War' (Bitdefender, 2012a). Kevin Haley, of Symantec, even quotes Winston Churchill's famous 'end of the beginning' speech, a speech that he feels is 'quite appropriate' in light of the Flame malware (Haley, 2012a). An ESET article on cybersecurity legislation references an event that is more prominent in American memories of the Second World War, arguing that we must be proactive in the face of cyber-threats and cannot simply sit around and 'wait for a cyber Pearl Harbor' (ESET Research, 2010b). The Pearl Harbor analogy is one that has remained extremely pertinent in the American consciousness, being used after the 11 September 2001 attacks as a means of comprehension: 'The Pearl Harbor analogy came to mind so readily because people needed familiar references, experiences, or examples from the past in order to understand the events they were facing' (Jespersen, 2005, p. 413).

However, the tendency of politicians and industry experts to readily and un-problematically use this event as a means of communicating the likely outcome of a cyber-attack has led to dissident voices, critical of the accuracy of such a comparison. Lisa Vaas is very critical of the way security experts choose to 'terrorise' people with a culture of fear in which terms such as '"Armageddon" and "digital Pearl Harbor" get tossed about and blazoned across headlines'. 'How much bloodshed', she asks, 'have we seen, exactly?' and 'how does it compare to a surprise military attack like Pearl Harbor?': 'Can hackers really cause as much bloodshed as 353 Imperial Japanese Navy fighters, bombers and torpedo planes launched from six aircraft carriers? Can hackers really kill 2,402 U.S. citizens, leave 1,282 wounded, lose 65 of their own attackers in the process, and plunge the United States into a World War?' (Vaas, 2012).

Vaas concedes that SCADA threats are real and could result in 'a body count', but she argues for a need to keep 'the rhetoric sane' so that a 'reasoned discussion of the threat' can take place which concentrates on how to 'secure the systems in question'. This plea to return to a 'reasoned discussion of the threat' implies a desire to 'return to reality', to get back to discussing cyber-threats as they *actually are* and not a hyperbolic version of them. Similar to critical voices in Chapter 3, Vaas levels another critique of a prevailing voice that does not deny the extra-discursiveness of cyber-threats but one that argues specific representations obscure these threats' reality. This is problematic for Vaas because primacy should be given to problem solving and therefore the industry should concentrate on 'making improvements instead of cooking up apocalyptic metaphors' (Vass, 2012).

The historical military metaphors and analogies referenced above liken aspects of the cybersecurity challenge, malware and potential cyber-attacks to war efforts that are thought to have shortened the biggest conventional war in human existence by two years (the Enigma code breakers), the closing stage of this war and a surprise physical attack that killed almost two and a half thousand US servicemen (Pearl Harbor). The use of these particular devices is important due to their signifying value within particular social contexts. Framed in a way that synonymises them with prominent and destructive military historical events, this contributes towards a particular construction of cyber-threats as being of the same order as those events cited above and accentuates their destructive capability and momentousness.

Comments such as those offered by Vaas reflect a general scepticism that, while observable, must be considered the exception as opposed to the rule. These moments of rupture that argue that terms such as cyber-war and cyber-terror are 'over-hyped' (Harley, 2009a) 'buzzwords' (ESET Global Threat Report, 2011) without 'real dimensions' and are 'too exaggerated' to characterise the examples of conflict in cyberspace (Panda, 2011a) stand out because they serve to puncture the apparent cohesiveness with which large sections of the industry use such terminology. Moreover, these characterisations do not challenge the extra-discursive reality of cyber-threats, but are, rather, criticisms related to the accuracy of others' assessments. Randy Abrams, for example, highlights 'misconceptions' that he feels surround the term 'cyber-war': 'There isn't going to be a war, at least anytime soon which is fought with only computers. Computers are simply being used as a weapon in conjunction with traditional warfare' (Abrams, 2009b).

A Securelist article[2] also hints at a certain scepticism surrounding terms like 'cyber-war' and 'cyber-terrorism', when Alexander Gostev comments that 'experts are doing all they can to create scenarios for real computer wars' (Gostev, 2007). Such perspectives are not as prevalent as those asserting that security companies are 'locked in combat' (Mashevsky, 2010) with malware and malicious actors, just as the traditional security actors (states) are also locked in a war of their own.

Perhaps the strongest critique that is offered from within the industry relating to the militarisation of cyberspace comes from Andrew Lee at ESET. Lee outright rejects the conventional wisdom that feels it appropriate to co-opt the use of military language at all:

> Over the last few years, in its insatiable thirst for the new, the security industry has increasingly co-opted military terminology for its marketing, and in return obliging government and military offices (particularly, but not exclusively in the western world) have predicted dire and terrifying scenarios. Couching the threats in the terms of modern warfare, spiced with the magic of 'Cyber', security wonks insist we exist in a new world of CyberWar, CyberTerrorism, Cyber-Attacks and CyberEspionage where devastation and carnage to our most sacred institutions lurk only a mouse-click away. (ESET Global Threat Report, 2012)

Lee questions whether we really exist in 'this strange new world' or whether it is 'simply a case of paranoia fuelled by undirected angst about real-world, boots-on-the-ground warfare and the endless "wars" on drugs and terror'. Has security dialogue been hijacked by 'hype and political expediency' and has

> [...] the constant exposure to the fantasy and science fiction novels fed into the security industry's hero complex wherein we become the fantastical knights in shining armour (or long leather coat, depending on your milieu), deploying our Low Orbit Ion Cannons against the evil (but faceless) phantoms of the global military industrial complex? (ESET Global Threat Report, 2012)

Lee's comments imply at least a deeper critique of this particular framing that alludes to an extension of the military–industrial complex in cyberspace and, while never explicit, appears to question the ontology of cyber-threats (at least specifically as cyber-war, cyber-terrorism, cyber-attacks and cyber-espionage) as having an extra-discursive existence.

Such alternative positions challenge us to question the common sense and consider just how appropriate it really is to talk of cyber-war, cyber-terror, cyber-arms races, cyber-Pearl Harbors and so on. Critiquing the discourse on its own terms, one could ask whether this analogising between cyberspace and physical space is 'accurate' but more significant, I think, are the productive connotations of this and the impact such knowledge has upon informing subsequent practices of government. If lines of code become weapons and those that write and deliver them soldiers, the destructiveness of these cyber-phenomena becomes a logical progression because we expect wars to be destructive. Moreover, this militarisation produces cyberspace as a legitimate security domain where war and cyber-war and terrorism and cyber-terrorism are comfortably analogous and ontologically stable.

Complexity and simplicity

The manner in which complexity *and* simplicity have been simultaneously written into these threats is another feature of the discourse and one that on the face of it might come across as contradictory. On the one hand, it has become something of a truism to point out that cyber-threats are continually becoming more complex; however, alongside this there is an understanding that despite their complexity in design the malware used to cause the destruction alluded to above is very user friendly.

Dwelling on complexity first, the consistent rate at which computing power increases, the rapid developments in the field of computing and improvement in individuals' ability to write novel code means that what is possible to achieve through the use of malware and other cyber-attacks increases over time. Occasionally, this is depicted as 'hacker gangs' painstakingly putting the 'finishing touches to their masterpieces' (Namestnikov, 2010b) but more often than not complexity is the rule and not the exception and there is a growing trend in which 'the most widespread malicious programs tend to be the most sophisticated' (Gostev, 2010). This complexity poses challenges for security companies (Avira, 2013) and the appearance of 'big and incredibly sophisticated' threats such as Flame have redefined 'the notion of cyberwar and cyberespionage' (Gostev, 2012), necessitating the expansion of these companies' product ranges (Namestnikov, 2010b).

The complexity that is overtly referenced above is also communicated to an audience via different discursive tactics – for example, the usage of a specialist and technical language. We have already considered Nissenbaum's notion of cybersecurity as a 'technified' field and the idea that it requires a specialist knowledge to be effectively understood (Nissenbaum, 2005, p. 72). When commenting on the threats, we get a sense of their complexity via the deployment of a particular vernacular that highlights a disconnect between expert and layperson when discussing and comprehending the nature of these threats. While the majority of the commentary found within the industry is written in such a way that the layperson can more easily understand, there are notable occasions where the audience is reminded of the complexity in a manner that is often linked to the severity of the threat posed.

Despite the claim I am making here, it may appear at first glance that much of the cyber-lexicon is not that specialist at all. For example, there are prominent examples of analogies such as 'virus', 'worm' and 'Trojan' that appear to be terms understood by the expert and layperson alike, as well as the abundance of terms that simply modify existing concepts with the addition of a 'cyber-' prefix. However, in the first instance it is worth noting that while the terminology of computer scientists and cybersecurity experts may have become shared with the wider population, it is, of course, a signifier that makes very complicated concepts more manageable and easier to communicate. For example, while computer viruses may be talked about with confidence by technical and non-technical people alike, the extent to which the general population fully understands[3] such terms is questionable:

> Indeed, the term computer virus, which appeared in 1986, has become familiar to the general public. This is not too surprising insofar as in present day society, computers are omnipresent in homes, at work and almost everyone which uses the Internet or any other network has been faced with a viral infection at least once. Nevertheless, it cannot be denied that user's knowledge of the word is incomplete. (Filiol, 2006, p. 81)

So I would argue that these more commonplace examples of cyber-parlance, while widely cited, are still poorly understood. Nevertheless, this language has become so prevalent in general non-specialist language that claiming its status as being exclusively expert terminology would be a stretch. This is why it is so interesting to explore where genuinely technical language is deployed to explain various phenomena in cyberspace and to convey the threat these phenomena present. With so many references to threats such as viruses and worms, the appearance of less mainstream elements of the industry's own lexicon stand out and effectively communicate a complexity that requires a detailed knowledge of computing to understand fully. Closing off the ability of the audience (or general users) to be able to fully engage in the understanding or discussion of the threat environment in this manner provides a timely reminder of the status of these speakers, their ability to speak on this subject and a privileged role in managing societal unease.

For example, a threat such as the software package 'Blackhole' (a ready-made 'exploit kit' available for purchase online) is described as being 'sophisticated and powerful', due to its 'polymorphic nature' and the fact that it is 'heavily obfuscated to evade detection by anti-malware solutions' (Ben-Itzhak, 2012). Similarly, the computer worm 'Koobface' is the subject of a study by Bitdefender within which they determine that there is more to the malware 'than meets the eye', with 'additional surprises' including 'CAPTCHA breakers, locally-installed HTTP servers, keyloggers and FTP file uploader components, as well as a rogue DNS changer and an advertisement pusher'

(Cosoi, 2011a). This discourse is explicit in explaining how malware has undergone a broad evolution, exploiting the full spectrum of operating systems on the market in so-called 'cross-platform attacks' (BullGuard, 2013a) as well as making use of 'metamorphic' code that allows the malware to 'encrypt or modify itself to distinguish its signature and thus evade antivirus programs' (Ben-Itzhak, 2013b). The upshot for the internet security industry is that experts now have to defend across multiple different operating systems while also no longer being able to rely on amassing a large list of 'blacklisted' signatures as the sole form of defence.

These threats have become so complex and 'multi-dimensional' that they now require equally 'multi-layered' solutions (Comodo, 2007) with a 'fully integrated layer of virus protection' (Avira, 2013). Metamorphic code is met with the addition of heuristic analysis as well as traditional behavioural scanning (Mustaca, 2010a), but other means of defence against malicious threats include 'intrusion detection/prevention, reputation, link scanning and other mechanisms such as firewalls, anti-phishing and anti-spam, all of which are commonplace' (Ben-Itzhak, 2013a). Comodo Internet Security offers a 'highly protective shield' that uses a combination of 'firewall, antivirus, host intrusion prevention, automatic sandboxing and behaviour analysis technologies to quickly and accurately identify safe, unsafe and questionable files' (Comodo, 2013). Writing in a blog post covering a controversial presentation at the 2010 Virus Bulletin conference on anti-virus testing, Sorin Mustaca opined that AV solutions should be held up against an 'in the wild' baseline check, as well as their ability to dynamically detect threats such as polymorphic malware and Java scripts, URL categorisation, the blocking of potential spam, malware and phishing links (Mustaca, 2010b). Check Point even provided 'tunnelling' within their SecuRemote 3.0 software to ensure that corporate users have 'new levels of assurance that their virtual private networks (VPNs) will be impervious to intruders' (Check Point, 1997).

The purpose of outlining all of this terminology is not simply to bombard the reader with a technical vernacular, but instead to point out that this discourse, much like many technical or expert discourses, does have a distinct terminology. Given the requirement for the industry to be able to meaningfully communicate to a non-expert audience, be that the general user, business or even government officials, the frequent usage of a non-technical language and perhaps even a tendency to prefix 'cyber-' to a host of other better known threats certainly makes sense. Even the most complex of these threats can have fairly straightforward effects and the intersection of the technical with everyday security practices means that it often pays for the industry to communicate the threat in such a way as to raise awareness, generate understanding and sell products.

Given this, the appearance of a more technical language is striking and its appearance can be explained, I think, by virtue of its ability to accentuate the risk found herein and to reassert the complexity of the field that may occasionally be lost, given the need to frequently speak to a non-specialist audience. I will dwell on this more as a tactic of the industry at the chapter's close; however, uncertainty and destructive capability can be brought out through complexity and all work well together as part of a mutually beneficial relationship that compounds the former and consequently enhances the threat. The unpredictability of a threat is a commonplace feature; there is often a latent but unknowable potential for harm whether it be a build-up of troops near our borders, terrorist organisations operating clandestinely or even tectonic plates shifting underneath our feet. However, what makes the *complexity* of cyber-threats quite unique is that it obfuscates *how* these threats might do us harm. Their complexity implies their ability to do tremendous damage and further entrenches the uncertainty via the difficulty of 'keeping up' with the rapid pace with which they are outsmarting and outmanoeuvring current defences.

We have seen earlier how the more media-friendly terms like 'cyber-war' and 'cyber-terrorism' have been the target of some resistance, with dissident voices in the industry describing them as 'buzzwords' (ESET Global Threat Report, 2011, p. 3) or, in the case of APTs, 'an overblown marketing term' (Waugh, 2013e). Such a critique does not exist in the same manner for the technical language highlighted here, but, given that this is the technical (scientific) vernacular associated with the domain, we should not be surprised by this. However, while the technical language appears free from controversy and is approached as neutral, we do witness contestation as to the extent to which the majority of the attacks constitute anything genuinely 'complex'.

In an article mainly dealing with internet spam, Graham Cluley argues that there is too great a focus on a very small fraction of cyber-threats that exhibit a high level of skill in how they have been written: '[…] so much attention is given by the-powers-that-be to the threat of cyberterrorists and rogue states launching attacks, but the fact is that it could be your sister-in-law Sandra who is helping the spammers without her knowledge, because her home PC is not properly defended' (Cluley, 2009a). He adds, 'of course, spam is not the only output from these compromised PCs. They can also be used to spread malware, steal identities and launch distributed denial-of-service attacks – all without the knowledge of the computer owner who doesn't even realise that their computer is infected' (Cluley, 2009a). The implication here is that, for all the focus given to the headline-grabbing malware, what is too often over-looked are the banal and commonplace exploits and the simple but effective techniques. In a similar vein, Roger Thompson dismisses the attention given to high-profile disruptive attacks such as those on US and South Korean web-sites in July 2009, challenging the purported technical complexity that sur-rounds such threats when he says 'it's obviously a great headline, but most actual security folk took the view that it's just a DDoS, for goodness sake' (Thompson, 2009). There appear to be a couple of criticisms here: first, that the vast majority of nefarious activity online is not complex malware but instead much simpler in its form and execution, and, second, that too much attention and significance is given to nefarious activity once it begins to garner more widespread attention in the media, for example.

However, as stated at the beginning of this section, complexity and simplic-ity are not a binary applied in an either/or fashion but, in fact, often applied simultaneously. The game changing complexity referenced above interlaces with a simplicity of usage and execution that means all manner of threatening actors, including hacktivists, terrorists and states, can exploit the weaknesses covered in the previous chapters to bombard systems with a diverse range of attacks. As one Symantec article outlines, cyber-attack can be simultaneously 'big and sophisticated' while also 'simple, easy, and very effective' for the mali-cious actor(s) conducting them. When focusing on the ease of these methods, the attention tends to be on those groups that do not have the same financial, expert and logistical muscle possessed by states. So, for example, the ease with which cyber-terrorism can be conducted has seen it become a 'mainstream' cybersecurity term and explains why it is a threat that is 'here to stay' (Granger, 2010). Cyber-terrorism has an 'extremely low' barrier of entry, making it a very attractive option, with the associated training for these kinds of attacks being 'cheap, fast, and effective' (Popp, 2010). Hacking and malware writing are not the domains of the genius alone and, in fact, the skills needed to gain unauthorised access to create malicious code are covered extensively in docu-mentation online, meaning that 'no sophistication or skill is required' (Raiu, 2009). The combination of the 'unprecedented growth of malicious code' and 'the degradation of virus writers' skills' has meant that 'today, to create a virus, one needs no special programming knowledge – to do so, he only needs to learn how to start up a computer and understand basic commands to manage a virus construction kit' (Kaspersky Labs, 2001a). It is argued that such positions are made credible with the reports of 'real-world terrorists' threatening to create disruption online through the use of software such as 'Electronic Jihad', which is capable of creating distributed denial-of-service attacks as well as offering the attacker flexibility and making it 'easy for cyber-terrorists to be more effective' (Paredes, 2007).

'Madi' was one example of a 'relatively unsophisticated' but effective piece of malware that was designed for cyber-espionage and was cited as strong evidence for what simplicity can achieve (Emm and Raiu, 2012), as are the slew of exploit kits that allow 'even a malicious novice to launch a cyberattack' (Symantec, 2011a). Toolkits such as Blackhole and Zeus 'lower the barrier of entry', leading to malware that is 'more sophisticated and more widespread … [enabling] … hackers to continuously generate new mutated malware variants, each targeting a different victim, making traditional discovery and finger-printing of these threats nearly impossible' (Symantec, 2011c). In fact, in one piece it is suggested that 'everybody with enough criminal energy is able to build his own botnet with this construction kit' (Avira, 2010).

Again, the ease with which such a broad array of actors can easily conduct complex attacks is met with scepticism elsewhere – for example, Faronics note that sub-state terrorists are 'usually affiliated with small, seditious political off-shoots' and therefore would lack the budget and expertise to cause disruption or destruction to 'grand institutions' (Beckham, 2012). Both of these points about budget and expertise are echoed at other junctures, leading to the conclusion that the most complex and destructive malware would be out of the question for those without the resources of a developed nation state (Sullivan, 2010; Cluley, 2011a; Panda, 2011a). Even when witnessing at the 2012 Breakpoint conference how a pacemaker could be tampered with to deliver an 830-volt shock to the body, the required set-up, scope for error and the necessary resources and technical expertise of this demonstration led Brian Donohue to the conclusion that, for terrorists, 'it's more effective to use good old bombs and guns' (Donohue, 2013).

One of the more difficult elements about the discussion that takes place surrounding simplicity is the aforementioned tension that appears to be at its heart: various forms of cyber-attack are said to be simultaneously complex and destructive, yet low-cost and easy. Conventional wisdom within the industry appears to be of the opinion that this is not really a tension at all because complexity of means does not necessarily equate to complexity of execution. However, this is not satisfactory for all. A piece by Trend Micro cites Eli Alshech, the Director of the Jihad and Terrorism Studies Project at the Middle East Media Research Institute, who asserts that the majority of cyber-attacks that we have seen that could be designated 'cyber-terrorism' have been simple and low-cost, but have only really constituted a 'nuisance' as opposed to a genuine 'threat' (Paredes, 2007).

Similarly, the characteristic of complexity as an apparent threat enhancer is interesting because it is hardly a characteristic distinct to cyber-threats and yet more appears to be made of it within this discourse as a reason to be fearful. Our inability to fully understand the inner workings of a gun, the processes involved in a bomb detonating or how a nuclear missile works are not common explanations for why we should be fearful of them. Two possible reasons for this are, first, that all of these weapons have been a common feature of domestic and international security discussion for a much longer period of time and therefore are more familiar to us. There is nothing cutting-edge and new about these weapons, whereas cyber-threats still often find themselves framed in terms of their unprecedented and ground-breaking nature, a trope that ties in well with a focus on their complexity. Second is that we can point towards clear empirical evidence that guns, bombs and nuclear weapons have caused significant destruction, a feature that surely 'trumps' the need to focus on their complexity? While cyber-threats continue to be discussed in terms of 'What if?', it follows that claims to their increased complexity could bolster their destructive capability – that is, their complexity increases the hypothetical risk and draws us closer to the actual. Weapons that have razed major cities to the ground have already shown their incredible destructive capability and therefore conversations of complexity are less necessary for asserting this characteristic.

Establishing credibility

In 2006, Mythen and Walklate said of the terrorist threat that while it is clearly not 'fictional' it 'is being fictionalised' (p. 389). Given some of the scepticism we have seen within even this site of discourse, perhaps a similar charge could be levelled at cyber-threats. Despite being overwhelmingly apprehensive in assessment, there do exist counter-currents of scepticism that offer everything from a raised eyebrow to an outright rejection, depending on the assessment being made. To refer back to Mythen and Walklate, while of course there is a slew of empirical evidence that demonstrates the nefarious cyber-activities of criminals, terrorists and states, there is also a striking amount of analogy, conjecture and hypothesising, in particular as we move up the scale from the more everyday towards the more complex and potentially catastrophic. Given the dearth of observable evidence at the more destructive end of the scale, as well as the propensity to focus on the hypothetical and the 'What if?' scenarios, one common charge levelled at the more apprehensive assessments is that major cyber-attacks are possible *in theory* but are not credible in reality. However, the industry does not leave these charges unanswered and looks to cement apprehensions about vulnerabilities and threats by solidifying the credibility of the risks it identifies against scepticism surrounding the validity of these assessments.

We have seen in the previous chapter how the industry uses an uncertainty/certainty binary to produce a foreboding and inevitable future. However, it is also at pains to stress that this is a threat to security *right now* rather than being exclusively tomorrow's threat. Cyber threats are already a 'viable option over conventional methods' and rather than this being a discussion for the future of what is yet to be, it is the case that 'countries are using malware to attack each other. The cyber warfare revolution is underway. It's happening right now' (F-Secure, 2012a). Almost all of the world's most developed nations have shown their willingness to use their 'cyber-arsenals' if necessary, a revelation that testifies to the fact that we are 'at the dawn of a new era of cyber-warfare' with 'cyber-espionage, cyber-sabotage and potentially even cyber-warfare' presenting as genuine threats (Kaspersky Labs, 2012a).

Broader intertextualities are evident in this effort to bolster claims to credibility and imminence, with individuals imbued with alternative forms of epistemic authority brought in to verify industry claims.[4] Former President Barack Obama, himself cautious to use the word 'war' when describing nefarious cyber-activity, did nevertheless stress the credibility of these threats and the fact they 'cost billions of dollars, lead to stolen industry secrets, and place the United States at a competitive disadvantage' (Waugh, 2013c). Such threats were considered so severe, the industry reports, that they were detailed as matters of US national security in the 2009 Annual Threat Assessment Intelligence Briefing to the Senate Intelligence Committee (ESET Research, 2009). Others, such as Richard Clarke, the former US Cybersecurity Advisor, and Admiral Jonathan Greenert, the US Navy Chief of Operations, are also quoted to convey the seriousness with which these threats are taken – apparently at the same level as strategic nuclear defence (Waugh, 2013a).

Clarke is quoted in one ESET article, talking about how we are at a 'very perilous point' now, with between twenty and thirty nations having formed 'cyberwar military units'. He goes on to say how our predictions from '10 or even 20 years ago' in terms of cybersecurity are now a reality, how other nations have begun 'preparing the battlefield' and the worrying fact that 'crazy' North Korea is 'taking over whole floors of hotels in cities in China to set up teams of cyberwarriors' (ESET Research, 2010c). The focus given here to China is reflective of what Jeffery Carr (cybersecurity expert and CEO of Taia Global) refers to as 'the China fallacy'. Carr does not dispute the credible threat posed by China but argues that undue attention given to China as the number one cyber-war belligerent risks missing 'what China is actually excelling at (cyber espionage)', as well as having the secondary effect of underestimating 'the authentic threats from other nation states that are busy eating your lunch without you knowing it' (ESET Research, 2010d). Outside of the US, we also see reports of international agreements between states that reflect the 'practical cooperation' that is underway in the face of the dangers posed online (Waugh, 2013f).

The Stuxnet effect

Between the years of 1997 and 2013 that make up the time period studied in this book, one piece of malware stands out against the rest: Stuxnet. The fact that Stuxnet was a complex piece of malware that caused destruction on a secure and critical network and involved two rival nation states meant that it garnered much attention. Subsequently, it did a lot to impact the perceived broader credibility of cyber-threats and how future stories were covered. Stuxnet and other malware from the same family, such as Flame and Duqu, were seen to 'highlight the technical sophistication of military-grade software able to damage large industrial installations and more' (Kaspersky Labs, 2012a). Indeed, the dominant cybersecurity knowledge, with all the qualities discussed in the previous two chapters, certainly appears to have been bolstered off the back of 'the mighty spectre of Stuxnet' (Hawes, 2013e).

As time has passed and the dust has settled on Stuxnet, its currency has waned and other malware have taken up the mantle. Indeed, the massive impact that Stuxnet had, as well as its historical significance, has seen it become a source of frustration for some on account of the trite and often well-trodden arguments that continue to go along with it (Rid, 2018). Nevertheless, in the wake of Stuxnet the breadth of discussion was phenomenal and often used in numerous different ways to provide empirical evidence of what malware can achieve. For example, Stuxnet was viewed as providing evidence for a raft of next generation threats:

> […] we are now witnessing new types of IT threats in the form of cyber terrorism. This is borne out by the malware that our company detected in 2010. The next generation of IT malware to be launched on an unsuspecting world will contain programs for commercial sabotage, or maybe even worse. Our experts are currently examining the situation in great detail and we are developing solutions that will provide our clients with the very best IT Security strategies available for countering cyber terrorism in the future. (Kaspersky Labs, 2010b)

This sort of coverage is reminiscent of Hagmann and Dunn Cavelty (2012, pp. 84–5), on how references to historically analogous events are made, extrapolated and projected into the future to aid in the assessment of societal and political risks. While Stuxnet would have been very recent history in the context of the above excerpt, we can observe here how this event is deployed to make possible a more threatening future. Symantec provided a more specific example of this practice when, a month after the malware was discovered, they covered the 'dark possibility' of Stuxnet being the work of terrorists, arguing that 'if the attacker gained control of a power station or another critical facility, they could wreak havoc, shutting down the facility or causing damage by disrupting the normal operations within the facility'. Echoing the earlier point about distancing these threats from fiction, the author stresses that while the scenario sounds like 'something out of a movie', given the situation, terrorism is within the 'realms of possibility' (Fitzgerald, 2010).

These malwares are depicted as a turning point[5] for the industry, opening 'a new chapter in cyber terrorism' (AhnLab, 2011b). Eugene Kaspersky, in the speech where he heralded the modern era as the age of 'cyber warfare and cyber terrorism', also focused on 'the infamous' Stuxnet and how its design for industrial sabotage marked 'a turning point in the history of malware evolution' (Kaspersky Labs, 2010c). Likewise Stuxnet, Flame and Duqu are all drawn upon when highlighting the vulnerability of 'critical energy, finance, telecommunication, and government cyber network infrastructures worldwide' to demonstrate the increased vulnerability of developed states to the threat of cyberterrorism (Kaspersky Labs, 2012c).

This complex group of malware has had an important impact on the industry; however, it is not the first instance of something new appearing and finding itself quickly heralded as transformative and signalling the existence of an apocalyptic new breed of threats. A 2003 piece on the Helkern malware (or the 'Helkern epidemic') shows how Kaspersky linked this particular piece of malware to the possible collapse of the internet: 'Is 'Helkern' an isolated event or unpremeditated attack? Or is it the next step for cyber-terrorists exposing network weaknesses that model the collapse of the Internet? What consequences will result from this epidemic have on the future of the Internet?' (Kaspersky Labs, 2003a). Reminiscent of John *Mueller*'s work on the overreaction to terrorism (Mueller, 2005, 2006), Kaspersky in this instance appears to have extrapolated in the face of uncertainty around a piece of malware to the existence of cyberterrorism and even the potential collapse of the internet. A similar thing has occurred with the more contemporary examples – their discovery has been touted as putting to bed scepticism around the existence of war, terrorism, espionage and/or sabotage in cyberspace and is said to pave the way for all manner of different hypothetical future threats.

Fact not fiction

One dilemma that potentially serves to undermine the credibility of cyber-threats is the problematic association 'cyber-' has with fiction. *Mr Robot*, *Die Hard 4*, *Skyfall* and earlier examples such as *WarGames* act as popular representations of cybersecurity that tend to couch the field within the confines of Hollywood as opposed to national security. While this certainly assists in placing the issues within the public consciousness, it also poses a problem for those within the internet security industry who are trying to communicate the *reality* of cyber-threats and the concern that should surround them. Cyber-attacks and infrastructure outages may be popular plotlines for directors of Hollywood movies and TV shows, but the industry is keen to establish in the minds of their audience that the kinds of scenarios outlined within fiction are not *purely* fictitious. The concept has undergone a change; what was once unthinkable is now a distinct possibility and a security concern. This technique demonstrates a desire to stop the association of cyber-threats with cinema, TV, fiction and fantasy and instead to consider their credibility as tangible security risks.

Alia at F-Secure highlights the connection that is often made between cybersecurity issues and fiction, stating that 'techies and non-techies have been debating about "cyberwar" – is there such a thing? Is it a threat? Who would do it? Who cares? – Since the movie *WarGames* came out in 1983' (Alia, 2009b). However, most are not so dismissive: 'A bit of news this week dealt with Cyberwarfare. Far from becoming part of the tinfoil hat crowd, cyberwarfare has been growing in real world relevance in the past eighteen months and is the primary impetus for pending legislation' (ESET Research, 2010c).

Such arguments are sometimes presented with an admission from the experts that these sorts of threats *were* at one stage purely fictional or hypothetical. However, this nostalgic point of view is quickly qualified with the assertion that this is no longer the case and that they have become 'genuine threats' (Paget, 2012; Trend Micro, 2012). Naively concluding that cyber-terrorism may only exist in fiction is understandable given that 'not long ago, things like terror cyber-attacks on critical infrastructure were something unthinkable'; however, recent events should have changed the mind of the public, as now cyber-terrorism represents 'a tangible threat' (Kaspersky Labs, 2013a). The desire to make clear that the threat from cyberspace is 'really there … [and] is extremely big and extremely sophisticated' is evident (Trend Micro, 2011a).

Melih Abdulhayoğlu, CEO of Comodo, takes a slightly different tack in his personal blog, appearing to suggest that cyber-terrorism as an empirical reality should be abundantly clear to us all. He compares those who do not believe this to ostriches with their heads firmly in the sand. Abdulhayoğlu argues that it is time to face up to the fact that this particular danger is an empirical reality, but after espousing this harsh reality explains that it is something 'we don't need to live through'. Abdulhayoğlu argues that considering cyber-threats such as those available to terrorists as an empirical reality is 'old news' to him and what we should be focusing on is how to prevent it becoming a personal reality for ourselves as internet users (Abdulhayoğlu, 2008a).

Staying with Comodo, the US TV show *Revolution* (which depicted Americans struggling to restore society in the wake of a complete national power outage) is the subject of one of their articles in which they consider the reality of what is being portrayed on the screen. The author acknowledges that the show's depiction of millions of deaths, government collapse and an ensuing survivor war is, of course, science fiction; however, 'all good science fiction has some basis in fact' (Admin, 2013). On the face of it, the author argues, it all may appear to be purely science fiction but, in reality, 'we need to be aware that there are people in this world who are working very hard to literally turn off the power in America'. These people include the Chinese and the Iranians as well as 'a host of anarchists and anti-capitalists' (Admin, 2013). This piece goes on to link the effects of a potential disruption of the electronic grid with the destruction caused by the natural disasters Hurricane Irene in 2011 and

Hurricane Sandy in 2013, linking the fictional scenario of *Revolution* to the tangible destruction caused by two hurricanes (Admin, 2013).

Constructing the objects of unease

In this chapter I have sought to demonstrate the tactics utilised within the internet security industry to identify a diverse range of cyber-threats as sources of insecurity and construct them as complex to defend against, simple to use and largely synonymous with the more familiar physical threats. Similar to the way the latent vulnerability of a settlement on a floodplain only experiences insecurity when the rain falls and the banks burst, users inhabit a vulnerable environment online that is rendered insecure by the presence of nefarious actors and malicious techniques. Consequently, what we see within the industry are efforts to clarify and accentuate the risks presented by these actors and techniques.

Just as we saw in relation to vulnerability, metaphor surfaced once again as a specific linguistic device utilised to translate the primary security impetus; namely, the destructiveness of threats and their linkage to phenomena in physical conflict. The use of military metaphors has been the subject of analysis elsewhere and a consensus reached as to their effectiveness in communicating particular sentiments. Cohen writes that 'the use of militaristic representations can be an effective device with which to convey seriousness of purpose, to marshal financial resources, to disable opponents, and to mobilise diverse constituencies behind a common banner' (Cohen, 2011, p. 200). It is pertinent to be cautious not to reduce a securitisation to any one thing and to recognise the inter-subjective nature of this process (Nyman, 2013, p. 59). However, it is also worth noting that the perceived effectiveness at least of this particular device may be evident given the number of diverse 'adversaries' different parties have been at war with in recent decades, including but not limited to: crime (Vorenberg, 1972), drugs (Blendon and Young, 1998), poverty (Zarefsky, 1986), homelessness (Breakey, 1997), corruption (Heineman and Heimann, 2006) and, of course, terror (Rothkopf, 2014). We can add to this list cyber-threats and consider cyberspace as the battlefield upon which a war is fought.[6]

Framing a topic in military terms 'concentrates on the physical, sees control as central, and encourages the expenditure of massive resources to achieve dominance'. This is a trifecta, Annas argues, that means such reasoning remains popular with policymakers (Annas, 1995, p. 746). Research by Dryzek points out that the use of metaphors that resonate strongly with the public, such as militaristic ones, becomes particularly pertinent and useful in situations where evidence is heavily contested and a particular group has sought to find another effective manner in which to make bold claims that will succeed in influencing the relevant audience (Dryzek, 2005). Given the role that anxious speculation and 'What if?' scenarios serve to illustrate the devastating potential of cyber-attack, Dryzek's point is of particular note here. These discursive tactics can assist in shaping the nature of the problem, compounding its seriousness as well as organising and rationalising potential solutions (Mutimer, 1997, p. 195).

For example, the aftermath of the 11 September 2001 attacks produced a distinctly military frame of language within disaster response literature (Tierney, 2005, p. 119), as did media discourse relating to the 2003 SARS (severe acute respiratory syndrome) epidemic. When exploring the media framing of the outbreak, Patrick Wallis and Brigitte Nerlich discovered that there was a distinct lack of war metaphors and analogies reported by UK outlets, where the threat of SARS was quite distant, contrasting heavily with the far greater prominence of war metaphors in Chinese reporting, where the threat was 'immediate'. The authors concluded that war metaphors 'are used more prominently when the relationship to the disease is either "personal" or perceived as a threat to a "nation"', such was the case with SARS and China (Wallis and Nerlich, 2005, p. 2633).

Such findings illuminate the currency of discursive tactics that take something 'beyond the established rules of the game and frames the issue either as a special kind of politics or as above politics' (Buzan *et al.*, 1997, p. 23). To pick just one aspect of this metaphorical reasoning, when a state is at war there is an expectation that further or indeed special powers will be required. The power alluded to above, when deployed by professionals of security with a particular authority vested in their expertise, results in another means by which these actors delimit the categories of security and insecurity and assert where and in what way intervention is required. The use of military metaphors and the synonymisation of cyberspace and physical space helps give form to the threats as well as the manner in which they present risk and can create harm. Orthodox cybersecurity knowledge operating as an extension of national security discourse is in part explained by these sorts of discursive tactics and the logics they appear to reinforce.

Staying with the language around different cyber-threats and the categorisation of particular actions it is apparent that a certain degree of homogeneity is retained from orthodox security discourse in that a fairly standard hierarchy of threats appears to operate within the industry. Within this hierarchy, phenomena such as (cyber)-war and (cyber)-terrorism take precedent over the likes of (cyber)-crime. The former of these could typically be linked more readily to their potential to disrupt critical infrastructure and possibly cause subsequent catastrophic damage. However, the existence of this hierarchy says nothing about the manner in which the specific terms are enacted and, in fact, two features of this operationalisation are the frequency and confidence with which powerful securitising language is used and the high degree of fluidity with which the terms are utilised.

This chapter, as well as the previous one, has demonstrated the prevalence of an apprehensive and fearful speculation around the existence of war, terrorism, sabotage and espionage on our networks. Such language has a high degree of securitising salience with the public, security professionals, the media and political professionals elsewhere. With significant security currency invested in this sort of language, its frequent usage within the industry reveals one of the more overt tactics found herein to securitise cyberspace in a manner that accentuates the probability of particular risks that bring this domain more comfortably in line alongside orthodox notions of realist security.

As Jackson *et al.* elaborate upon in relation to the word 'terrorism':

> Because the word brings with it condemnation, its employment also triggers the feeling that something important and dramatic has happened when we hear it. In other words, the term 'terrorism' conjures up an impression not only of immorality, but also of the spectacular and exciting. For political actors searching for votes, and for media and cultural elites searching equally hard for consumers, it therefore offers a power tool to elicit and maintain the public's attention. (Jackson *et al.*, 2011, p. 103)

More than just frequency, however, there is also significant fluidity and ambiguity around this language, and an apparent inability to clearly categorise events or define categories. Along similar lines to what was written above, such fluidity/ambiguity is significant because even if terrorism, crime, etc. are not used precisely within the industry, this is not to say that they do not have stable meanings outside of this discourse or that they have not demonstrated a high degree of securitisation salience elsewhere. This manifests not just as seemingly distinct events or actions being included under a single heading like 'cyberterrorism', but that the same event or action can be labelled using multiple different categories.

The industry spends very little time considering how terms should be defined and so establishing the characteristics of one class of act over another is not particularly easy, but an illustrative example of the sort of ambiguity/ fluidity I am referring to comes in relation to the manner in which Stuxnet was presented as evidence of an ongoing cyberwar (Panda, 2011a), as an example of an isolated 'state-sponsored cyber-attack' (Cluley, 2010), as a cyber-terrorist attack (Penn, 2012) and, in one instance, as an unclear combination of espionage, sabotage and war (Kaspersky Labs, 2012a). Not only, then, was Stuxnet understood in quite different and contradictory ways across the industry, but this ambiguity was also set against a broader context in which universal definitions for the overarching categories were not agreed upon.[7]

The use of such terminology in this manner, without any sort of wider analytical engagement, ignores the broader meaning that terms like 'terrorism' and 'war' have and couches debate within an apprehensive and fearful context. There is little engagement by the industry in what it is that makes particular events examples of cyber-war, cyber-terrorism, cyber-espionage, hacktivism, etc. and thus the contestability of these terms goes largely unheralded within the discourse. Perhaps understandably the industry appears more interested in saying 'this is cyberwar' or 'this is hacktivism' than 'What is cyberwar?' or 'What is hacktivism?' The rationale for this appears to be that such assessments are self-evident, that cyber-war and cyber-terrorism (whatever they are) are realities that are presently occurring (Abdulhayoğlu, 2008a).

There is evidence within the industry that the picture I paint above is not lost on everyone. Scepticism around the use of terms such as 'cyber-war' is linked into an appreciation of the media-friendly nature of such language: 'the media wants a cyberwar … cyberwar is dark, sexy, mysterious' (Abrams, 2010). Perhaps the characterisation of such events within the confines of a mysterious war fought using 'bits and bytes' explains why Stuxnet 'may have sold more newspapers than it damaged nuclear centrifuges' (Kováč, 2011). When dealing with a complex subject such as this, the ability to easily draw on better understood, more evocative language (even if these are enacted in a largely metaphorical sense) affords these speakers a tremendous utility that can be more readily picked up by other actors such as the news media (Jewkes, 2011, pp. 47–9) and political professionals. The locating of nefarious cyber-activity within the framework of 'Tier 1' national security threats (HM Government, 2010, p. 30) may be done with alarming frequency and significant ambiguity, but the willingness to frame it as such not only demonstrates one way in which expert knowledge contributes to a stock exchange of fear and uncertainty but also to the construction of a vague and amorphous external enemy or enemies.

Finally, efforts to link cyber-threats to users' everyday online experience operates alongside the construction of cyber-threats as complex and existing within a technified field. Frequent reference to the everyday experience of the audience aids in securing the partnership of these individuals and groups in the pursuit of securing networks as well as 'making hypersecuritisation scenarios more plausible by linking elements of the disaster scenario to experience familiar from everyday life' (Hansen and Nissenbaum, 2009, p. 1165). I am not arguing that this is a precise calculation, but, rather, it is a tactic designed to link cyber-threats to the individual's lived experience online, prominent events or the broader security imaginary. Through this combination a technified field that would be closed off to the layperson can be more readily comprehended and the security implications of it better understood with the effect of accentuating the threat and entrenching the place of the industry within the broader security *dispositif.*

My reference to a specific and technical language that is occasionally utilised within the discourse may appear to contradict this conclusion; however, I think this language has an important function allowing speakers to give specific meaning to a particular phenomenon. Authorities of delimitation make use of these sorts of tools in the formation of objects of discourse; however, the use of the technical language does not just convey a specific technical meaning but, in the case of these threats, helps make them possible. Francois Debrix, drawing upon Carol Cohn's examination of the 'techno-strategic' (Cohn, 1987) language of nuclear weapons used by defence intellectuals, talks about the technical language associated with cyber-terrorism and used by experts:

> The language of cyberterrorism mobilized by the media and its so-called experts is quite technical for sure. But this technicality, far from de-realizing the threat, makes it possible. It realizes it in the mind/psyche of the public who is subjected to the simulated scenarios and mediations. The taxonomy of cyber-terrorism and its technocratic language allow the public to recognize that there *is* a threat, and that this threat, as presented to them by the media, will surely cause serious casualties within the population. (Debrix, 2001, p. 164)

In the manner that Debrix suggests here, the use of a technical language that could potentially detach the audience from the threat instead 'realises it' when mobilised alongside everyday security practices and references to war, crime and terrorism. It exacerbates the sense of uncertainty and seriousness rather than de-realising it. Moreover, this terminology gives those speakers (classified as experts), who already speak from a unique position of authority regarding the complexity of cybersecurity and its associated threat, the ability to re-assert the technified nature of the field and close off the discussion to non-experts when they choose, essentially leaving the audience to rely on faith in their expertise.

A return to Cohn's 1987 article helps clarify this effect: '[…] one of the most important functions of an expert language is exclusion – the denial of a voice to those outside the professional community' (Cohn, 1987, p. 708).[8] What this means is that meaningful engagement outside of these expert communities on issues such as threat assessment and response is very difficult, if not impossible. This language serves to reassert the complexity of the field that may be lost within a discourse that is often required to talk in layperson's terms to effectively communicate the threat. Communicating and assessing the threat relies on more than the ability to deploy a particular language, but it does serve as an indicator of these speaker's role as insiders and their special position within the field of cybersecurity. By simultaneously making references to everyday security practices as well as technical expertise (as evidenced, in part, through the deployment of a particular language), experts can cement these threats as complex and threatening but also as relatable, while maintaining their ability to make accurate knowledge claims.

Building upon the vulnerability and uncertainty established in Chapter 3, this chapter has demonstrated how these characteristics are given potentially catastrophic significance through the construction of malicious actors with complex and destructive means whose effects will be felt across the full spectrum of users and referents. This represents the second broad theme by which industry expertise looks to define and demark (in)security within cyberspace. In the next chapter, I will be considering these findings together with those from Chapter 3 to assess how the knowledge found looks against the dominant frame. I will explain how the re-appearance of broadly similar tropes and tactics herein, when taken alongside relationships of mutual recognition and benefit across the *dispositif*, can help explain the production of a sedimented cybersecurity knowledge as well as the decision making and security practices that have emerged from it.

Chapter 5

Constructing cybersecurity

In the previous two chapters I have explored the tropes and tactics contained within a series of dominant themes to demonstrate some of the ways in which security professionals of the internet security industry have constructed a particular cybersecurity risk knowledge and, in doing so, contributed to a 'stock exchange of threats, fears and uneases' (Bigo, 2008, p. 45). Across these two chapters I have been primarily responding to my second research question concerning *how* cybersecurity has been constructed within this discursive site. Given the theoretical context within which I situated my analysis, I understand what has been discovered here as an effect of power relations as well as recognising that the knowledge is produced by a source that demonstrates a novel epistemic authority on account of its own technical know-how and the special information it is privy to. Rather than simply being viewed as benign or neutral elements of a discourse, the various features I have unearthed should be understood as intentional actions, operationalised within determinate political contexts (Heller, 1996, p. 87). In surveying this expert knowledge I have charted the characteristics of this discourse, revealing how various discursive tactics manifest and what these help to make real. In this chapter I turn my attention to my final research goal, namely establishing the significance and impact of internet security discourse as part of the broader inter-subjective process of knowledge construction.

Consequently, in this chapter, I begin by reviewing the character of the expert discourse that I have studied and draw attention to the broad homogeneity that exists between this and the 'dominant threat frame' identified by others such as Dunn Cavelty (2008). I then move on to theorise as to why this homogeneity exists and consider the impact upon the broader process of knowledge construction. In this endeavour, I pay particular attention to the position and *raison d'être* of the industry and the forging of relationships between this sort of expertise and the professionals of politics. I argue that the strengthening of the linkages between these sources contributes to the sedimentation of cybersecurity as analogous with national security and to the formation of important communities of mutual recognition that have provided mutual benefit for both the industry and the state. I conclude that the arrival of the 'technological age' that poses challenges to the traditional Weberian relationship between the state, security and the population has brought about an expansion and reorganisation of the security *dispositif* as a means of overcoming a sovereignty gap and allowing for the continuation of a strategy of neoliberal governance.

Before considering the 'Why?' and 'To what effect?' questions, it is first worth reflecting on what has come to the fore across the previous two chapters. Considering the particular construction that is constituted across this expert discourse, and the particular discursive tactics deployed, is necessary to help situate the position of the industry within the security *dispositif* and its situation and linkages relative to other sources.

Homogeneity and heterogeneity with the 'dominant threat frame'

In her analysis of US cybersecurity discourse, Dunn Cavelty (2008, pp. 98–101) considers the emergence of a 'dominant threat frame' that she locates as crystallising during the Clinton administration and that, in large part, stems from the publication of a report entitled *Critical Foundations: Protecting America's Infrastructure* by the President's Commission on Critical Infrastructure Protection in 1997 (President's Commission on Critical Infrastructure Protection, 1997). Cavelty identifies how a number of different phenomena come together in this important document to sediment this framing, including an expanded vocabulary of cybersecurity to include threats such as cyber-war and cyber-terrorism; the recognition that cyber weapons are available to 'everyone'; the uncertainty around the attackers and their ability to conceal themselves; the creation of new dimensions of vulnerability brought about by breadth of the internet and the subsequent broadening of referent objects; the 'newness' of the threat such that it renders old defences 'useless'; and the necessity for interdependence between public and private actors given the shared nature of the risk. This framing becomes 'set in stone' (Dunn Cavelty, 2008, p. 99), in part through the consistency of message and the buy-in of specific security and political professionals, but does undergo some change during the Bush administration with regard to the tendency to focus on catastrophic potential and the inevitability of this, rather than focusing on whether this *would* happen (p. 120).

If we reflect upon Dunn Cavelty's conclusions in 2008, and what my own analysis has identified, it is apparent that the internet security discourse, despite not being a site of discourse Dunn Cavelty focuses on, shares a lot with the 'dominant frame' that she describes. Coincidently the beginning of the period of time studied in this book coincides exactly with the year that the *President's Commission on Critical Infrastructure Protection* was published, upon which Dunn Cavelty puts such emphasis but continues its analysis five years after the publication of her book. While Dunn Cavelty's 2008 contribution remains a seminal one which retains its importance in relation to the construction of cybersecurity in political discourse, we saw in Chapter 1 that other examples of research have corroborated features of this dominant knowledge or unearthed additional tropes/tactics. Briefly reflecting upon what has been unearthed in my own analysis and taking these findings alongside similarly motivated constructivist research provides a useful exercise in informing where agreement and variance are present.

Much has already been written about the use made of metaphor and analogy within cybersecurity discourse as a means to aid in the communication of cyber-threats and responding to them (Dunn Cavelty, 2008; Lawson, 2012; Betz and Stevens, 2013; Wolff, 2014; Quigley *et al.*, 2015; Stevens, 2016). Following suit, private-sector internet security discourse shares this common trope and employs various spatial, temporal, medical, biological, historical, mythological and militaristic metaphors to convey threat but also the fraught nature of the space itself. On this latter point, while considerable attention has been given to the metaphor of cyberspace itself in the wider literature (Gozzi, Jr, 1994; Adams, 1997; Cohen, 2007), the focus on metaphor and the construction of threat within cybersecurity discourse has tended to focus on actions (as bullets, bombs, etc.) rather than the environment itself. The obvious exception to this is the metaphor of cyberspace as battlefield (Lawson, 2012), one that was also apparent in the internet security discourse. Less commonplace metaphors likening the milieu to a perilous Hobbesian state of nature (wilderness) or a lawless Western Frontier *have* received coverage (Yen, 2002), but were noteworthy against a focus that has typically been about the metaphorical militarisation of cybersecurity. These metaphors speak to a space inhabited by predators or bandits, as well as the isolation and vulnerability users will experience without the security afforded by a strong posse.

There is also a commonality between industry discourse and the wider dominant threat frame when it comes to uncertainty and apprehension. Sometimes these appear as worst-case 'nightmare scenarios' that are often predicated upon specific conceptualisations of time. For example, Stevens (2016) writes in *Cybersecurity and the Politics of Time* about how past, present and future time all contribute towards a foreboding construction of threat, whether it be with reference to dangerous lessons from the past, the revolutionary and unprecedented present or the unknown dystopic future. All of these temporal tropes are in evidence within the industry, as are moments of radical discontinuity or 'game changing' events that sit atop an undercurrent of precedented continuity of the ever-increasing cyber-threat (Jarvis, 2009). As Stevens puts it, 'in the cybersecurity imaginary … the future looks almost nothing like the past and has become not only threatening but also catastrophic in an existential register' (Stevens, 2016, p. 102). The industry, given its claims to expert status, is particularly well placed at this juncture to engage in the sorts of fearful predictions that have been a feature of the dominant cybersecurity discourse (Conway, 2008; Dunn Cavelty, 2008; Brito and Watkins, 2011; Lawson, 2013) and likewise, these perform an important function in depicting risk.

Significant pains were also taken within the industry to establish the credibility of the cyber-threat alongside the characteristics and nature of the risks it presents. Claims to the seriousness of the threat came in the form of straightforward assertions, the use of statistics/threat assessment reports, as well as efforts to distance cybersecurity from a potentially unhelpful association with fictional depictions. As pointed out by Quigley *et al.* (2015) in their work exploring cybersecurity 'gurus', there is also a tendency within the industry to mobilise particular high-profile events to 'serve as a framing event that can seem to validate many exaggerated claims' (p. 115).

Finally, in evidence across both of the previous two chapters was an undercurrent of scepticism as to the dominant discourse put forward within the industry. While this never threatened to rival the dominant threat frame, these dissident accounts touch on the 'hype' that has surrounded both broad categories such as cyber-war (Ducklin, 2011; Abrams, 2009a) or cyber-terrorism (Hyppönen, 2007, 2008) and specific events such as Stuxnet (Kováč, 2011; Harley, 2010) or the 'Millennium Bug' (Kaspersky Labs, 1999b). The latter of these examples indicates that this has been a feature for some time. However, over the course of the time period studied in this book, examples of these alternative accounts have become more frequent as the discourse and the attention cybersecurity itself has received has burgeoned. The temptation is to conclude that these dissident accounts provide explicit examples of the lines of creativity Deleuze spoke of within the *dispositif* (1992). However, while they certainly puncture any notion of a totally homogenous discourse, the examples unearthed in this study are overwhelmingly charges against the accuracy or categorisation of particular events or acts understood in orthodox terms. Whether or not it is predominately on account of my desire to look for these sorts of sceptical readings where others have not, or whether it represents a theme that is more prominent in this discursive space, this sustained thread of scepticism represents a feature that does not appear so prominently elsewhere.

While my own research has identified specific and novel discursive tactics and techniques over the previous two chapters, reflecting on the broad framing of such knowledge makes it apparent that this site of discourse still operates in a way that resonates with the dominant threat frame. Expert knowledge is a special kind of knowledge, but in this instance it does not appear to be one that offers a radically different assessment of the situation. We should be wary of interpreting the duplication of a cyber-(national) security knowledge as corroborating evidence for its 'accuracy', as this is contingent and must be 'forged, argued, and accepted in the political process' (Dunn Cavelty, 2013, p. 105). The features of this discourse are only part of their importance and rather than simply concluding as to the broad homogeneity that can be found between expert industry discourse and wider cybersecurity knowledge, it is at the site of the 'forging', in the crucible of knowledge construction, where the greatest significance is to be found.

The *dispositif* exhibits lines of sedimentation and creativity, the linkages and intertextualities unearthed here between different sources reveal to us the breadth and depth of the sedimentation. These similarities can be found across politics, the media and fiction and my own analysis has revealed that they are also shared by the security professionals of the internet security industry. Through the production and reproduction of a particular knowledge across multiple sources of the *dispositif* (with its specific constitutive logics), a dominant knowledge has been elevated to the status of truth. If the 'apparatus itself is the system of relations that can be established between these elements' (Foucault, 1980b, p. 194), then the continuity observed here helps to explain the formation of a stable common-sense knowledge. Everybody is pulling in the same direction, so to speak, and the epistemic authority brought by expert professionals of security should not be understated in its ability to imbue this framing with a scientific/technical validity.

This risk knowledge has produced, and is the product of, a successful securitisation that has delimited the particularities of cyber-(in)security and served to duplicate the established realist national security framework. The fear and anxiety produced in this system of relations comes across clearly. Private industry co-produces and reinforces the dominant frame, amplifying the message that cyberspace is inhabited by all the same nefarious actors we are familiar with, as well as harbouring a new breed of cyber-specific actors. The net result of this is that, in cyberspace, hostile states, terrorists and criminals pose a threat to referents as wide ranging as the individual home user, the nation state and even the networked world itself. Uncertainty and anonymity are also features and shroud the full extent of the threat to compound anxiety and danger, clearing the way for (informed/expert) speculation. More importantly than this, though, is that the framing of cyberspace/cybersecurity in this manner legitimises the extension of a pre-emptive security logic and delimits where and in what form this occurs.

The sedimentation between sources reveals to us the means by which a stable and 'objective' cybersecurity knowledge has formed and represents one area of significance as to what is occurring here, in particular between expert and political knowledge. The correlation between different sources provides answers as to the speed with which a stable knowledge has been produced but important questions regarding the power relations, motivations and politics contained within and concealed by the maintenance of this construction remain unaddressed. After all, Bigo reminds us that security professionals claim they are only responding to 'new threats requiring exceptional measures beyond the normal demands of everyday politics' but all further their own immediate interests, be they resources or responsibility (Bigo, 2002, pp. 63–4). To my mind, there are three further important aspects to glean from the construction of cybersecurity as national security and the role of expert knowledge in this process. First, what private industry immediately serves to gain in material terms from the maintenance of this knowledge. Second, how the industry has sought to carve out its role as security guarantor within the frenetic and uncertain world of cyberspace. Important here is how the industry has formed communities of mutual recognition, in particular with political professionals, with the effect of strengthening the knowledge claims of both parties and legitimising the policies and security practices both want to enact in light of this knowledge. And linked to this, finally, is the manner in which all of this has allowed for the expansion of the security *dispositif* and the continuation of a strategy of neoliberal governance. I will address each of these in turn.

Profitable panacea

That the internet security industry has a stake in the continued interest with and recognition of cyber-threats as a serious but manageable risk may not come as a complete surprise for two reasons. First, and most straightforwardly, private industry's *raison d'être* is symbiotically linked to the continued existence and credibility of these threats. As private companies, they compete in the marketplace with each other for similar clients and ultimately have to generate profit if they wish to survive or grow. If the threat were to 'go away', or more likely if a particular company was unable to convince its client base that its products and services were the best defence against the threat, then that company would see profits fall and it would eventually go under. Bigo's metaphor of the stock exchange of fear and unease is doubly pertinent here as there is a literal stock exchange at work within that which he theorised about. The second reason that is perhaps less forthcoming without prior theorising around security professionals and their role, is that a defining aspect of these actors is their claim only to be responding to new threats, when they are actually furthering their own immediate interests and staking a bigger claim within the marketplace/*dispositif* (Bigo, 2002, pp. 63–4).

The internet security industry shares something fundamental in this regard with other security professionals. Whether it is the police requesting greater resources to deal with cyber-crime, the intelligence community demanding a wider surveillance remit, or the internet security industry trying to sell more of their products, each stands to gain something from the continued acceptance of an existential threat and the appropriateness of these stakeholders to mitigate against it. There is a vested interest here, then, and the industry serves not only as a regime of truth within the security *dispositif* but also stands to benefit inside it because of a preconceived understanding of cybersecurity as extra-discursive, destructive, uncertain and credible, etc. Paul Virilio once said that 'to invent the sailing ship or steamer is to invent the shipwreck' (Virilio, 2006, p. 10). Extending this metaphor further, the invention of the shipwreck also creates a marketplace for more seaworthy boats, experienced crews and an insurance industry to mitigate against treacherous voyages. Without cyber-threats there is no industry, so not only does the continued existence of companies such as those studied here require an audience to accept the seriousness of risks in cyberspace, the severity with which potential customers come to understand these risks will likely impact upon the products and services they can sell.

This reminds us of the importance of the power/knowledge relationship and what in this instance the particular contingent framing of actors and actions online can mobilise. Framing a subject or a discussion as a particular kind of security issue, and possibly even allowing for particular behaviour or actions in light of this, involves an inter-subjective process of securitisation and knowledge sedimentation that requires a receptive audience. As Mark Salter points out, the public is not always the audience being appealed to in securitising moves (2008, pp. 327–8) and within the internet security companies studied in this volume, we see the breadth of this audience and the casting of a very wide net that targets the general public, business of all sizes, the public sector and even other experts/companies.

The breadth of the messaging here tells us something about the companies' status within the security community. Notwithstanding what was covered in the Introduction regarding the ever-increasing role of the private sector in providing security, these internet security companies are 'outsiders' when compared to the traditional public-sector agencies/institutions, as well as being a relatively new development within the broader private security industry itself. The most established internet security companies typically go back no further than the 1980s (McAleavey, 2011). This means that stakes need to be claimed and connections within the *dispositif* established between companies, security professionals, regimes of truth, etc. The sheer volume of material being produced by these companies tells us something about their efforts to communicate to an audience and in turn stake their place within the industry, just as the industry looks to stake a wider influence within the *dispositif*.

The discourse I have studied represents one channel of communication and demonstrates audience-specific tailoring as mentioned; however, far more common is the adoption of default position that speaks to the general user. I view this generic messaging less as an example of ambiguity on the part of the industry and more as a demonstration of the apparent universal applicability of cybersecurity across society and the manner in which it speaks to 'everyday security practices' (Hansen and Nissenbaum, 2009, p. 1165). The industry recognises the potential breadth of its client base in an increasingly computerised world. On occasion we see this more generic position being eschewed and deliberate efforts being made to hone in on specific audiences. Notable examples include the way in which business (in particular small and medium business), parents/families and smartphone users are addressed directly within the discourse.

The size of each company often tells us something about the range of the services offered, with some smaller companies being known almost exclusively for one piece of off- the-shelf anti-virus software and others offering a whole raft of products across a range of clients. Typically, however, each aims to provide security, not just for the home user's desktop PC, tablet or smartphone but also to organisations including businesses of all sizes. We see evidence of this across the time span of data collected. Check Point offered 'peace of mind' to network managers in 1997 by ensuring protection against new privacy threats to Netscape products (Check Point, 1997). Fifteen years later, Bitdefender continues to stress the need for such solutions, warning that consistent under-spending on security within IT budgets by corporations endangers significant risk (Bitdefender, 2012b). In a piece paying particular attention to the tech sector, Sophos Labs picked up on a report by BitSight that rated seventy Fortune 200 companies over a twelve-month period to determine their protection against security risk, concluding that 'at a corporate level we're just not giving security the importance it merits, unless forced to do so by strict regulation' (Hawes, 2013f).

Clearly, home users are also a very important focus for each of these companies and they make up a vital portion of their customer base. Promoting their off-the-shelf anti-virus products is a crucial aspect of this and, unsurprisingly, each claimed theirs offered something over the competitor and was quick to report on industry awards won (Admin, 2012; Business Wire, 2011). Another example of where we witness the more universal position eschewed in favour of an audience-specific message comes in relation to a particular sort of home user – parents and the family. AVG were particularly forthcoming in their efforts to reach this population, but across the industry there were also tailored messages stressing the need to keep children safe online from bullying (Anscombe, 2013; BullGuard, 2013d; AVG, 2011f) or 'Internet pornographers' (Comodo, 2005), as well as efforts to engage with 'mobile moms' (AVG, 2013) and 'baby boomers' (AVG, 2012a) to pass on good cybersecurity practice.

Finally, smartphone and mobile users provide an example of an audience defined by a technology/platform. Smartphone penetration rates continue to increase, and a 2015 study by the Pew Research Centre found smartphone ownership was above 70 per cent in Australia, the US, Spain and Israel, with many other European nations not far behind (Pew Research Centre, 2016). In 2018, within the US, that percentage was 77 per cent, up from 35 per cent in 2011 (Pew Research Centre, 2018). That is a very significant increase in smartphone ownership in less than a decade and as owning a smartphone increasingly becomes 'the norm' in the advanced Western economies, we can chart the manner in which this new platform and its operators have been singled out for messaging in relation to cyber-threats. Highlighting the vulnerabilities of mobile platforms (Ostache, 2013; Redfield, 2012), charting the upturn in attacks targeting mobile devices (Dunlaevy, 2013b; Bell, 2013a) and exploring novel modes of attack such as via malicious QR codes (AVG, 2012b) are all examples of the specific attention given to this platform/threat.

Where particular audiences have been spoken to, we typically witness that company offering a tailored security solution for their situation. In relation to the specific audiences covered above, this could look like offering robust and 'resource-friendly' software to small business (AVG, 2011g) or defence against threats incurred in an increasingly virtualised and cloud-based corporate environment (Doherty, 2012). Kaspersky's 'PURE Total Security' offers, among other benefits, 'control for parents like never before' to prevent children straying onto gambling websites, adult content and message boards (Kaspersky, 2011b) just as 'AVG Family Safety' provides a 'virtual guardian' to prevent online abuse 'before it develops into a potentially harmful situation' (AVG, 2011f). In recognition of their increased market share, mobile users are offered 'lightweight' anti-malware solutions to keep them safe from the latest attacks (ESET Research, 2008) and to protect tablets and smartphones from 'highly professional cybercriminals' and their 'sophisticated operations' (Kaspersky Labs, 2013c).

These examples that speak to specific sections of the client base are nuances that provide evidence of how particular threats are covered, how particular audiences are communicated with and how the two come together to promote and sell particular solutions. These more tailored messages and products should not obscure the fact that, as mentioned above, the dominant voice is a broader one that speaks to a more general user. Equally important is recognising that it is far from the case that every single white paper, blog, article or threat report analysed was essentially a sale pitch. Nor in fact was it the case that in every situation where the industry had tailored their message, a security product was promoted. Most of the materials analysed were not explicitly trying to sell a product or service but rather contributed in some manner to a body of expertise that assessed and constituted the threat. So while the sales pitch was a distinct and important feature of this discourse and while products and services *were* explicitly promoted, it was often the case that these products were coupled with threat assessments or emerging trends reassuring customers or potential customers of their safety if making use of the company's security.

Given the *raison d'être* of the companies studied here, the efforts to promote their wares makes sense. Those points within the discourse that look most like 'sales pitches' remind us of the way in which the industry, rather than being a 'neutral' source of expert knowledge in this domain, does of course benefit from continued attention and apprehension around cyber-threats. In fact, given the relationship that exists between the continued existence of the industry and the collective understanding of cyber-threats as salient risks, it is perhaps surprising that more of the discourse was not explicit in its promotion of products and services. One explanation I would offer here returns us to the industry's security professional status and the fine line these companies walk between wanting to be viewed as credible and neutral expert voices that are simply responding to emergent and developing threats, but also recognising the need to promote their services and distinguish themselves from market competitors. The industry may purport to be simply responding to this emergent and rapidly developing threat, but it directly benefits from a construction that accentuates destructiveness, uncertainty and credibility in two predominant ways.

First, it generates financial benefits for the industry. At the broadest level, as the salience and importance afforded to cybersecurity has increased so too have estimations of the market value of the industry as well as projections for future worth. Estimations of the current value as well as that of the future do vary quite significantly, in part due to the variable breadth of different studies. However, it is not uncommon to read of global valuations either in the tens or hundreds of billions of dollars (Gartner, 2018; Market Research Engine, 2018; Allied Market Research, 2016). Recent figures published in a report commissioned by the UK Government estimated the contribution of the UK cybersecurity industry alone as £5.7 billion across 846 firms (RSM, 2018). Focusing more specifically on the sorts of companies studied in this research, we can see how many of those publicly traded, while experiencing different degrees of price volatility, have seen an upwards trend in value going back further than ten years where the data are available (NASDAQ, 2018). Finally, it is worth noting that just as has been evidenced in the wider defence industry (Apergis and Apergis, 2016), recent research focusing specifically on high-profile examples of cyber-attack, such as WannaCry, has begun to provide empirical evidence that links the occurrence of such events with positive excess returns for the stock of cybersecurity firms (Castillo and Falzon, 2018). Across these various different sources we can see how the value and scale of the industry has increased alongside the emphasis placed upon the threat posed in cyberspace and where, therefore, the industry stands to gain from (re)producing a particular cybersecurity knowledge. As important as this feature is, there is more at stake here than financial gain and position within the marketplace.

I mentioned earlier that when assessing and analysing the *dispositif*, Foucault was not interested so much in individual sources as much as the connection between sources across the *dispositif*. By studying the internet security industry in the manner I have, I have shown a specific interest in this source for reasons laid out most explicitly in the Introduction and Chapter 2. However, I am also interested in the connection between private industry and other, more established, sources across the security *dispositif* and the enhanced impact these companies are having here. It is true that this industry has benefited financially by offering diagnosis and cure as part of its conflation of national security and cybersecurity, which resonates with an already entrenched discourse delimited similarly narrowly. But, second, it has also seen its influence and importance grow within the security *dispositif* through the formation of stronger links between other professionals of security as part of an expanding community of mutual recognition.

Communities of mutual recognition

In addition to the overt manner in which these companies stand to benefit financially from the increasing salience of cyber-threats, this discourse also reveals how these professionals of security have developed the connections between themselves and other sources, notably within the public political sphere. A prominent explanation for this trend is that there exists a need to ensure greater cooperation between the public and the private sector in order to be more effective in combining the manpower and resources of the former with the innovation and flexibility of the latter (McAfee, 2018; Stackpole, 2018). Such sentiments are reflected in the way in which law enforcement often finds itself 'hampered by bureaucracy' when dealing with counterparts overseas, whereas 'large global security firms, on the other hand, are able to operate across borders much more easily, and have deep expertise often unavailable to law enforcement' (Hawes, 2013b).

Steps taken to rectify this problem have been met with effusive praise by prominent professionals of politics and security, including ex-presidents, who have responded positively to the efforts made to coordinate existing mechanisms while continuing to stress that this is an ongoing process which requires that 'federal decision makers and public officials must continue engaging with

IT security professionals and defense experts' (ESET Research, 2010a; Kaspersky Labs, 2013b). The desire to develop these connections is overt and forthcoming, as the above indicates. However, what a general language of cooperation and coordination perhaps plays down is the extent to which aspects of the private sector are already conducting important functions within the formal political process when it comes to cybersecurity.

The influence of private industry upon issues of national security is well documented, probably most notably in relation to the military–industrial complex (Ledbetter, 2011; Der Derain, 2009). The particular section of the industry I have focused upon makes evidencing something as extensive as this difficult. However, what *is* revealed upon studying the discourse of private industry and the corresponding political discourse is the manner in which a community of mutual recognition has formed between particular internet security companies and professionals of politics.

Mutual recognition is a principle that explains cooperation between competent authorities within a particular area or domain – for example, trade or justice (European Commission, 2018; Taupiac-Nouvel, 2012; Valdes, 2015). These communities provide a means of governance and standardisation around areas and issues (Nicolaidis and Shaffer, 2005), and their formation between professionals of security and/or professionals of politics in this instance means the coming together of different regimes of truth to produce an even more acute delimiting function and the sedimentation of a particular, cyber-(national) security knowledge.

> This ethos of a shared knowledge between the professionals, a knowledge beyond the grasp of people who do not have the know-how about risk assessment and proactivity, is also an ethos of secrecy and confidentiality. It creates a community of mutual recognition and governs a logic of implicit acceptance of claims made by other professionals, not only with respect to the substance of these claims but also to the forms and technologies of knowledge acquisition. (Bigo, 2012, pp. 74–5)

Political professionals have shown their willingness to let the more established internet security companies into their fold to perform a range of functions, including providing expert testimony, representation on committees, supporting legislation and initiatives, organising and financing networking events and being beneficiaries of government funding for technical cybersecurity solutions or mutually beneficial research and development. These diverse contributions have been assimilated into the network of power/knowledge, giving additional epistemic credibility to the knowledge claims and practices made herein while also bolstering the status and credibility of the private companies given their closer association to salient and established institutions of security. In what follows, I will provide evidence of this.

On 13 May 2011, Congressman Peter Welch for Vermont gave a short speech in Congress in which he simply pointed Representatives towards a 2010 article published in *The Washington Post*. In this article, the authors highlight the reliance the intelligence community has upon private contractors, an issue Welch described as 'critical' and that caused him 'great concern' (House of Representatives, 2011d). The article Welch was referencing, penned by Dana Priest and William M. Arkin, is an eye-opening one and, despite casting its net much wider than internet security companies alone, the authors concede that 'of all the different companies in Top Secret America, the most numerous by far are the information technology, or IT, firms. About 200 firms do nothing but IT'. The US Government is 'nearly totally dependent on these firms' and the closeness of the relationship is evidenced in one excerpt that explains how these IT companies who are looking for government funding, in this instance McAfee, are expected to finance and organise networking conferences:

> The McAfee network security company, a Defense Department contractor, welcomed guests to a Margaritaville-themed social on the garden terrace of the hotel across the street from the convention site, where 250 firms paid thousands of dollars each to advertise their services and make their pitches to intelligence officials walking the exhibition hall. Government officials and company executives say these networking events are critical to building a strong relationship between the public and private sectors. 'If I make one contact each day, it's worth it', said Tom Conway, director of federal business development for McAfee. (Preist and Arkin, 2010)

These sorts of events are a critical aspect of the networked learning environment and help to galvanise the formation of a 'knowledge consensus' (Haas, 1992, p. 23). Symantec's recent 'Government Symposia', provides a contemporary example of the mutual recognition that exists between these parties, in which high-ranking members of various bodies within the US Government, including the Department of Homeland Security (DHS) and the Office of the Director of National Intelligence spoke alongside senior staff at Symantec (Symantec, 2018). Returning to the example cited in *The Washington Post*, members of the US intelligence community walk the halls and corridors listening to pitches from various private firms, each identifying how national security is compromised in various different ways as well as offering up their company's technical solutions to secure against such threats. The knowledge consensus here is acute, all speak the same security language and both recognise the importance of the other party's role as guarantor/provider of security.

For the governmental professional, either of politics or security, cybersecurity knowledge homogenises in these spaces around a familiar agenda. Meanwhile, these private firms offer technical solutions that budget can be allocated towards in fitting with developed nations' penchant for high-tech solutions to issues of security. For companies like McAfee and others, the cost of hosting or attending such events offers tremendous return on investment, be it in working towards securing new government contracts or making contacts that allow for the opportunity to exert a little more policy influence.

On this latter point, we see a range of alternative means by which internet security companies have been welcomed or, indeed, relied upon to speak directly upon issues of national security. Concentrating on the Anglosphere, it is apparent how frequently the bigger companies have been called in to offer testimony in front of government committees. The nature of this testimony ranges from discussing specific high-profile examples of malware (House of Representatives, 2000), the importance of cybersecurity specific users such as small businesses or the home user (House of Representatives, 2004, 2011a) and the impact of cyber-attack on particular industries and targets, including the financial sector or critical national infrastructure (Australian Parliament, 2003; House of Representatives, 2011b). Such testimony provides some idea of the breadth of areas in which representatives of these companies are called upon not only to report on but also to offer their own assessments and recommendations.

In an early instance of representatives from these companies giving testimony on a specific malware, in this case the Love Bug virus, ex-Senior Vice President of McAfee, Sandra England, laments the lack of a coherent policy response to viruses of this sort, agreeing with the Committee of Science that stiffer punishments were required for virus writers (House of Representatives, 2000). England goes beyond speaking about the topic of Love Bug and provides assessment on government policy and punitive measures associated with coordinating malware such as this. Offering broader national security relevant assessments or making policy recommendations becomes a more frequent occurrence as we move forward in time.

Committee and subcommittee hearings across a range of domains from National Security to Technology and Innovation call upon industry experts to help assess the 'immediate threat to the United States' (House of Representatives, 2011c) and the efforts of departments such as Homeland Security and the National Institute of Science and Technology (House of Representatives, 2009). In the latter of these examples, Mark Bregman, then executive vice president and chief technology officer of Symantec, commended the efforts made by the DHS to engage more with the private sector but argued that the National Institute of Standards and Technology's (NIST) funding was 'inadequate', required further investment and that their efforts should be focused on ensuring that 'agreed-upon standards, protocols, and requirements are accomplished in reasonable timelines' (House of Representatives, 2009). Similar instances in the Australian Parliament give the private sector an opportunity to quantify the level of threat ('scary' according to one lawmaker), clarify technical terminology such as 'blended threat' and stress the need to go beyond technical solutions to incorporate wider cybersecurity education within any government strategy (Australian Parliament, 2003, pp. 70–82).

McAfee's written evidence, provided to the Commons Select Committee on Defence, provides the government with a private-sector assessment of the UK's National Security Strategy. In it they also talk up the 'best-in-class' tools their company has developed that, they believe, can enable the UK Government to develop a robust posture in cyberspace against 'crippling' cyber-attacks such as the 'game changing' Stuxnet, that 'threaten real loss of property and life'. Such tools, they stress, have already been utilised by the US Department of Defense. Of the UK's approach, McAfee welcomed the government's assessment of cyber-crime as a 'Tier 1' threat, but warned against a patchwork approach to cybersecurity, recommending instead that a single uniformed approach is 'the desired outcome' in terms of delivering value for money and comprehensive protection. Crucially, all of this can be better achieved with a closer and more effective relationship between the public and private sector. McAfee stress this is not tantamount to a reliance on one company, but a warning that if the government wishes to provide a more secure environment, it 'cannot afford not to cooperate with technology security companies such as McAfee and draw on their extensive experience and knowledge to meet the ever-evolving nature of the cyber-threat' (House of Commons, 2013).

These testimonies provide rich examples of the sorts of expertise, insight and assessment offered up by the industry to professionals of politics and speak to the ability of this technical expertise to provide 'tangible and undisputed guidance for policy design in the form of "actionable knowledge"' (Hagmann and Dunn Cavelty, 2012, p. 84). These examples are, however, to be taken alongside the more straightforward ways in which industry expertise overlaps with political professionals. Industry expertise is often drawn upon in the form of direct citation by political professionals – for example, using a relevant research report to verify statements in formal political spaces such as when debating legislation. Expertise here occasionally goes beyond that which is specifically security oriented (House of Commons, 2012) but much more familiar are threat assessments (Australian Parliament, 2010, 2011; House of Lords, 2010), information pertaining to cyber-crime (Australian Parliament, 2007) and its financial cost (Senate, 2010), as well as threats posed from specific adversaries such as China (Senate; 2012; House of Representatives, 2007).

As with the majority of expert testimony considered above, this expertise tends to be understood as 'politically neutral'. It is deployed in such a way that accentuates a largely bipartisan national security agenda by virtue of the ability of these companies to provide the most accurate reading of how things 'actually' are and subsequently has clear implications for how national interests are understood and acted upon (Leander, 2005, pp. 815–16). Exceptions to this norm are apparent though. Republican Representative Vicky Hartzler, of Missouri, when discussing the 'great challenge' of Obamacare, lists seven significant problems she has with the law. Number four on her list is how Obamacare jeopardises personal security and privacy. Hartzler asks the House, 'How would you like to have your social Security number made available to everybody?' before citing how McAfee ('one of the nation's premier Internet security companies') had described Obamacare as a 'hacker's dream' (House of Representatives, 2013).

If this is one example of industry expertise being used (indirectly) to criticise a particular law, there are others where industry leaders are included as supports for particular pieces of legislation, including the Cybersecurity Enhancement Act (House of Representatives, 2010) and the Electronic Communications Privacy Act (Senate, 2013). The former of these is interesting for what it inscribes in law vis-à-vis implementing public–private partnership in the areas of 'coordinating and prioritizing the Federal cybersecurity portfolio, improving the transfer of cybersecurity technologies to the marketplace, and training an IT workforce that can meet the growing needs of both public and private sectors' (House of Representatives, 2010, p. 495).

As well as being called upon to offer their expertise in front of policymakers, there have also been a number of instances where individuals representing these companies have been asked to serve as permanent members of influential committees. Rather than being on the 'outside' and speaking 'in', here we see external expertise being brought directly into the fold and sitting on the 'other side of the table' as a member of a team tasked with providing policy advice to government. Both David DeWalt and Steve Bennett, ex-presidents of McAfee and Symantec respectively at the time of appointment, were among the 'impressive' (The White House, 2011a) 'talented and dedicated' (The White House, 2013) individuals who took up positions on Obama's National Security Telecommunications Advisory Committee. Chris Young, former CEO of McAfee, maintains the company's presence on the Committee (Department of Homeland Security, 2018). Ex-leadership of these companies has also been represented on George W. Bush's National Infrastructure Advisory Committee (The White House, 2002) and Barack Obama's Management Advisory Board (The White House, 2011b).

Along similar lines, Symantec's ex-CEO, John W. Thompson, also sat on the International Multilateral Partnership Against Cyber-terrorism (IMPACT) board, an institution that strives for 'proactive security' through the coordination of private and government resources and expertise (Symantec, 2006). The invitations to impart knowledge go further and include speaking roles at such high-profile gatherings as the G-8 conference, where Symantec were present to promote 'exchanges between public and private entities, commercial and administrative sectors, and between countries' and to strengthen the G-8 countries' fight against 'cyber-terrorism and information warfare' (Symantec, 2000).

The extent to which private industry actors are called upon to provide expert testimony, is cited as valid knowledge, or plays a direct role in helping to shape and direct decision making speaks to the reliance placed upon them to provide a more accurate picture of the realities of cybersecurity. Private security experts have 'established themselves as interlocutors in debates about insecurity and protection' (Leander, 2010, p. 213) and government increasingly looks to them to make legible the uncertainties of cybersecurity and reveal the various objects of knowledge that are obscured to the layperson. It is not just mutual recognition that is on display here, but also mutual *benefit*. Professionals of security benefit directly by securing investment from the state to provide software solutions, training, consultancy and research and development

(Panda, 2010, 2018; Business Wire, 2018; Australian Parliament, 2009). However, alongside this they also position themselves closer to the levers of power by speaking directly to or alongside those tasked with strategising, making policy, allocating budgets, etc. Through this, they can simultaneously verify the quality of their own knowledge as something that is sought after by the actor that has the ultimate security mandate: the state. In this respect private firms such as those studied here are becoming more political as they 'increasingly take on strategic, ethical, and foreign-policy alignment issues that were previously outside their purview' (Collier, 2018, p. 15).

For government, as we have seen, this knowledge exchange occurs within the narrow confides of a national security framework. Private expertise may very well be useful in revealing the extent of an established cyber-threat, or providing insight into the most effective responses to them, but these exchanges always operate in a way that reproduces the orthodoxies of security. In this regard the private sector reveals the unknowns of cybersecurity or elaborates around the periphery of what is known. However, it does this within familiar confines that entrench the national security frame and close off alternative conceptualisations.

Governance through security

To briefly summarise, then, we have seen how a particular cybersecurity knowledge has formed that has comfortably conflated cybersecurity with a more familiar *national security*. In seeking to understand how this process has been achieved, I have revealed the role that expert discourse has played in (re)producing a knowledge that shares many features of the dominant threat frame; a frame that draws from wider national security discourse and understands cybersecurity as security *of* cyberspace. The strong networks that have formed between these professionals of security and other political professionals are important, in particular given the complex technical nature of the domain and the need for expertise to translate 'the reality'. My analysis does not stop here though, but rather it argues that while these links help consolidate a stable notion of cybersecurity, they also serve to benefit the industry both financially and by allowing greater access to the levers of political power. However, this is not a one-way process and what has developed is a community of mutual recognition and benefit. As part of this process, companies enhance their status within the security *dispositif* and exert influence on decision making, while professionals of politics benefit from the epistemic credibility and validity that these actors bring to the continued relevance of the state within issues of cybersecurity.

The mutual recognition and benefit between these sources within the *dispositif* bring us back to questions of power and governmentality. The security *dispositif* provides the mechanism by which governance is achieved and what I have demonstrated over the course of this book shows how expertise found in the private sector has provided one source within a wider assemblage (Stevens 2016, pp. 181–6) that has been embraced/co-opted by the state as a means of maintaining its centrality at the heart of cybersecurity. This comes against the backdrop of unique challenges facing the state that threaten traditional Weberian notions of its role within all things 'security', given the inability for issues of cybersecurity to fit neatly within the confines of the Westphalian model. The security *dispositif* provides the means by which governmentality is achieved and yet, with the emergence of a new milieu, the organisation of this mechanism is threatened, as are sovereign and disciplinary modalities of power, to create what Kello (2017) refers to as a 'sovereignty gap'.

With the emergence of this gap, private companies with a clear stake in this domain, as well as expertise and abilities that in some cases go beyond that of the state, have the potential to widen or bridge this gap; they can interject with lines of sedimentation or lines of creativity (Deleuze, 1992, p. 165). Such developments will never be wholly one way or the other and these relationships can be competitive as well as cooperative (Collier, 2018, p. 15). What my analysis has revealed, however, is a site of expert discourse that has largely settled in line with a version of cybersecurity that echoes the logic of national security and reasserts the centrality of the state, albeit while also giving privileged status to private companies and the expertise and flexibility they bring. Indeed, in a similar vein to Leander's observations about private military companies (2005, p. 824), the private internet security industry not only (unsurprisingly) approaches issues as *security* issues but also follows this assumption with another by prioritising the suitability of 'technico-managerial' solutions to these issues. Private companies such as those studied in this book have therefore been brought into the fold, interjecting new sources within the expanded mechanism of the security *dispositif*, but doing so in such a way that the fundamental organisation remains in place and familiar solutions are implemented.

Citing Lawrence Lessig, Coles-Kemp *et al.* (2018) point out that 'real space sovereigns' (Lessig, 1999) 'will respond to the threat of cyberspace by attempting to ensure that their regulatory power encompasses virtual spaces, and, by framing cyberspace as a spatial domain analogous to land, sea and air'

(Coles-Kemp *et al.*, 2018, p. 47). This is precisely what we have seen play out here in the construction of cybersecurity as national security and as the protection of 'things' against a familiar range of nefarious actors. Moreover, the strength of the links between security professionals of the internet security industry and political professionals/public-sector security professionals also provides insight into the *how* of this process and the manner in which Kello's 'sovereignty gap' dilemma has been overcome. Mutual recognition becomes mutual benefit, with private-sector groups benefiting both financially and in their transformation into more political entities with greater agenda setting/policy influence. The state, on the other hand, cedes some of the monopoly it typically has as guarantor and regime of truth by acknowledging the role of private-sector expertise and capability, but, as a consequence, succeeds in subsuming this new source within the predefined organisation of the security *dispositif* and mobilising this expertise as capital in securitising moves (Berling, 2011, p. 390). This means that cybersecurity becomes comfortably conflated with national security and the securitisation and militarisation we witness here overlap comfortably with more familiar security domains in which the state's role has been longstanding.

Rather than being reflective of an extra-discursive reality, such a construction is contingent upon various power relations, some of which I have sought to outline in my mapping of a small corner of this *dispositif*. Social knowledge, in whatever form, can only ever become partially fixed, even if it may appear as a 'brute fact' given the multiplicity of lines of sedimentation converging from across the *dispositif*. Not only is this knowledge contingent, it is also not neutral and nor is the state (McCarthy, 2018, p. 9). The state is not only able to bridge the sovereignty gap through the formation of these communities of mutual recognition, rebuffing assertions that this domain falls outside its traditional remit, but it also allows for cybersecurity to become subsumed within a broader strategy of neoliberal governance. Consequently, the state's continued relevance in this emergent domain provides it with a 'natural' mandate to deal with the (in)security posed by cyberspace. This context shapes and orders political, social and economic priorities (read as: neoliberalism) as well as explicit security practices used to respond to the risks to circulation that present (read as: governmentality).

As has already been seen, there are challenges and opportunities for the neoliberal project pursued by states but as the 'ultimate symbol of globalisation' (Bendrath *et al.*, 2007, p. xix), the internet has already demonstrated its ability to further the objectives of neoliberalism. As we saw in Chapter 2, though, such a logic relies on circulation; it relies on *letting things happen* (Foucault, 2007, p. 45). Strengthening the links across the *dispositif* between technical expertise and political professionals has helped solidify the traditional importance of the state as co-guarantor of cybersecurity and subsequently provides the conditions of possibility through which the strategy of governmentality can be expanded into this domain.

As ever, it is important to note that this is never all one way or the other. For example, contemporary discussions between the state and prominent technology companies over encryption provide a high-profile example of instances of antagonism and disagreement. While the state has access to and utilises robust forms of encryption to protect its sensitive information, political professionals have spoken critically about the availability of strong end-to-end encryption for the general public. The rationale is a national security one; that with readily available encryption for all, we allow those who wish to do us harm to communicate and plot in anonymity and confidence (Yadron *et al.*, 2016; Price, 2017).

'Real people' (Rudd, 2017) do not want nor require such technology and so its availability to all does more harm than good. In the wake of the 2015 terrorist attacks in Paris, former UK Prime Minister David Cameron claimed a future Conservative government would push for legislation granting the state the ability to break into encrypted communication and for the powers to read the content of these messages 'in extremis' so that terrorists had no safe space to communicate (Watt *et al.*, 2015). This approach has been strongly resisted by private companies such as WhatsApp and Telegram, who consider this assurance of privacy to be a major selling point (Wakefield, 2015) as well as civil liberty advocates who argue that the national security argument must be considered alongside the defence of civil liberties and human rights around privacy.

However, as McCarthy points out nor should the relationship be thought of as one where these parties are exclusively at odds with one another:

> Instead liberal state institutions are used to create the conditions for the market to operate. A range of tasks, such as protecting and enforcing property rights, providing basic research and development for technological innovation, and correcting market-failures when they arise, as in the provision of cybersecurity, are undertaken because specific interest groups that control the state apparatus view these policies as valuable, necessary or desirable. (McCarthy, 2018, p. 9)

The dominant cybersecurity knowledge that conflates as national security consequently prioritises strategies such as the protection of infrastructure and

legitimises the accumulation of data and techniques of surveillance to mitigate against the uncertainty posed by a multiplicity of risks online. However,
it can hardly be said that the sorts of infrastructure protection we have witnessed serve as a universal public good. Rather, what emerges 'mainly benefits
a few and already powerful entities and has no, or even negative effects for the
rest' (Dunn Cavelty, 2014, p. 707). It maintains a status quo that disproportion-
ately distributes economic benefits, in this case securing a cluster of private
infrastructure companies. The requirement of circulation sees that these sorts
of actors and institutions receive special treatment, justified by what is required
to achieve 'cybersecurity', and avoid the sort of destruction discussed in particular in Chapters 1 and 4.

Achieving these objectives has clear budgetary consequences also and as a
'Tier 1' threat with 'untold human cost' (HM Government, 2010, p. 30), cybersecurity is primarily the responsibility of GCHQ in the UK. However, this does
not adequately reflect a vast array of different agencies and bodies that are
tasked with various elements of the cybersecurity remit. CERT-UK, the Centre for Cyber Assessment, the Joint Forces Cyber Group, the Defence Cyber
Protection Partnership, the National Cyber Crime Unit, the Centre for the
Protection of National Infrastructure and a Cyber Reserve have all staked a
claim on the subject of protecting cyberspace and have been beneficiaries of
£860 million (HM Government, 2015) that was freed up in 2011 and £1.9 billion
in the 2016 Strategy (HM Government, 2016). This network of public-sector
institutions tasked with responding to the threats in cyberspace and protecting
critical infrastructure (re)produce the dominant cybersecurity knowledge and
obtain central funding to achieve objectives informed by this logic.

Governmentality aims to allow for circulation like this, but it also looks to
manage populations. It looks to demark (in)security, acting upon that which is
deviant. In this regard the uncertainty of cyber-risks, as seen across Chapters
1 and 3, justifies further intervention in the form of surveillance and monitoring by the state and the intelligence community. While sifting presents significant challenges to the intelligence community, the sheer volume of data online
allows for tremendous surveillance potential. As more people migrate online,
more intelligence can be gleaned from these spaces; however, increased internet penetration rates and the ubiquity of connected devices means that rather
than just targeting the 'bad guys' these institutions can broaden their gaze to
surveil, monitor and manage entire populations.

Covert programmes of mass surveillance, including the NSA-run Prism and
GCHQ's Tempora provide empirical examples of this very phenomenon.

Both of these formerly secret projects amassed citizens' data by default, as well as appearing to allow access of this data to their respective trans-Atlantic partners (*BBC News*, 2013). A national security logic within cybersecurity has helped produce the conditions for such processes and demonstrates the manner in which the information age has facilitated new techniques of governmentality. Mass surveillance may not be new, but the scale of the monitoring made possible by this technology, combined with the slew of new types of data available, certainly is. Prism and Tempora are two high-profile examples of formerly secret mass surveillance projects, but where the state is not so constrained by scrutiny attached to major infringements of human rights and civil liberties there are more overt examples of mass surveillance such as the Chinese Golden Shield and Russia's SORM.

A cybersecurity knowledge has been elevated to the status of truth, in part, because technical expertise found in companies such as those I have studied in this book 'was aligned with and influenced by political reasoning' (Dunn Cavelty, 2018, p. 28). This has not been a chance phenomenon but the result of a process of mutual recognition and benefit that serves both parties. What I have sought to show in this final section is the way that the construction of a particular cybersecurity knowledge and the sedimentation of this knowledge has had implications on the extension and expansion of techniques of governance in furtherance of a particular form of political economy. The effectiveness of this sort of power is 'proportional to its ability to hide its own mechanisms' (Foucault, 1986, p. 86). The complex ensemble of the *dispositif* conceals its governmental operation and the manner in which linkages established between sources help to delimit (in)security, allowing that which is permissible and acting upon the deviant that threatens circulation.

Conclusion

Michel Foucault's work, in particular during his genealogical phase, was at its heart a problem-solving endeavour. He sought to identify a problem 'expressed in the terms current today' (Foucault, 1988, p. 262) and then tried to make sense of it through analysing the descent of the object, identifying the finger-prints of power, explaining why the problem is constituted a certain way in the present and considering what alternative knowledge has been rejected in this process. In Foucault's own words the role of the 'intellectual', therefore, was to uncover the 'specificity of the mechanisms of power' that produce these ways of thinking (Foucault, 1980c, p. 145). I have attempted to do something very similar in this piece of work in order to further contribute to the field of critical cybersecurity studies. My constructivist analysis has drawn heavily on Foucauldian 'tools' (Foucault, 2001, p. 1391) as well as the work of those who have sought to develop these ideas as a means of providing a unique theorisation of cybersecurity knowledge.

My starting point, the problem I was facing, was trying to understand why swathes of this relatively new domain had become so rapidly and seemingly unanimously understood as analogous with national security. In one sense this did not surprise me, given the power of this discourse to subsume all things 'security', but the more I considered it the less comfortably the conflation with physical space seemed to fit and the more striking the lack of alternative frames became. Over the previous five chapters, therefore, I have sought to isolate this problem, demonstrate its features and then shed a critical light upon it to explain its connection to the nexus of power/knowledge across society and the importance that flows from this.

Achieving this would not have been possible without bringing to bear a number of theoretical tools and applying these to my object of study. In par-ticular, I have worked with specific notions of power, knowledge and security as a means to try and illuminate the functioning of power within the hetero-geneous assemblage – the *dispositif* – and the constitutive effect particular sources have within and across it. Others will have their own take on how valuable or effective these conceptual and theoretical tools are to conduct the sort of work I have done within this book. However, I argue that these have been uniquely valuable in their ability to explain the sedimentation of knowl-edge claims, the importance of relationships between sources and the manner in which these come together to extend a particular power/knowledge as well as a strategy of governmentality.

My primary task has been to clarify the role that expertise contained within the internet security industry has had on the sedimentation of a particular form of cybersecurity knowledge and thus the construction of popular under-standings of the 'cyber security imaginary' (Stevens, 2015). Such a position is predicated on the idea that, rather than existing as a purely extra-discursive reality, cyber-threats are constituted as part of an inter-subjective process of social construction. Clearly, this does not preclude the material existence of the networks, computers, software, actors, etc. that makes up the substance of some of the discussions I have engaged in over the course of this book. Rather than arguing that the social world is discourse 'all the way down', I conceptualise of knowledge as a product of power that emerges, changes and settles as lines of creativity and sedimentation interact across the network of the *dispositif*.

In the furtherance of this primary task, I have conducted an in-depth overview of cybersecurity research to date to identify the form and structure found herein. I identified three organising themes around which an over-whelmingly problem-solving orthodox knowledge has formed (Cox, 1981). If my motivation has been to address what I see as an issue with the manner in which cybersecurity has been unproblematically conflated with national security, then it was first necessary to characterise this issue. Much of the research and commentary on cybersecurity purports to reflect that which it in fact it 'makes real'. It focuses on defining acts and actors, assessing threats and responding to risks in a manner that conceals a number of assumptions and that, at the very least, implicitly prioritises knowledge that can better inform policy.

In an effort to broaden the narrow confines of this knowledge and the deci-sion making and practices that subsequently flow from it, I have drawn atten-tion to a counter-hegemonic constructivist research agenda and situated my own study within this broader academic tradition. The connecting tissue between the problem I identified in Chapter 1 and the constructivist analysis I subsequently conducted was the interjection of Foucauldian theory that formed the basis to my argument about the relationships between private-sector expertise, political professionals, security imaginaries and neoliberal governmentality.

I have argued that despite the increased role of the private sector upon issues of cybersecurity this industry remains an understudied one, as does the productive relationship formed both within and outside of this sector. The effect of expertise within a technified field such as this (Hansen and Nisenbaum, 2009, p. 1157) requires recognition on account of its ability to speak with enhanced epistemic authority on matters that are largely incomprehensible to the layperson, and for which evidence or reference points that can serve as social moorings are not particularly forthcoming.

My focus has been upon one corner of the industry – those companies who are probably best known for their anti-virus products, but many of which offer products and services that go much further than this. Having argued for the unique importance of the sort of knowledge, what my analysis has revealed is something that shares broad features of the dominant threat frame as identified elsewhere (Dunn Cavelty, 2008). The discourse *is* unique in its specificity and it makes use of common tropes in ways that are different to the other sources that have been previously studied. However, on a broader level we see many of the same tactics, themes, techniques and tropes here as have been used in other discursive sites to achieve a broadly similar construction. The comfortable conflation between cybersecurity and national security that provided the impetus for this study plays out here too – in a space where knowledge claims come with a reinforced epistemic credibility and authority to speak the 'truth'. My interest, therefore, is with this source and how it constructs cybersecurity, but also with the networks that have formed between this source and others and how this sediments the 'direction' of the *dispositif*.

I have sought to argue for the importance of the source I have studied here and, through the use of the theoretical tools I mention above, demonstrate how powerful, constitutive relationships have formed between these security professionals and professionals of politics. I am not looking to establish who or what 'came first', but rather to identify the homogeneity of knowledge claims between technical cybersecurity expertise and those of the political professionals. This alignment between technical expertise and political reasoning provides a salient explanation for the entrenchment of a partial knowledge that conflates cybersecurity with national security (Dunn Cavelty, 2018, p. 28).

Conclusion

To understand how cyber-threats have been constructed, we need to investigate different sites of discourse but we also need to study the linkages, relationships and intertextualities that exist between different sources. When changes occur, such as the emergence of a 'technological age', this will pose challenges to the existing societal power diagram and alter or reformulate it, interjecting lines of creativity. My analysis has mapped one small aspect of the *dispositif* and shown how relationships of not only mutual recognition but also mutual benefit have developed between private-industry expertise and political professionals. There has been disruption to a governance status quo and the potential for a great deal more with the arrival of ubiquitous computing, the increased role of the private sector in this domain and the emergence of the network as the primary organising principle (Harknett, 2003, p. 18). However, despite all of this the state has been able to maintain its centrality and its role of security guarantor by strengthening links with new sources (e.g. the internet security industry) but by doing so within the established power/knowledge framework.

The industry I have studied has benefited from the strengthening of ties with the state in terms of material gain and influence over political decision making. For the state, the shift in the power diagram has seen an expansion and reformulation of the network of power relations that cedes some of its monopoly, but that aligns these new actors and institutions with a logic of cybersecurity that is largely analogous with national security. The cohesiveness of the knowledge claims between technical expertise and the state provide an explanation as to why certain sorts of cyber-incidents become visible, why certain actors have authority to make claims about cybersecurity and why certain accounts are elevated to the status of 'truth' (Dunn Cavelty, 2018, p. 27).

With an entrenched knowledge achieved, in part, on account of the sorts of relationships I have laid out over the course of this book, the state in particular can begin determine how to manage circulation and impose on the deviant margins of (in)security. A strategy of governance remains in place, where the rapidity and freedoms associated with cyberspace continue but where the established national security logic of this domain still requires that the state adopts its traditional position as guarantor of security. The formation of a knowledge that conflates national and cybersecurity produces a logical and traditional role for the state, where a form of security can be achieved even if this version has a dubious claim always to act in the public good. The state is not neutral, just as the dominant version of cybersecurity is not; both serve to maintain the conditions conducive to the continuation of a dominant political-economic logic.

The potential contributions of this book, therefore, are to be found in the empirical and theoretical depth that I believe I have brought to cybersecurity studies and the manner in which I have usefully developed upon the constructivist literature that currently exists. However, this is not to say that my own study does not suffer from its own limitations and I would identify four such areas where I think similarly inclined studies could usefully develop upon what I have laid out here.

First, while the companies I studied were certainly international in nature, it is the case that my analysis has very much taken place within a Western context. The companies studied were often operating from a Western or even more specifically North American perspective. As I reflected upon in my Introduction, one purposive factor for my decision to focus on the companies that I did was on account of their having available materials written in English. This undoubtedly influences the conclusions drawn. Given both the indication at points within Chapter 1 as to alternative models of governance in places like China and Russia and the increasing evidence of a dominant threat frame within Western discourse, I believe that constructivist analysis into discourses situated within different political/security contexts would add considerable value to this discussion.

Second, it has become something of a truism to note the fast pace of technology and the speed with which new developments become history. This is a particular challenge when combined with academic research, which is often painstakingly drawn out over a period of time and requires drafting and redrafting. While I have not sought to define this study by its ability to commentate on the most recent developments, but rather capture a period of recent history, I do recognise that the fifteen-year period I have studied here inevitably misses more recent developments and will not be able to capture possible changes of direction in the discourse I have studied. Unfortunately, this will never be something that authors can wholly respond to given the practicalities of research and the academic publishing timeline. However, if I have achieved my goal of asserting the importance of private industry expertise and convinced others as to the value that exists here, then future analyses that respond to more contemporary events and perhaps use studies such as this as a comparative point will be beneficial to see whether constructions and relationships I have sought to chart remain consistent or not.

Third, while the companies that I studied as part of my analysis generated hundreds of items of text and provided a large corpus, these are only one aspect of a much larger industry. I hope I have been able to demonstrate the value there is in studying technical expertise within the private sector and, with this in mind, I foresee this being a particularly fruitful domain for which further study could generate greater insight. For example, it would be very interesting to see how some of the major technology firms such as Microsoft, Google, Apple, etc. have conceptualised of cybersecurity and how their relationships with professionals of politics have developed. As I noted in Chapter 5, there have been high-profile examples of public disagreement between the state and these companies around security and privacy, and a cursory reading of this relationship seems to imply that there may be a very different relationship here. There is a far more extensive industry out there than that which I have analysed in this book, and comparing my findings and testing my conclusions across different aspects of this industry would help to continue the process of mapping this increasingly important aspect of the *dispositif*.

Finally, I have sought across my empirical analysis to not only identify the homogeneity across internet security discourse but also to draw out where there have been moments of rupture with a conventional knowledge. In my own empirical analysis this has tended to look like a sceptical retort to the orthodoxy – for example, questioning the alarmist tone of a threat assessment or the characterisation of an event as 'war', 'terrorism', etc. While these instances were less forthcoming, they were not absent and this leads me to believe that another route forward for this sort of constructivist research would be to try and capture these dissident forms of knowledge. Typically, we have been interested in the assumptions inherent in a dominant knowledge and what these accounts make possible. I wonder, having conducted my own research and identified some examples of 'dissidence', whether attempts to consider in more depth what these accounts look like, and in particular what it is that prevents them from meaningfully challenging hegemonic accounts, could be a useful next step in this research agenda.

To close, my aim in this book has been to highlight the effects of the expanding influence of private-sector internet security expertise upon the construction of a widely held cybersecurity knowledge that understands this as analogous to national security. The effects of this co-construction and the relationships that have been formed within the security *dispositif* have provided the conditions of possibility for the continuation and extension of neoliberal governance. The conflation with national security is not chance but the effect of the capillary functioning of power across the *dispositif*, including between industry expertise and the state. The effects of this conflation have been to produce a familiar foundation to how security looks and to imbue this domain with the same logics that inform the state's position on land, in the air and at sea. Having delimited the categories of (in)security, the majority can experience the managed circulation that is the lifeblood of a specific political/economic logic while particular subjects and actions can be rendered justified targets of intervention where they threaten this status quo.

Notes

Introduction

1   Definitional issues around the term 'cyber-threats' and other closely related terms will
be addressed in Chapter 1. However, when used in this book, I am referring to the
entire spectrum of techniques and tools designed to achieve unauthorised access to
confidential information, compromise the integrity of systems, obscure authenticity, or
deny or slow availability. See Hollis (2011, p. 380).

2   A note of clarification before going any further. The analysis that proceeds over the following chapters is based on the materials produced by a number of private-sector internet
security companies. These companies make up a prominent aspect of the wider internet security industry but are not reflective of the entire industry, which consists of a host
of private-, public- and third-sector entities offering products and services, research and
development, regulation and governance, etc. The companies I have studied are primarily
known for their anti-virus software; however, between different companies there exists
quite a high degree of variation with regard to the size and reach of the companies, the
products and the services they offer, as well as the sorts of customers and clients they compete for. For example, some are much more reliant on their internet security software and
primarily focus on the typical end-user or small/medium business, but the larger companies operating in this marketplace have the resources to sell to large organisations as well
as bidding for and winning major government contracts. I wanted to provide this clarification in the Introduction because, over the course of this book, I often use short-hand
terms such as 'the industry' or 'industry expertise', etc., when referring to these companies
I have studied and the knowledge they produce. However, I do recognise that these sorts
of companies are but one aspect of a wider and more complex industry.

3   The eighteen companies were: AhnLab; Avast; AVG; Avira; Bitdefender; BullGuard;
Check Point; Comodo; ESET; Faronics; F-Secure; K7; Kaspersky; McAfee; Panda;
Sophos; Symantec; and Trend Micro.

1 Cybersecurity knowledge: cohesion, contestation and constructivism

1   See Shanahan (2010) and Lord Carlile (2007).

Notes

2 Embar-Seddon comments that 'by simply placing the word cyber, computer or information before another word … this can seem to denote an entirely new thing, but often, it does not. These neologisms can create confusion'. See Embar-Seddon (2002, p. 1034).

3 Roland Heickerö also defines cyber-terrorism using an effects-orientated approach when he writes: 'For an attack to be regarded as cyber terrorism, the intended effect has to be serious human and economic casualties, intense fear and anxiety—terror—among the citizens'. See Heickerö (2014, p. 555).

4 Of course, all these definitional questions will have ramifications on legal definitions as set out by States. Keiran Hardy and George Williams in their chapter investigating legal definitions of cyber-terrorism note that the UK, Australia, Canada and New Zealand have the same 'general thrust', but also note that of these definitions only Canada requires that infrastructure targeted be 'essential' and only New Zealand requires the act of cyber-terrorism to be 'likely to endanger life'. See Hardy and Williams (2014).

5 See Decker (2008, p. 964); Esen (2002, p. 269); Furnell (2002); Jones (2007, p. 605); Zhang *et al.* (2012, p. 423).

6 It is important to note, however, that there is opposition to the idea that different cyber-threats can be differentiated solely in terms of the 'attacker's intent'. Audrey Guinchard (2011, p. 79), for example, argues that it is too simplistic to ascribe crime to financial gain and terrorism to ideological ends when many terrorists are motivated by monetary gain 'in order to finance political actions'.

7 The use of 'non-cyber-crimes' to refer to cyberterrorism is slightly confusing here but this category simply refers to traditional crimes facilitated through computers or networks. See Zhang *et al.* (2012, p. 423).

8 Moonlight Maze was a cyber-espionage campaign discovered by US officials that targeted critical systems in the US, including the Pentagon, the Department of Defense and a number of universities and research institutes.

9 See also Valeriano and Maness (2014, p. 347).

10 Despite receiving significant coverage, the report and its headline £27 billion estimate was met with 'widespread scepticism and seen as an attempt to talk up threat' (Anderson *et al.*, 2012, p. 2).

11 To read about this in the Canadian context, see Platt (2012, p. 165).

12 There is also mention of cooperation between the State and so called 'white hat' and 'grey hat' hackers. See Milone (2003).

13 For an overview of the core commitments of constructivist international relations, see Hopf (1998); Copeland (2005); Theys (2017); and Williams and McDonald (2018).

2 Security *dispositifs* and security professionals

1 Hagmann and Dunn Cavelty (2012, p. 88) draw our attention to one important ethical consequence of this when they say 'the authority of popular legitimacy is effectively discounted' in the face of the high validity benchmark set by scientific expert knowledge claims. Consequently, 'an agenda is empowered in which insecurity is articulated on behalf of populations rather than by populations'.

3 Constructing the milieu

1   A programmable logic controller is a 'special form of microprocessor-based controller that uses a programmable memory to store instructions and to implement functions such as logic, sequencing, timing, counting and arithmetic in order to control machines and processes'. See Bolton (2011, p. 3).

2   This web browser has now been discontinued but is still being maintained by Microsoft, despite being officially replaced by their new browser Microsoft Edge.

3   'Zero-day vulnerabilities are vulnerabilities against which no vendor has released a patch. The absence of a patch for a zero-day vulnerability presents a threat to organizations and consumers alike, because in many cases these threats can evade purely signature-based detection until a patch is released.' See Symantec (2015).

4   The 'Internet of Things' refers to the move towards a larger more integrated "smart world" where 'environmental and daily life items, also named "things", "objects", or "machines" are enhanced with computing and communication technology and join the communication framework'. In this world not only would computers as we traditionally understand them (PC, laptop, tablet, smartphone) be connected via the internet but so too would everyday household items – televisions, fridges, boilers, for example – allowing for them to be managed remotely by the user. See Chaouchi (2013, p. 1).

5   Here, I am referring to two metaphorical usages of 'the wild'; however, it is important to note that in the technical vernacular of the internet security industry, 'the wild' does have a specific meaning: the state in which malware is discovered. Specifically, it refers to discovering malware for the first time. This specific use of 'the wild' is not the focus here, but for more information see Mashevsky (2010).

6   A drive-by download refers to a download in which the user is either misled into clicking a link authorising a download – for example, through an illicit popup, or where the user has malware downloaded onto their device surreptitiously, perhaps when visiting an 'infected' website.

7   It is important to note the murmuring of scepticism that had already begun to occur by the late twentieth and early twenty-first centuries surrounding this metaphor. Kathleen Olson argues that the Western Frontier/cyberspace metaphor did not survive intact into the twenty-first century and that it, instead, 'represented an early way of thinking about the internet'. See Olson (2005, p. 15).

8   URL redirection refers to the process of a user accessing a URL and being redirected to an alternative page with a different URL. This is a not an inherently malicious function; however, the ability to redirect a user to a malicious site has made it a popular technique for phishing (attempting to gain sensitive information by masquerading as a legitimate or trustworthy source) attacks.

9   Hard-to-detect external access points allowing the attacker to gain unauthorised access even after the original zero-day exploit has been patched.

10 GhostNet managed to infect 1,295 computers, 30 per cent of which were determined to be 'high-value targets' across 103 different countries (TheSecDev Group, 2009).

11 Cofer Black is the former head of the CIA's counter-terrorism centre and one of the individuals who is credited for his foresight, prior to 11 September 2001, into the threat Al-Qaeda presented to the US.

Notes

12 Metaphor analysis has been used extensively within the field of security studies and international relations on topics such as war, security policy and terrorism. See, respectively, Paris (2002), Thornborrow (1993) and Lakoff (2001).

4 Constructing cyber-threats

1 For other examples of definition, see Skoudis and Zeltset (2004, p. 3), and Kramer and Bradfield (2010).
2 Securelist is a separate website operated by Kaspersky Labs, where many of their articles and blogs on 'Viruses, hackers and spam' are posted. See Securelist (2019).
3 As a point of clarification, the use of the word 'understand' in this context is a qualified one; the suggestion is not that the general population could accurately describe how biological viruses operate in the same way a medical doctor or virologist could. Analogies and metaphors such as these are always acting as sort of linguistic 'shortcuts'; they take the core features, observable qualities or the manner in which something operates (say, the common cold) and extend these features to something else in some other domain. The cold virus is an illness (harmful); it is contagious and it requires a host in order to live and propagate – it is these characteristics that are understood. The general population's understanding of computer viruses, therefore, is an extension of this (qualified) understanding of a virus such as the common cold into the world of computer technology.
4 See Jarvis *et al.* (2016).
5 In this vein, see also Jarvis (2009, pp. 44–62) on 9/11 as 'rupture' and Stevens (2016, pp. 68–72) on the 'revolutionary present' that cybersecurity communities are keen to emphasise.
6 The militarisation of cyberspace links into a pre-existing literature on the militarisation of 'everyday life'. Drawing upon the Foucauldian notion of biopolitics, authors such as Henry Giroux have written about the 'biopolitics of militarisation' that exerts an influence over various domains, spaces and peoples, particularly in the US. For examples of this, see Feldman (2002), Giroux (2006, 2008) and Bernazzoli and Flint (2010). However, outside of this distinct literature there is also a range of other examples where military metaphors have been used. See, for example, Parameswaran (2006), Marland (2003), Reisfield and Wilson (2004), Howe (1988) and Thornburg (1995).
7 On the topic of cyber-war, compare F-Secure (2012a) ESET Research (2010c) and Paget (2012) with Abrams (2009a) and Ducklin (2011).
8 See also Brown (1986).

Bibliography

Abdulhayoğlu, M. (2008a) *Cyber Terrorism*. Melih.com blog. Available at www.melih. com/2008/11/19/cyber-terrorism/ (accessed 29 August 2015).

Abdulhayoğlu, M. (2008b) *Machine vs Human – A War Underway*. Melih.com blog. Available at www.melih.com/2008/05/04/machine-vs-human-a-war-underway/ (accessed 29 August 2015).

Abdulhayoğlu, M. (2009) *Comodo TV: Cyber-Militias in Action –Who's Next?* Comodo. Available at www.comodo.tv/m-vision/cyber-militias-in-action-whos-next/ (accessed 29 August 2015).

Abraham, S. and Chengalur-Smith, I. (2010) 'An overview of social engineering malware: trends, tactics, and implications', *Technology in Society*, 32(3), 183–96.

Abrams, R. (2009a) *Cyber War or Cyber Hype*. Available at www.welivesecurity.com/ 2009/07/10/cyber-war-or-cyber-hype/ (accessed 29 August 2015).

Abrams, R. (2009b) *Cyberwar Exposed*. Available at www.welivesecurity.com/2009/11/13/ cyberwar-exposed/ (accessed 29 August 2015).

Abrams, R. (2010) *Who Wants a Cyberwar?* Available at www.welivesecurity.com/2010/09/30/ who-wants-a-cyberwar/ (accessed 29 August 2015).

Adams, J. (2001) 'Virtual defence', *Foreign Affairs*, 80(3), 98–113.

Adams, P. C. (1997) 'Cyberspace and virtual places', *Geographical Review*, 87(2), 155–71.

Adler, E. (1997) 'Seizing the middle ground: constructivism in world politics', *European Journal of International Relations*, 3(3), 319–63.

Adler, E. and Haas, P. M. (1992) 'Conclusion: epistemic communities, world order, and the creation of a reflective research program', *International Organisation*, 46(1), 367–90.

Admin (2012) *AVG Awarded Best in Class For Management Usability in Tolly Group Tests*. AVG. Available at https://now.avg.com/avg-awarded-best-in-class-for-management-usability-in-tolly-group-tests (accessed 27 March 2019).

Admin (2013) *Where Will You Be When the Lights Go Out?* Comodo. Available at https://blogs. comodo.com/it-security/where-will-you-be-when-the-lights-go-out/ (accessed 29 August 2015).

AhnLab (2008a) *AhnLab Announces Seven Security Issues for 2007*. AhnLab. Available at www. ahnlab.com/company/site/eng/pr/comPressReleaseEng/comPressReleaseEngView. do (accessed 22 May 2014).

AhnLab (2008b) *AhnLab Exports A Vaccine for Mobile Phones Overseas for the First Time*. AhnLab. Available at www.ahnlab.com/company/site/eng/pr/comPressReleaseEng/com PressReleaseEngView.do (accessed 22 May 2014).

Bibliography

AhnLab (2011a) *Ahnlab Announces Its Top 7 Security Threat Predictions for 2012*. AhnLab. Available at www.ahnlab.com/company/site/eng/pr/comPressReleaseEng/comPressReleaseEng View.do (accessed 22 May 2014).

AhnLab (2011b) *AhnLab Announces Security Prediction 2011: Threats Getting Socialized and Diversified*. AhnLab. Available at www.ahnlab.com/company/site/eng/pr/comPressReleaseEng/comPressReleaseEngView.do (accessed 22 May 2014).

Akdag, Y. (2019) 'The likelihood of cyberwar between the United States and China: a neo-realism and power transition theory perspective', *Journal of Chinese Political Science*, 24(2), 225–47.

Aleks (2011) *The Mystery of Duqu: Part One*. Kaspersky Labs. Available at www.securelist.com/en/blog/208193182/The_Mystery_of_Duqu_Part_One (accessed 29 August 2015).

Algani, A. F. (2013) 'Policing internet fraud in Saudi Arabia: expressive gestures or adaptive strategies?', *Policing and Society: An international Journal of Research and Policy*, 34(4), 498–515.

Al-Garni, T. and Chen, T. H. (2015) 'An updated cost-benefit view of cyberterrorism', in T. Chen, L. Jarvis and S. Macdonald (eds) *Terror Online: Politics, Law and Technology*. London: Routledge, pp. 72–85.

Alia (2009a) *Cyberwar Crops Up Again*. F-Secure. Available at www.f-secure.com/weblog/archives/00001788.html (accessed 29 August 2015).

Alia (2009b) *Taking Cyberwar Seriously?* F-Secure. Available at www.f-secure.com/weblog/archives/00001667.html (accessed 29 August 2015).

Allied Market Research (2016) *Internet Security Market by Type (Hardware, Software, Services), Technology (Authentication, Access Control Technology, Content Filtering and Cryptography) and Application (BFSI, IT & Telecommunications, Retail, Government, Education and Aerospace, defense & intelligence) – Global Opportunity Analysis and Industry Forecast, 2014–2021*. Allied Market Research. Available at www.alliedmarketresearch.com/world-internet-security-market (accessed 14 January 2019).

Anderson, B. (2010) 'Security and the future: anticipating the event of terror', *Geoforum*, 41(2), 227–35.

Anderson, R., Barton, C., Böhme., Clayton, R., van Eeten, M. J. G., Levi, M., Moore, T. and Savage, S. (2012) *Measuring the Costs of Cybercrime*. The Workshop on the Economics of Information Security. Available at www.econinfosec.org/archive/weis2012/papers/Anderson_WEIS2012.pdf (accessed 8 August 2019).

Annas, G. (1995) 'Reframing the debate on health care reform by replacing our metaphors', *New England Journal of Medicine*, 332(11), 744–7.

Anscombe, T. (2013) *In the Digital Age, What Really Keeps Parents Up at Night?* AVG. Available at http://blogs.avg.com/news-threats/one-parent-to-another-tony-ansombe/ (accessed 24 March 2016).

Antón, P. S. (2003) *The Vulnerability Assessment and Mitigation Methodology*. Santa Monica, CA: RAND.

Apergis, E. and Apergis, N. (2016) 'The 11/13 Paris terrorist attacks and stock prices: the case of the international defense industry', *Finance Research Letters*, 17, pp. 186–92.

Aquilla, J. (2000) 'Screen saver', *The New Republic*, 1 May, 16–18.

Arachchilage, N. A. G. and Love, S. (2013) 'A game design framework for avoiding phishing attacks', *Computers in Human Behavior*, 29(3), 706–14.

Aradau, C. (2010a) 'Security that matters: critical infrastructure and objects of protection', *Security Dialogue*, 41(5), 491–514.

Aradau, C. (2010b) 'The myth of preparedness', *Radical Philosophy*, 161(May/June), 2–7.

Bibliography

Aradau, C. and Van Munster, R. (2007) 'Governing terrorism through risk: taking precautions, (un)knowing the future', *European Journal of International Relations*, 13(1), 89–115.

Aradau, C. and Van Munster, R. (2012) 'The time/space of preparedness: anticipating the "next terrorist attack"', *Space and Culture*, 15(2), 98–109.

Archer, E. (2014) 'Crossing the Rubicon: understanding cyber terrorism in the European context', *The European Legacy: Toward New Paradigms*, 19(5), 606–21.

Arizona Department of Public Safety (2011) *DPS Victim of Cyber Attack*. Arizona Department of Public Safety. Available at www.azdps.gov/media/news/View/?p=316 (accessed 29 August 2015).

Aseev, E., Gostev, A. and Maslennikov, D. (2010) *Kaspersky Security Bulletin 2009. Malware Evolution 2009*. Kaspersky Labs. Available at www.securelist.com/en/analysis/204792100/Kaspersky_Security_Bulletin_2009_Malware_Evolution_2009 (accessed 29 August 2015).

Asokhia, M. O. (2010) 'Enhancing national development and growth through combatting cybercrime/internet fraud: a comparative approach', *Journal of Social Sciences: Interdisciplinary Reflection of Contemporary Society*, 23(1), 13–19.

Australian Parliament (2003) *Cybercrime*, testimony before the Joint Committee on the Australian Crime Commission, July 18 2003. Available at https://parlinfo.aph.gov.au/parlInfo/download/committees/commjnt/6728/toc_pdf/2674–2.pdf;fileType=application%2Fpdf#search=%22committees/commjnt/6728/0014%22 (accessed 15 November 2018).

Australian Parliament (2007) *Future Impact of Serious and Organised Crime on Australian Society*, Joint Committee on the Australian Crime commission, 5 July 2007. Available at https://parlinfo.aph.gov.au/parlInfo/download/committees/commjnt/10329/toc_pdf/5551–2.pdf;fileType=application/pdf (accessed 15 November 2018), p. 92.

Australian Parliament (2009) *The Senate Questions on Notice, Treasury: Consultants*, 14 September 2009. Available at https://parlinfo.aph.gov.au/parlInfo/genpdf/chamber/hansards/2009–09–14/0158/hansard_frag.pdf;fileType=application/pdf (accessed 17 November 2018).

Australian Parliament (2010) 'Crimes Legislation Amendment (Sexual Offences against Children) Bill 2010 (Second Reading)', speech by Nola Marino, 9 March 2010. Available at https://parlinfo.aph.gov.au/parlInfo/genpdf/chamber/hansardr/2010–03–09/0071/hansard_frag.pdf;fileType=application/pdf (accessed 21 November 2019).

Australian Parliament (2011) 'Cybercrime Legislation Amendment Bill' (Second Reading)', speech by Luke Simpkins MP, 23 August 2011. Available at https://parlinfo.aph.gov.au/parlInfo/genpdf/chamber/hansardr/18675d35-aa1f-4f94–8672-a196b5fc3901/0102/hansard_frag.pdf;fileType%3Dapplication%2Fpdf (accessed 21 November 2018).

AVG (2011a) *Cybercrime Risk A Perfect Storm Brewing, Warns AVG Report*. AVG. Available at http://now.avg.com/cybercrime-risk-a-perfect-storm-brewing-warns-avg-report/ (accessed 1 September 2015).

AVG (2011b) *AVG Unveils Global Community Powered Threat Report – Q2–2011*. AVG. Available at http://mediacenter.avg.com/news/threat-report-q2–2011 (accessed 29 August 2015).

AVG (2011c) *AVG Technologies Presents Global Q1–2011 Security Threat Report*. AVG. Available at http://now.avg.com/avg-technologies-presents-global-q1–2011-security-threat-report/ (accessed 29 August 2015).

AVG (2011d) *Cyber Attacks Costs Billions to UK Economy*. AVG. Available at http://blogs.avg.com/news-threats/cyber-attacks-cost-billions-uk-economy/ (accessed 21 May 2014).

AVG (2011e) *Cybercrime at Street Level: the Reality, the Threat and the Future*. AVG. Available at http://blogs.avg.com/news-threats/cybercrime-street-level-reality-threat-future/ (accessed 9 April 2014).

Bibliography

AVG (2011f) *AVG Launches 'AVG Family Safety'*. AVG. Available at http://mediacenter.avg.com/news/avg-launches-avg-family-safety (accessed 7 February 2016).

AVG (2011g) *AVG Business Edition 2012 Unveiled*. AVG. Available at http://mediacenter.avg.com/news/avg-business-edition-2012-unveiled (accessed 3 March 2019).

AVG (2012a) *Baby Boomers Need to Become More Educated about Digital Technology*. AVG. Available at http://mediacenter.avg.com/news/baby-boomers-need-to-become-more-educated-about-digital-security (accessed 16 August 2016).

AVG (2012b) *AVG Technologies Unveils Global Community Powered Threat Report – Q4–2011*. AVG. Available at https://now.avg.com/avg-technologies-unveils-global-community-powered-threat-report-q4–2011 (accessed 2 April 2019).

AVG (2013) *AVG Technologies Shares Five Mother's Day Tips for Mobile Moms*. AVG. Available at http://mediacenter.avg.com/news/avg-technologies-shares-five-mothers-day-tips-for-mobile-moms (accessed 15 May 2016).

AVG Web Threats Research (2012) *What Threats Will Web Users Face in 2012?* AVG. Available at http://blogs.avg.com/news-threats/threats-web-users-face-2012/ (accessed 22 May 2014).

Avira (2010) *Botnets Evolving: Spy Eye vs Zeus*. Ariva. Available at https://aviratechblog.wordpress.com/2010/04/26/botnets-evolving-spy-eye-vs-zeus/ (accessed 29 August 2015).

Avira (2013) *Libra ESVA Integrates Avira Scanning Engine to Improve Virus Protection*. Avira. Available at www.avira.com/en/press-details/nid/763/news/libra-integrates-avira-scanning-engine (accessed 29 August 2015).

Bachrach, P. and Baratz, M. S. (1970) *Power and Poverty: Theory and Practice*. Oxford: Oxford University Press.

Baldwin, D. A. (1997) 'The concept of security', *Review of International Studies*, 23(1), 5–26.

Ballard, J. D., Hornik, J. G. and McKenzie, D. (2002) 'Technological facilitation of terrorism: definitional, legal and, policy issues', *American Behavioral Scientist*, 45(6), 989–1016.

Bambauer, D. E. (2012) 'Conundrum', *Minnesota Law Review*, 96(2), 584–674.

Barnard-Wills, D. and Ashenden, D. (2012) 'Securing virtual space: cyber war, cyber terror, and risk', *Space and Culture*, 15(2), 1–14.

Barnes, J. (2009) 'A "universal metaphor" for the user interface for an internet based health support website', in P. A. van Brakel (ed.) *Proceedings of the 11th Annual Conference on World Wide Web Applications*, Port Elizabeth, 2–4 September. Cape Town, South Africa: Cape Peninsula University of Technology, pp. 4–15.

Barthes, R. (1993) *Image, Music, Text*. Translated from French by S. Heath. London: Fontana Press.

Bauer, J. M. and van Eeten, M. J. G. (2009) 'Cybersecurity: stakeholder incentives, externalisites and policy options', *Telecommunications Policy*, 33(10–11), 706–19.

BBC News (2013) *GCHQ Use of Prism Surveillance Data Was Legal, Says Report*. London: BBC. Available at www.bbc.co.uk/news/uk-23341597 (accessed 29 August 2015).

Beaumont, C. (2008) 'Bill Gate's dream: a computer in every home', *The Telegraph*. Available at www.telegraph.co.uk/technology/3357701/Bill-Gatess-dream-A-computer-in-every-home.html (accessed 29 January 2018).

Beck, U. (1992) *Risk Society: towards A New Modernity*. London: Sage.

Beck, U. (2008) *World at Risk*. Cambridge: Polity Press.

Beck, U. (2009) 'World risk society and manufactured uncertainties', *IRIS: European Journal of Philosophy and Public Debate*, 1(2), 291–9.

Beckham, K. (2012) *Cyberterrorism: Cutting through the Hype*. Faronics. Available at www.faronics.com/en-uk/news/blog/cyberterrorism-cutting-through-the-hype/ (accessed 22 August 2014).

Bibliography

Bell, S. (2013a) *Hackers Target Financial Apps on Apple and Google Platforms*. BullGuard. Available at http://blog.bullguard.com/2013/12/hackers-target-financial-apps-on-apple-and-google-platforms.html (accessed 29 August 2015).

Bell, S. (2013b) *How Real-Life Pickpocketing Equals Identity Theft in the Online World*. BullGuard. Available at www.bullguard.com/blog/2013/09/how-real-life-pickpocketing-equals-identity-theft-in-the-online-world.html (accessed 29 August 2015).

Bendrath, R., Eriksson, J., and Giacomello, G. (2007) 'From "cyberterrorism" to "cyber-war", back and forth: how the United States securitized cyberspace', in J. Eriksson and G. Giacomello (eds) *International Relations and Security in the Digital Age*. Abingdon: Routledge, 57–82.

Ben-Itzhak, Y. (2012) *Threat Report – Analysis of the First Three Months of 2012*. AVG. Available at http://blogs.avg.com/news-threats/threat-report-analysis-months-2012/ (accessed 16 April 2014).

Ben-Itzhak, Y. (2013a) *Do You Really Need Anti Virus Protection? Go On, Uninstall It Then*. AVG. Available at http://blogs.avg.com/news-threats/anti-virus-protection-uninstall/ (accessed 29 August 2015).

Ben-Itzhak, Y. (2013b) *Privacy – the New Security*. AVG. Available at http://blogs.avg.com/news-threats/is-privacy-the-new-security/ (accessed 29 August 2015).

Berling, T. V. (2011) 'Science and securitization: objectivation, the authority of the speak and mobilization of scientific facts', *Security Dialogue*, 42(4–5), 385–97.

Berling, T. V. and Bueger, C. (2015) 'Security expertise: an introduction', in T. V. Berling and C. Bueger (eds) *Security Expertise: Practice, Power, Responsibility*. Abingdon: Routledge, pp. 1–18.

Bernazzoli, R. M. and Flint, C. (2010) 'Embodying the garrison state? Everyday geographies of militarization in American society', *Political Geography*, 29(3), 157–66.

Bernick, J. (2013) *Knowing Is Half the Battle for Today's CISOs*. Symantec. Available at www.symantec.com/connect/blogs/knowing-half-battle-today-s-cisos (accessed 29 August 2015).

Betz, D. J. and Stevens, T. (2013) 'Analogical reasoning and cyber security', *Security Dialogue*, 44(2), 147–64.

Bigo, D. (2001) 'The Mobius ribbon of internal and external security(ies)', in M. Albert, D. Jacobsen and Y. Lapid (eds) *Identities, Borders, Orders – Rethinking International Relations Theory*. London: University of Minnesota Press, pp. 91–116.

Bigo, D. (2002) 'Security and immigration: toward a critique of the governmentality of unease', *Alternatives: Global, Local, Political*, 27(1 – Supplement), 63–92.

Bigo, D. (2004) 'The globalization of (in)security and the ban-opticon', in N. Sakai and J. Solomon (eds) *Translation, Biopolitics, Colonial Difference*. Hong Kong: Hong Kong University Press, pp. 109–55.

Bigo, D. (2008) 'Globalized (in)security: the field and the ban-opticon', in D. Bigo and A. Tsoukala (eds) *Terror, Insecurity and Liberty. Illiberal Practices of Liberal Regimes after 9/11*. Abingdon: Routledge, pp. 10–48.

Bigo, D. (2011) 'Security: a field left fallow', in M. Dillon and A. W. Neal (eds) *Foucault on Politics, Security and War*. Basingstoke: Palgrave Macmillan, pp. 93–114.

Bigo, D. (2012) 'Globalisation and security', in E. Amenta, K. Nash and A. Scott (eds) *The Wiley-Blackwell Companion to Political Sociology*. Chichester: Blackwell Publishing, pp. 204–213.

Bigo, D. and Guittet, E. (2011) 'Northern Ireland as metaphor: exception, suspicion and radicalization in the "war on terror"', *Security Dialogue*, 42(6), 483–98.

Bitdefender (2012a) *UK to Recruit Cyber-Spies from Gaming Communities*. Bitdefender. Available at www.bitdefender.co.uk/security/uk-to-recruit-cyber-spies-from-gaming-communities.html (accessed 29 August 2015).

Bibliography

Bitdefender (2012b) *UK Companies Spending Billions on Security Threats*. Bitdefender. Available at www.bitdefender.co.uk/security/uk-companies-spending-billions-on-security-threats. html (accessed 2 February 2016).

Bitdefender (2013) *UK Targeted by 120,000 Cyber-Hits a Day*. Bitdefender. Available at www. bitdefender.co.uk/security/uk-targeted-by-120–000-cyber-hits-a-day.html (accessed 29 August 2015).

Blendon, R. J. and Young, J. T. (1998) 'The public and the war on illicit drugs', *The Journal of the American Medical Association*, 279(11), 827–32.

Bolton, W. (2011) *Programmable Logic Controllers*. Oxford: Newnes.

Bourdieu, P. (2004) *Science of Science and Reflexivity*. Cambridge: Polity.

Boyle, P. and Haggerty, K. D. (2009) 'Spectacular security: mega-events and the security complex', *International Political Sociology*, 3(3), 257–74.

Breakey, W. R. (1997) 'It's time for the public health community to declare war on homelessness', *American Journal of Public Health*, 87(2), 153–5.

Brenner, J. (2013) 'Eyes wide shut: the growing threat of cyber attacks on industrial control systems', *Bulletin of Atomic Scientists*, 69(5), 15–20.

Brenner, S. (2006a) 'Cybercrime, cyberterrorism and cyberwarfare', *International Review of Penal Law*, 77(3), 453–71.

Brenner, S. (2006b) 'Cybercrime jurisdiction', *Crime, Law and Social Change*, 46(4–5), 189–206.

Brenner, S. (2007) '"At light speed": attribution and response to cybercrime/terrorism/ warfare', *The Journal of Criminal Law and Criminology*, 97(2), 379–476.

Brenner, S. and Schwerha, J. J. (2007) 'Cybercrime havens: challenges and solutions', *ABA Journal*, 17(2), 49–52.

Brito, J. and Watkins, T. (2011) 'Loving the cyber bomb? The dangers of threat inflations in cybersecurity policy', *Harvard National Security Journal*, 3(1), 39–84.

Brown, J. (1986) 'Professional language: words that succeed', *Radical History*, 34(3), 33–51.

Bueger, C. (2014) 'From expert communities to epistemic arrangements: situating expertise in international relations', in M. Mayer, M. Carpes and K. R. Wiesbaden (eds) *International Relations and the Global Politics of Science and Technology*. Berlin: Springer, VS, pp. 39–54.

BullGuard (2013a) *'The safer you feel, the more vulnerable you are' – Alex Balan, Product Manager at BullGuard*. BullGuard. Available at http://blog.bullguard.com/2013/09/the-safer-you-feel-the-more-vulnerable-you-are-alex-balan-product-manager-at-bullguard.html (accessed 29 August 2015).

BullGuard (2013b) 'BullGuard launches free online virus scan to detect the latest threats'. BullGuard. Available at www.bullguard.com/press/latest-press-releases/2013/07–11. aspx (accessed 28 January 2015).

BullGuard (2013c) *Bigger than the Drugs Trade*. BullGuard. Available at http://blog. bullguard.com/2013/07/bigger-than-the-drugs-trade.html?utm_source=feedburner& utm_medium=feed&utm_campaign=Feed:+BullGuardBlog+(BullGuard+Blog) (accessed 28 January 2015).

BullGuard (2013d) 'Protect sensitive data and keep kids safe online 24/7 with BullGuard Identity Protection'. BullGuard. Available at www.bullguard.com/press/latest-press-releases/2013/12–09.aspx (accessed 28 January 2015).

Burton, J. (2013) 'Small states and cybersecurity: the case of New Zealand', *Political Science*, 65(2), 216–38.

Bibliography

Business Wire (2006) *Check Point to Acquire NFR Security; Expands Intrusion Prevention Capabilities to Fortify Enterprise Networks.* Business Wire. Available at www.businesswire.com/news/home/20061219005384/en/Check-Point-Acquire-NFR-Security-Expands-Intrusion#.VeMsmCVViko (accessed 30 August 2015).

Business Wire (2010) *McAfee, Inc. Report Reveals Cyberwar, with Critical Infrastructure under Constant Cyberattack Causing Widespread Damage.* Business Wire. Available at www.businesswire.com/news/home/20100128005408/en/McAfee-Report-Reveals-Cyber-Coldwar-Critical-Infrastructure#.VJFoYdKsXeo (accessed 30 August 2015).

Business Wire (2011) *Avira Earns Top Certification in AV-Comparatives Malware Test.* Business Wire. Available at www.businesswire.com/news/home/20110601005135/en#.Usa5H_RdWSo (accessed 22 February 2016).

Business Wire (2018) *U.S. Department of Defense Awards $551 Million Enterprise-Wide Contract for McAfee Products and Services.* Business Wire. Available at www.businesswire.com/news/home/20180730005016/en/U.S.-Department-Defense-Awards-551-Million-Enterprise-Wide (accessed 7 February 2019).

Bussolini, J. (2010) 'What is a dispositive?', *Foucault Studies*, 10, 85–107.

Buzan, B., Wæver, O. and de Wilde, J. (1997) *Security: A New Framework for Analysis.* London: Lynne Rienner.

Calderoni, F. (2010) 'The European legal framework on cybercrime: striving for an effective implementation', *Crime, Law and Social Change*, 54(5), 339–57.

Camp, C. (2011a) *North Korea's Overseas Cyber Warrior Training.* Available at www.welivesecurity.com/2011/06/03/north-koreas-overseas-cyber-warrior-training/ (accessed 28 January 2015).

Camp, C. (2011b) *U.S. Standard Agency Warns Energy Producers of Cyber Attacks.* Available at www.welivesecurity.com/2011/08/08/us-agency-warns-energy-producers-of-cyber-attacks/ (accessed 28 January 2015).

Camp, L. J. (2011) 'Reconceptualizing the role of security user', *Daedalus*, 140(4), 93–107.

Carr, J. (2010) *Inside Cyber Warfare: Mapping the Cyber Underworld.* California, CA: O'Reilly Media Publishing.

Carr, M. (2016) 'Public–private partnerships in national cyber-security strategies', *International Affairs*, 92(1), 43–62.

Carrapico, H. and Barrinha, A. (2017) 'The EU as a coherent (cyber)security actor', *Journal of Common Market Studies*, 55(6), 1254–72.

Carveth, R. and Metz, J. (1996) 'Frederick Jackson Turner and the democratization of the electronic frontier', *The American Sociologist*, 27(1), 72–90.

Cassim, F. (2009) 'Formulating specialised legislation to address the growing spectre of cybercrime: a comparative study', *Potchefstroom Electronic Law Journal*, 12(4), 36–79.

Cassim, F. (2011) 'Addressing the growing spectre of cyber crime in Africa: evaluating measures adopted by South Africa and other regional role players', *The Comparative and International Law Journal of Southern Africa*, 44(1), 123–38.

Cassim, F. (2012) 'Addressing the spectre of cyber terrorism: a comparative perspective', *Potchefstroom Electronic Law Journal*, 15(2), 381–415.

Castillo, D. and Falzon, J. (2018) 'An analysis of the impact of WannaCry cyberattack on cybersecurity stock returns', *Review of Economics & Finance*, 13(3), 93–100.

Cerf, V. G. (2011) 'Safety in cyberspace', *Dædalus*, 140(4), 59–69.

Cetron, M. J. and Davies, O. (2009) 'World War 3.0: ten critical trends for cybersecurity', *The Futurist*, 43(5), 40–9.

Chaikin, D. (2006) 'Network investigations of cyber attacks: the limits of digital evidence', *Crime, Law and Social Change*, 46(4–5), 239–56.

Chaouchi, H. (2013) *The Internet of Things: Connecting Objects*. Hoboken, NJ: John Wiley & Sons.

Checkel, J. T. (1998) 'The constructivist turn in international relations theory', *World Politics*, 50(2), 324–48.

Check Point (1997) *Check Point Software Brings New Levels of Security and Confidence to Virtual Private Networks*. Check Point. Available at www.checkpoint.com/press/1997/newlevel0902.html (accessed 17 April 2014).

Check Point (2006) *Media Alert: Check Point to Enter Beta for New ZoneAlarm Internet Security Suite 7.0*. Check Point. www.checkpoint.com/press/2006/zonealarmbeta111706.html (accessed 24 August 2014).

Chilton, P. (2004) *Analysing Political Discourse: Theory and Practice*. London: Routledge.

China Copyright and Media (2016) *Chinese National Cyberspace Security Strategy* (unofficial translation by R. Creemers). Available at https://chinacopyrightandmedia.wordpress.com/2016/12/27/national-cyberspace-security-strategy/ (accessed 6 September 2017).

Chittister, C. G. and Haimes, Y. Y. (2011) 'The role of modelling in the resilience of cyber infrastructure systems and preparedness for cyber intrusions', *Journal of Homeland Security and Emergency Management*, 8(1), 1–19.

Chourcri, N. and Goldsmith, D. (2012) 'Lost in cyberspace: harnessing the internet, international relation, and global security', *Bulletin of the Atomic Scientists*, 68(2), 70–7.

Christensen, K. K. and Petersen, K. L. (2017) 'Public–private partnerships on cyber security: a practice of loyalty', *International Affairs*, 93(6), 1435–52.

Cilluffo, F. J. and Pattak, P. B. (2000) 'Cyber threats: ten issues for consideration', *Georgetown Journal of International Affairs*, 1(1), 41–50.

Clarke, L. B. (2006) *Worst Cases: Terror and Catastrophe in the Popular Imagination*. Chicago, IL: University of Chicago Press.

Clarke, R. (2009) 'War from cyberspace', *The National Interest*, November/December (104), 31–6.

Clarke, R. (2010) *Cyber War: The Next Threat to National Security and What to Do about It*. New York, NY: Harper Collins.

Clem, A., Galwankar, S. and Buck, G. (2003) 'Health implications of cyber-terrorism', *Prehospital and Disaster Medicine*, 18(3), 272–5.

Clifford, M. (2001) *Political Genealogy after Foucault: Savage Identities*. London: Routledge.

Clinton, L. (2015) 'Best practices for operating government industry partnerships in cyber security', *Journal of Strategic Security*, 8(4), 53–68.

Cluley, G. (2009a) *America! Stop Helping Spam Spread and Clean Up Your Computer*. Sophos. Available at http://nakedsecurity.sophos.com/2009/07/20/spam-stats-q2-2009/ (accessed 29 August 2015).

Cluley, G. (2010) *Stuxnet, Vancouver, and Virus Bulletin*. Sophos. Available at http://nakedsecurity.sophos.com/2010/09/24/stuxnet-vancouver-virus-bulletin/ (accessed 29 August 2015).

Cluley, G. (2011a) *'Foreign Government' Hackers Steal Secret Pentagon Plans*. Sophos. Available at http://nakedsecurity.sophos.com/2011/07/15/hackers-governmentsecret-plans-pentagon/ (accessed 29 August 2015).

Cluley, G. (2011b) *Lessons to Learn from the HBGary Federal Hack*. Sophos. Available at https://nakedsecurity.sophos.com/2011/02/16/lessons-to-learn-from-the-hbgary-federal-hack/ (accessed 29 August 2015).

Cobb, S. (2013) *2013 Forecast: Malware, Scams, Security and Privacy Concerns*. Sophos. Available at www.welivesecurity.com/2013/01/03/2013-forecast-malware-scams-security-and-privacy-concerns/ (accessed 29 August 2015).

Cohen, J. E. (2007) 'Cyberspace as/and space', *Columbia Law Review*, 107(210), 201–56.

Bibliography

Cohen, L. and Manion, L. (2008) *Research Methods in Education. 6th Edition.* Abingdon: Routledge.

Cohen, M. J. (2011) 'Is the UK preparing for "war"? Military metaphors, personal carbon allowances, and consumption rationing in historical perspective', *Climatic Change*, 104(2), 199–222.

Cohn, C. (1987) 'Sex and death in the rational world of defense intellectuals', *Signs*, 12(4), 687–718.

Coles-Kemp, L., Ashenden, D. and O'Hara, K. (2018) 'Why should I? Cybersecurity, the security of the state and the insecurity of the citizen', *Politics and Governance*, 6(2), 41–8.

Collier, J. (2018) 'Cyber security assemblages: a framework for understanding the dynamic and contested nature of security provision', *Politics and Governance*, 6(2), 13–21.

Collin, B. C. (1997) 'The future of cyberterrorism', *Crime and Justice International*, 13(2), 15–18.

Comer, D. E. (2007) *The Internet Book: Everything You Need to Know about Computer Networking and How the Internet Works. 4th Edition.* London: Pearson.

Comodo (2005) *Protect Your Family from Nefarious Email.* Comodo. Available at www.comodo.com/news/press_releases/01_06_05.html (accessed 28 January 2015).

Comodo (2007) *Comodo Helps Consumers Stay Safe Online with New Website Visual Trust Indicator and Free Desktop Security Tools.* Comodo. Available at www.comodo.com/news/press_releases/27_09_07.html (accessed 28 January 2015).

Comodo (2013) *Browsing the Sandbox: Its Time Has Come with Comodo.* Comodo. Available at https://blogs.comodo.com/pc-security/browsing-in-the-sandbox-its-time-has-come-withcomodo/ (accessed 30 August 2015).

Comodo (n.d.) *Product Portfolio.* Hacker Guardian. Available at www.hackerguardian.com/partners/products/comodo-product-portfolio-full.pdf (accessed 27 March 2019).

Conway, M. (2002) 'Reality bytes: cyberterrorism and terrorist "use" of the internet', *First Monday*, 7(11), n.p.

Conway, M. (2004) 'Cyberterrorism: media myth or clear and present danger?', in J. Irwin (ed.) *War and Virtual War: The Challenges to Communities.* Amsterdam: Rodopi, pp. 79–98.

Conway, M. (2008) 'Media, fear and the hyperreal: the construction of cyberterrorism as the ultimate threat to critical infrastructure', in M. A. Dunn and K. S. Kristensen (eds) *Securing 'the Homeland': Critical Infrastructure, Risk and (In)security.* London: Ashgate, pp. 109–29.

Conway, M. (2014) 'Reality check: assessing the (un)likelihood of cyberterrorism', in T. Chen, L. Jarvis and S. Macdonald (eds) *Cyberterrorism: Understanding, Assessment and Response.* London: Springer, pp. 103–22.

Copeland, D. C. (2005) 'The constructivist challenge to structural realism: a review essay', in S. Guzzini and A. Leander (eds) *Constructivism and International Relations: Alexander Wendt and His Critics.* Abingdon: Routledge, pp. 1–20.

Corrons, L. (2009) *Computer Threat Trend Forecast for 2010.* Panda. Available at www.pandasecurity.com/mediacenter/security/computer-threat-trend-forecast-for-2010-2/ (accessed 28 January 2015).

Cosoi, C. (2011a) *BitDefender on Social Media Threats.* Bitdefender. Available at www.bitdefender.co.uk/blog/BitDefender-on-Social-Media-Threats-15.html (accessed, 16 April 2014).

Cosoi, C. (2011b) *Possible Aftermath of the Recent Gmail Accounts Hacking Incident.* Bitdefender. Available at www.bitdefender.co.uk/blog/Possible-Aftermath-of-the-recent-gMail-accounts-hacking-incident-019.html (accessed 19 May 2014).

Cox, R. W. (1981) 'Social forces, states and world orders: beyond International Relations theory', *Millennium: Journal of International Studies*, 10(2), 126–55.

Cronin, A. K. (2002–2003) 'Behind the curve: globalisation and international terrorism', *International Security*, 27(3), 30–58.

Cross, M. K. D. (2013) 'The military dimension of European security: an epistemic community approach', *Millennium: Journal of International Studies*, 42(1), 45–64.

Cross, M. K. D. (2015) 'The limits of epistemic communities: EU security agencies', *Politics and Governance*, 3(1), 90–100.

Dahl, R. A. (1957) 'The concept of power', *Systems Research and Behavioral Science*, 2(3), 201–15.

De Bruijn, H. and Janssen, M. (2017) 'Building cybersecurity awareness: the need for evidence-based framing strategies', *Government Information Quarterly*, 34(1), 1–7.

De Larrinaga, M. and Doucet, M. G. (2008). 'Sovereign power and the biopolitics of human security', *Security Dialogue*, 39(5), 517–37.

Dean, M. (1994) *Critical and Effective Histories: Foucault's Methods and Historical Sociology*. London: Routledge.

Debrix, F. (2001) 'Cyberterror and media-induced fears: the production of emergency culture', *Strategies: Journal of Theory, Culture & Politics*, 14(1), 149–68.

Debrosse, J. (2009) *Cybersecurity Awareness Month – Awareness for the Next Generation*. Available at www.welivesecurity.com/2009/10/01/cybersecurity-awareness-month-awareness-for-the-next-generation/ (accessed 30 August 2015).

Decker, C. (2008) 'Cyber crime 2.0: an argument to update the United States criminal code to reflect the changing nature of cyber crime', *Southern California Law Review*, 81(5), 959–1016.

Deibert, R. J. and Rohozinski, R. (2010) 'Risking security: policies and paradoxes of cyberspace security', *International Political Sociology*, 4(1), 15–32.

Deleuze, G. (1988) *Foucault*. Minneapolis, MN: University of Minnesota Press.

Deleuze, G. (1992) 'What is a Dispositif?', in T. Armstrong (ed.) *Michel Foucault Philosopher*. Translated from French by T. Armstrong. Hemel Hempstead: Harvester Wheatsheaf, pp. 159–68.

Denning, D. (2000) *Cyberterrorism: Testimony before the Special Oversight Panel on Terrorism Committee on Armed Service U.S. House of Representatives*. Available at www.stealthiss.com/documents/pdf/CYBERTERRORISM.pdf (accessed 30 August 2015).

Denning, D. (2001a) 'Activism, hacktivism and cyberterrorism: the internet as a tool for influencing foreign policy', in J. Aquilla and D. Ronfeldt (eds) *Networks and Netwars. The Future of Terror, Crime, and Militancy*. Santa Monica, CA: RAND Corperation, pp. 239–88.

Denning, D. (2001b) 'Cyberwarriors', *Harvard International Review*, 23(2), 70–5.

Denning, D. (2010) 'Terror's web: how the internet is transforming terrorism', in Y. Jewkes and M. Yar (eds) *Handbook of Internet Crime*. Abingdon: Routledge, pp. 194–213.

Denscombe, M. (2007) *The Good Research Guide. 3rd Edition*. New York, NY: McGraw-Hill Education.

Department for Digital, Culture, Media and Sport (2019) *Cyber Security Breaches Survey 2019*. Available at https://assets.publishing.service.gov.uk/government/uploads/system/uploads/attachment_data/file/813599/Cyber_Security_Breaches_Survey_2019_-_Main_Report.pdf (accessed 6 September 2019).

Department of Defense (2015) *The Department of Defense Cyber Strategy*. Department of Defense. Available at www.dtic.mil/doctrine/doctrine/other/dod_cyber_2015.pdf (accessed 6 September 2017).

Bibliography

Department of Homeland Security (2018) *NSTAC Members*. Department of Homeland Security. Available at www.dhs.gov/nstac-members (accessed 2 January 2019).

Der Derain, J. (2009) *Virtuous War: Mapping the Military-Industrial-Media-Entertainment Network*. Abingdon: Routledge.

deSouza, F. (2012) *Driving Growth with a Relentless Focus on Information Protection*. Symantec. Available at www.symantec.com/connect/blogs/driving-growth-relentless-focus-information-protection (accessed 22 May 2014).

Desouza, K. C. and Hensgen, T. (2003) 'Semiotic emergent framework to address the reality of cyberterrorism', *Technological Forecasting and Social Change*, 70(4), 385–96.

Detica (2011) *The Cost of Cyber Crime*. Surrey: Detica.

Devost, M. G., Houghton, B. K. and Pollard, N. A. (1997) 'Information terrorism: political violence in the information age', *Terrorism and Political Violence*, 9(1), 72–83.

Dillon, M. (2003) 'Virtual security: a life science of (dis)order', *Millennium*, 32(3), 531–58.

Doherty, S. (2012) *Security in the Cloud*. Symantec. Available at www.symantec.com/connect/blogs/security-cloud (accessed 22 January 2019).

Donohue, B. (2013) *Hacking Humans*. Kaspersky. Available at https://blog.kaspersky.com/hacking-humans/ (accessed 30 August 2015).

Downing, R. W. (2005) 'Shoring up the weakest link: what lawmakers around the world need to consider in developing comprehensive laws to combat cybercrime', *Columbia Journal of Transnational Law*, 43(3), 705–62.

Droege, C. (2012) 'Get off my cloud: cyber warfare, international humanitarian law, and the protection of civilians', *International Review of the Red Cross*, 94(886), 533–78.

Dryzek (2005) *The Politics of the Earth: Environmental Discourse*. Oxford: Oxford University Press.

Ducklin, P. (2011) *Memories of the Nimda Virus*. Sophos. Available at http://nakedsecurity.sophos.com/2011/09/16/memories-of-the-nimda-virus/ (accessed 30 August 2015).

Dunlaevy, K. (2013a) *Phishers Want Your Facebook Password!* BullGuard. Available at http://blog.bullguard.com/2013/07/phishers-want-your-facebook-password.html (accessed 30 August 2015).

Dunlaevy, K. (2013b) *Mobile Malware Has Seen an Increase by 614% This Year*. BullGuard. Available at www.bullguard.com/blog/2013/08/mobile-malware-has-seen-an-increase-by-614-this-year (accessed 2 April 2019).

Dunlop, C. (2000) 'Epistemic communities: a reply to Toke', *Politics*, 20(3), 137–44.

Dunn Cavelty, M. (2008) *Cyber-security and Threat Politics: US Efforts to Secure the Information Age*. London: Routledge.

Dunn Cavelty, M. (2013) 'From cyber-bombs to political fallout: threat representations with an impact in the cyber-security discourse', *International Studies Review*, 15(1), 105–22.

Dunn Cavelty, M. (2014) 'Breaking the cyber-security dilemma: aligning security needs and removing vulnerabilities', *Science and Engineering Ethics*, 20(3), 701–15.

Dunn Cavelty, M. (2016) 'Cyber-security and private actors', in R. Abrahamsen and A. Leander (eds) *The Routledge Handbook of Private Security Studies*. Abingdon: Routledge, pp. 89–99.

Dunn Cavelty, M. (2018) 'Cybersecurity research meets science and technology studies', *Politics and Governance*, 6(2), 22–30.

Dysart, J. (2011) 'The hacktivists', *ABA Journal*, 97(12), 40–8.

Efremoy, A. (2012) *Kaspersky Lab Report: 23% of Users Are Running Old or Outdated Web Browsers, Creating Huge Gaps in Online Security*. Kaspersky. Available at www.kaspersky.com/about/news/virus/2012/Kaspersky_Lab_report_23_of_users_are_running_old_or_outdated_web_browsers_creating_huge_gaps_in_online_security (accessed 30 August 2015).

Eichenseher, K. E. (2015) 'The cyber-law of nations', *The Georgetown Law Journal*, 103(2), 317–80.

Elliot, D. (2009) 'Weighing the case for a convention to limit cyberwarfare', *Arms Control Today*, 39(9), n.p.

Embar-Seddon, A. (2002) 'Cyberterrorism: are we under siege?', *The American Behavioral Scientist*, 45(6), 1033–43.

Emm, D. and Raiu, C. (2012) *Kaspersky Security Bulletin 2012. Malware Evolution.* Kaspersky Labs. Available at http://securelist.com/analysis/kaspersky-security-bulletin/36732/kaspersky-security-bulletin-2012-malware-evolution/ (accessed 30 August 2015).

Epstein, C. (2013) 'Constructivism or the enteral return of universal in International Relations. Why returning to language is vital to prolonging to owl's flight', *European Journal of International Relations*, 19(3), 499–519.

Erlanger, L. (2012) *How Likely Is a Cyber Sandy?* McAfee. Available at https://blogs.mcafee.com/business/security-connected/how-likely-is-a-cyber-sandy (accessed 30 August 2015).

Esen, R. (2002) 'Cybercrime a growing problem', *The Journal of Criminal Law*, 66(3), 269–83.

ESET Global Threat Report (2011) *Feature Article: Stuxnet: Conspiracy or Sensationalism?* Available at www.eset.com/us/resources/threat-trends/Global_Threat_Trends_January_2011.pdf (accessed 28 January 2015).

ESET Global Threat Report (2012) *Feature Article: Cyberwar: Reality, or a Weapon of Mass Distraction?* Available at www.eset.com/us/resources/threat-trends/Global_Threat_Trends_September_2012.pdf (accessed 30 August 2015).

ESET Research (2008) *ESET Announces Availability of Antivirus for Smartphones.* Available at https://www.eset.com/int/about/newsroom/press-releases/announcements/press-eset-announces-availability-of-antivirus-for-smartphones/ (accessed 2 April 2019).

ESET Research (2009) *Cybersecurity Awareness Month – Awareness for the Next Generation.* Available at www.welivesecurity.com/2009/10/01/cybersecurity-awareness-month-awareness-for-the-next-generation/ (accessed 28 January 2015).

ESET Research (2010a) *Securing our eCity Listed as Winner of National Cybersecurity Awareness Challenge.* Available at www.welivesecurity.com/2010/07/15/securing-our-ecity-listed-as-winner-of-national-cybersecurity-awareness-challenge/ (accessed 29 August 2015).

ESET Research (2010b) *Cyberwarfare and Music: It's All Tempo.* Available at www.welivesecurity.com/2010/04/15/cyberwarfare-and-music-its-all-tempo/ (accessed 29 August 2015).

ESET Research (2010c) *Debate Heating Up: Cybersecurity Act of 2010 S. 773.* Available at www.welivesecurity.com/2010/05/22/773-debate-pt-1/ (accessed 29 August 2015).

ESET Research (2010d) *From Megatons to Megapings: Cyberwarfare.* Available at www.welivesecurity.com/2010/04/11/from-megatons-to-megapings-cyberwarfare/ (accessed 29 August 2015).

ESET Research (2012) *May Threats: INF/Autorun Returns to Top Spot.* Available at www.eset.com/gr-en/about/press/articles/article/may-threats-infautorun-returns-to-top-spot/ (accessed 30 September 2015).

Eun, Y. and Aßmann, J. S. (2015) 'Cyberwar: taking stock of security and warfare in the digital age' (pre-print). Submitted to *International Studies Perspectives*. Available at http://onlinelibrary.wiley.com/doi/10.1111/insp.12073/pdf (accessed 30 August 2015).

European Commission (2018) *Mutual Recognition.* European Commission. Available at http://ec.europa.eu/growth/single-market/goods/free-movement-sectors/mutual-recognition_en (accessed 2 April 2019).

Bibliography

Evans, R. (2015) 'What is expertise? Technical knowledge and political judgement', in T. V. Berling and C. Bueger (eds) *Security Expertise: Practice, Power, Responsibility*. Abingdon: Routledge, pp. 19–36.

Evron, G. (2008) 'Battling botnets and online mobs Estonia's defense efforts during the Internet War', *Georgetown Journal of International Affairs*, 9(1), 121–6.

Eyal, G. and Pok, G. (2015) 'What is security expertise? From the sociology of professions to the analysis of networks of expertise', in T. V. Berling and C. Bueger (eds) *Security Expertise: Practice, Power, Responsibility*. Abingdon: Routledge, pp. 37–59.

Faarshchi, J. (2003) *Statistical-Based Intrusion Detection*. Symantec. Available at www.symantec.com/connect/articles/statistical-based-intrusion-detection (accessed 30 August 2015).

Faleg, G. (2012) 'Between knowledge and power: epistemic communities and the emergence of security sector reform in the EU security architecture', *European Security*, 21(2), 161–84.

Farmer, B. (2017) 'Defending UK "digital homeland" from cyber attack as important as spying and counter terrorism, says new GCHQ director', *The Telegraph*. Available at www.telegraph.co.uk/news/2017/10/08/defending-uk-digital-homeland-cyber-attack-important-spying/ (accessed 19 December 2018).

Farrell, T. (2002) 'Constructivist security studies: portrait of a research program', *International Studies Review*, 4(1), 49–72.

Farwell, J. P. and Rohozinski, R. (2011) 'Stuxnet and the future of cyber war', *Survival*, 53(1), 23–40.

Farwell, J. P. and Rohozinski, R. (2012) 'The new reality of cyber war', *Survival: Global Politics and Strategy*, 54(4), 107–20.

Feldman, A. (2002) 'X–children and the militarisation of everyday life: comparative comments on the politics of youth, victimage and violence in transitional societies', *International Journal of Social Welfare*, 11(4), 286–99.

Ferguson, D. (2013) *Looking Back at the AVG 2014 Launch in London*. AVG. Available at http://blogs.avg.com/news-threats/avg-2014-launch-london-2/ (accessed 30 August 2015).

Filiol, E. (2006) *Computer Viruses: From Theory to Applications*. New York, NY: Springer.

Finkel, E. (2010) 'Cyber space under siege', *ABA Journal*, 96(11), 39–43.

Finnemore, M. and Hollis, D. B. (2016) 'Constructing norms for global cybersecurity', *The American Journal of International Law*, 110(3), 425–79.

Fitzgerald, P. (2010) *The Hackers behind Stuxnet*. Symantec. Available at www.symantec.com/connect/blogs/hackers-behind-stuxnet (accessed 30 August 2015).

Flew, T. (2014) 'Six theories of neoliberalism', *Thesis Eleven*, 22(1), 49–71.

Flick, U. (2002) *An Introduction to Qualitative Research. 4th Edition*. London: Sage.

Ford, R. and Spafford, E. H. (2007) 'Happy birthday, dear virus', *Science*, 317 (5835), 210–11.

Foucault, M. (1972) *The Archaeology of Knowledge*. London: Tavistock Publications.

Foucault, M. (1977) *Discipline and Punish: The Birth of the Prison*. Translated from French by A. Sheridan. London: Penguin Books.

Foucault, M. (1980a) 'The eye of power', in C. Gordon (ed.) *Power/Knowledge: Selected Interviews and Other Writings 1972–1977*. Translated from French by C. Gordon, L. Marshall, J. Mepham and K. Soper. London: Harvester Wheatsheaf, pp. 146–65.

Foucault, M. (1980b) 'The confessions of the flesh', in C. Gordon (ed.) *Power/Knowledge: Selected Interviews and Other Writings 1972–1977*. Translated from French by C. Gordon, L. Marshall, J. Mepham and K. Soper. London: Harvester Wheatsheaf, pp. 194–228.

Foucault, M. (1980c) 'Power and strategies', in C. Gordon (ed.) *Power/Knowledge: Selected Interviews and Other Writings 1972–1977*. Translated from French by C. Gordon, L. Marshall, J. Mepham and K. Soper. London: Harvester Wheatsheaf, pp. 134–45.

Bibliography

Foucault, M. (1981) *The Will to Knowledge: The History of Sexuality Volume 1*. Translated from French by R. Hurley. Harmondsworth: Penguin.

Foucault, M. (1984) 'Truth and power', in P. Rabinow (ed.) *The Foucault Reader: An Introduction to Foucault's Thought*. London: Penguin, pp. 51–75.

Foucault, M. (1986) *The History of Sexuality: The Use of Pleasure. Volume 2*. Translated from French by R. Hurley. New York: Random House.

Foucault, M. (1988) 'The concern for truth', in L. Kritzman (ed.) *Politics, Philosophy, Culture: Interviews and Other Writings*. London: Routledge, pp. 255–70.

Foucault, M. (1991) 'Governmentality', in G. Burchell, C. Gordon and P. Miller (eds) *The Foucault Effect: Studies in Governmentality*. London: Harvester Wheatsheaf, pp. 87–104.

Foucault, M. (1994) 'An interview with Michel Foucault', in J. D. Faubion (ed.) *Power*. Translated from French by R. Hurley and others. London: Allen Lane, pp. 239–97.

Foucault, M. (2001) *Dits et ecrits I, 1954–1975*. Paris: Quatro Gallimard.

Foucault, M. (2004) *Society Must Be Defended: Lectures at the College de France*. A. Fontana and M. Bertani (eds). Translated from French by D. Macey. London: Penguin.

Foucault, M. (2007) *Security, Territory, Population: Lectures at the College de France 1977–1978*. Michel Senellart (ed.). Translated from French by G. Burchell. Basingstoke: Palgrave Macmillan.

Fraser, N. (1981) 'Foucault on modern power: empirical insights and normative confusions', *Praxis International*, 3(1), 272–87.

F-Secure (2012a) *Cyber Warfare Is Reality Now, Says F-Secure*. F-Secure. Available at www. f-secure.com/es_MX/web/press_mx/news/news-archive/-/journal_content/56/ 1075444/1104320?p_p_auth=NmY1A6cZ (accessed 30 August 2015).

F-Secure (2012b) *Top 7 Predictions for 2013 (if the Internet as We Know It Still Exists)*. F-Secure. Available at http://safeandsavvy.f-secure.com/2012/12/12/top-7-predictions-for-2013-if-the-internet-as-we-know-it-still-exists/#.U3Mvw4FdWuK (accessed 30 August 2015).

Furnell, S. (2002) *Cybercrime: Vandalizing the Information Society*. Boston, MA: Addison-Wesley.

Gartner (2018) *Gartner Forecasts Worldwide Information Security Spending to Exceed $124 Billion in 2019*. Gartner. Available at www.gartner.com/newsroom/id/3135617 (accessed 15 January 2019).

Geers, K. (2010) 'The challenge of cyber attack deterrence', *Computer Law and Security Review*, 26(3), 298–303.

Geers, K. (2012) 'Strategic cyber defence: which way forward?', *Journal of Homeland Security and Emergency Management*, 9(1), 1–10.

Giacomello, G. (2007) 'Bangs for the buck: a cost–benefit analysis of cyberterrorism', *Studies in Conflict and Terrorism*, 27(5), 387–408.

Gieryn, T. E. (1999) *Cultural Boundaries of Science: Credibility on the Line*. Chicago, IL: University of Chicago Press.

Gilmore, G. J. (2001) *U.S. 'Will Hunt Down and Punish' Terrorists, Bush Says*. US Department of Defense. Available at www.defense.gov/news/newsarticle.aspx?id=44914 (accessed 1 August 2015).

Giroux, H. A. (2006) 'War on terror: the militarising of public space and culture in the United States', *Third Text*, 18(4), 211–21.

Giroux, H. A. (2008) 'The militarization of US higher education after 9/11', *Theory Culture & Society*, 25(5), 56–82.

Gjelten, T. (2010) *Extending the Law of War to Cyberspace*. NPR. Available at www.npr.org/ templates/story/story.php?storyId=130023318 (accessed 30 August 2015).

Bibliography

Glennon, M. J. (2012) 'State level cyber security', *Policy Review*, 171 (February/March), n.p.

Goodman, S. E., Kirk, J. C. and Kirk, M. H. (2007) 'Cyberspace as a medium for terrorists', *Technological Forecasting & Social Change*, 74(2), 193–210.

Gordon, S. and Ford, R. (2003) *Cyberterrorism?* Cupertino, CA: Symantec. Available at www.symantec.com/avcenter/reference/cyberterrorism.pdf (accessed 30 August 2015).

Gostev, A. (2007) *Malware Evolution: April–June 2007*. Kaspersky Labs. Available at http://securelist.com/analysis/quarterly-malware-reports/36163/malware-evolution-april-june-2007/?print_mode=1 (accessed 30 August 2015).

Gostev, A. (2010) *Outcomes for 2010 and Predictions for 2011*. Kaspersky Labs. Available at http://securelist.com/analysis/36334/outcomes-for-2010-and-predictions-for-2011/ (accessed 30 August 2015).

Gostev, A. (2011) *Kaspersky Security Bulletin. Malware Evolution 2010*. Kaspersky Labs. Available at http://securelist.com/analysis/kaspersky-security-bulletin/36343/kaspersky-security-bulletin-malware-evolution-2010/#0 (accessed 30 August 2015).

Gostev, A. (2012) *The Flame: Questions and Answers*. Kaspersky Labs. Available at http://securelist.com/blog/incidents/34344/the-flame-questions-and-answers-51/ (accessed 30 August 2015).

Gozzi Jr, R. (1994) 'The cyberspace metaphor', *ETC: A Review of General Semantics*, 51(2), 218–23.

Grabosky, P. N. (2001) 'Virtual criminality: old wine in new bottles?', *Social and Legal Studies*, 10(2), 243–9.

Graham, L. J. (2005) 'Discourse analysis and the critical use of Foucault'. *The Australian Association of Research in Education Annual Conference*, 27 November – 1 December, Parramatta, Sydney. Available at http://eprints.qut.edu.au/2689/1/2689.pdf (accessed 2 August 2019).

Granger, S. (2010) *Social Engineering Reloaded*. Symantec. Available at www.symantec.com/connect/articles/social-engineering-reloaded (accessed 30 August 2015).

Green, P. (1966) *Deadly Logic: The Theory of Nuclear Deterrence*. Columbus, OH: Ohio State University Press.

Grogan, S. (2009) 'China, nuclear security and terrorism: implications for the United States', *Orbis*, 53(4), 685–704.

Guinchard, A. (2011) 'Between hype and understatement: reassessing cyber risks as a security strategy', *Journal of Strategic Security*, 4(2), 75–96.

Guzzini, S. (2005) 'The concept of power: a constructivist analysis', *Millennium*, 33(3), 495–521.

Haas, P. (1992) 'Introduction: epistemic communities and international policy co-ordination', *International Organisation*, 46(1), 1–35.

Hagmann, J. and Dunn Cavelty, M. (2012) 'National risk registers: security scientism and the propagation of permanent insecurity', *Security Dialogue*, 43(1), 79–96.

Haley, K. (2012a) *Collateral Damage*. Symantec. Available at www.symantec.com/connect/blogs/collateral-damage (accessed 30 August 2015).

Haley, K. (2012b) *The 2011 Internet Security Threat Report – There Is No Panacea to Protect against All Attacks*. Symantec. Available at www.symantec.com/connect/blogs/2011-internet-security-threat-report-there-no-panacea-protect-against-all-attacks (accessed 30 August 2015).

Haley, K. (2012c) *Top 5 Security Predictions for 2013 from Symantec*. Symantec. Available at www.symantec.com/connect/blogs/top-5-security-predictions-2013-symantec-0 (accessed 30 August 2015).

Bibliography

Hannah, M. (2007) 'Formations of "Foucault" in Anglo-American geography: an archaeological sketch', in J. W. Crampton and S. Elden, (eds) *Space, Knowledge and Power: Foucault and Geography*. Abingdon: Routledge, pp. 83–106.

Hansen, L. and Nissenbaum, H. (2009) 'Digital disaster, cyber security, and the Copenhagen School', *International Studies Quarterly*, 53(4), 1155–75.

Hardy, K. (2015) 'Resilience in UK counter-terrorism', *Theoretical Criminology*, 19(1), 77–94.

Hardy, K. and Williams, G. (2014) 'What is cyberterrorism? Computer and internet technology in legal definitions of terrorism', in T. Chen, L. Jarvis and S. Macdonald (eds) Chen, *Cyberterrorism: Understanding, Assessment and Response*. London: Springer, pp. 1–23.

Harknett, R. (2003) 'Integrated security: a strategic response to anonymity and the problem of the few', *Contemporary Security Policy*, 24(1), 13–45.

Harknett, R. J. and Stever, J. A. (2011) 'The new policy world of cybersecurity', *Public Administration Review*, 71(3), 455–60.

Harley, D. (2009a) *Botnets, Complacency and the UK Government*. Available at www.welivesecurity.com/2009/11/16/botnets-complacency-and-the-uk-government/ (accessed 30 August 2015).

Harley, D. (2009b) *Cyberhype*. Available at www.welivesecurity.com/2009/11/17/cyberhype/ (accessed 30 August 2015).

Harley, D. (2010) *Stuxnet Code: Chicken Licken or Chicken Run?* Available at www.welivesecurity.com/2010/11/26/stuxnet-code-chicken-licken-or-chicken-run/ (accessed 30 August 2015).

Harris, P. (2013) *Cyber Defense vs. Cyber Vigilante – Part 2 – Hacking Back*. Symantec. Available at www.symantec.com/connect/blogs/cyber-defense-vs-cyber-vigilante-part-2-hacking-back (accessed 30 August 2015).

Hart, C., Jin, D. Y. and Feenberg, A. (2014) 'The insecurity of innovation: a critical analysis of cybersecurity in the United States', *International Journal of Communications*, 8(1), 2860–78.

Harvey, D. (2005) *A Brief History of Neoliberalism*. Oxford: Oxford University Press.

Harwood, V. (2000) *Truth, Power and the Self: A Foucaultian Analysis of the Truth of Conduct Disorder and the Construction of Young People's Mentally Disordered Subjectivity*. PhD thesis, University of South Australia.

Hathaway, O. A., Crootof, R., Levitz, P., Nix, H., Nowlan, A., Perdue, W. and Spiegel, J. (2012) 'The law of cyber-attack', *California Law Review*, 100(4), 817–85.

Hawes, J. (2013a) *Cyber Security in US Power System Suffering from Reactive, Self-policed Rules*. Sophos. Available at http://nakedsecurity.sophos.com/2013/05/23/cyber-security-us-power-system/ (accessed 30 August 2015).

Hawes, J. (2013b) *Cybercrime Fighters Ready to Up Their Game, but Will It Be Enough?* Sophos. Available at http://nakedsecurity.sophos.com/2013/11/18/cybercrime-fighters-ready-to-up-their-game-but-will-it-be-enough/ (accessed 30 August 2015).

Hawes, J. (2013c) *Stock Exchanges of the World Form Central Cyber Security Working Group*. Sophos. Available at http://nakedsecurity.sophos.com/2013/12/18/stock-exchanges-of-the-world-form-central-cyber-security-working-group/ (accessed 30 August 2015).

Hawes, J. (2013d) *Tech Firms Way behind the Curve on Handling Cybersecurity*. Sophos. Available at http://nakedsecurity.sophos.com/2013/11/25/tech-firms-way-behind-the-curve-on-handling-cybersecurity/ (accessed 30 August 2015).

Hawes, J. (2013e) *Why Must Political Chiefs Keep Pushing the Cyberwar Alert Button*. Sophos. Available at http://nakedsecurity.sophos.com/2013/07/22/why-must-political-chiefs-keep-pushing-the-cyberwar-alert-button/ (accessed 30 August 2015).

Hay, C. (1997) 'State of the art: divided by a common language: political theory and the concept of power', *Politics*, 17(1), 45–52.

Hay, C. (2002) *Political Analysis*. Basingstoke: Palgrave.

Hear4U (2009a) *Endpoint Security–A Necessary Addition to Antivirus!* Symantec. Available at www.symantec.com/connect/articles/endpoint-security-necessary-addition-antivirus (accessed 30 August 2015).

Hear4U (2009b) *TechTip: Protecting Your SharePoint Environment by 'Defense in Depth'*. Symantec. Available at www.symantec.com/connect/articles/techtip-protecting-your-sharepoint-environment-defense-depth (accessed 30 August 2015).

Heath-Kelly, C. (2013) 'Counter-terrorism and the counterfactual: producing the 'radicalisation' discourse and the UK PREVENT Strategy', *The British Journal of Politics and International Relations*, 15(3), 394–415.

Heath-Kelly, C. and Jarvis, L. (2017) 'Affecting terrorism: laughter, lamentation, and detestation as drives to terrorism knowledge', *International Political Sociology*, 11(3), 239–56.

Heickerö, R. (2014) 'Cyberterrorism: electronic jihad', *Strategic Analysis*, 38(4), 554–65.

Heineman, B. W. Jr. and Heimann, F. (2006) 'The long war against corruption', *Foreign Affairs*, 85(3), 75–86.

Heller, K. J. (1996) 'Power, subjectification and resistance in Foucault', *SubStance*, 25(1), 78–110.

Henrie, M. (2013) 'Cyber security risk management in the SCADA critical infrastructure environment', *Engineering Management Journal*, 25(2), 38–45.

Herrington, L. and Aldrich, R. (2013) 'The future of cyber-resilience in an age of global complexity', *Politics*, 33(4), 299–310.

Herzog, S. (2011) 'Revisiting the Estonian cyber attacks: digital threats and multinational responses', *Journal of Strategic Security*, 4(2), 49–60.

Hiller, J. S. and Russell, R. S. (2013) 'The challenge and imperative of private sector cyber-security: an international comparison', *Computer Law & Security Review*, 29(3), 236–45.

Hirshleifer, J. (1983) 'From weakest-link to best-shot: the voluntary provision of public goods', *Public Choice*, 41(3), 371–86.

HM Government (2010) *A Strong Britain in an Age of Uncertainty: The National Security Strategy*. HM Government. Available at http://webarchive.nationalarchives.gov.uk/20121018134855/ http://www.direct.gov.uk/prod_consum_dg/groups/dg_digitalassets/@dg/@en/documents/digitalasset/dg_191639.pdf (accessed 2 February 2018).

HM Government (2015) *National Security Strategy and Strategic Defence and Security Review 2015: A Secure and Prosperous United Kingdom*. HM Government. Available at www.gov.uk/government/uploads/system/uploads/attachment_data/file/555607/2015_Strategic_Defence_and_Security_Review.pdf (accessed 2 February 2018).

HM Government (2016) *National Cyber Security Strategy 2016–2021*. Available at www.gov.uk/government/uploads/system/uploads/attachment_data/file/567242/national_cyber_security_strategy_2016.pdf (accessed 6 September 2017).

Hollis, D. B. (2011) 'An e-SOS for cyberspace', *Harvard International Law Journal*, 52(2), 373–432.

Holsti, K. J. (1964) 'The concept of power in the study of international relations', *Background*, 7(4), 179–94.

Holt, T. (2012) 'Exploring the intersections of technology, crime, and terror', *Terrorism and Political Violence*, 24(2), 337–54.

Home Office Science Advisory Council (2018) *Understanding the Costs of Cyber Crime: A Report of Key Findings from the Costs of Cyber Crime Working Group*. Home Office. Available at https://

assets.publishing.service.gov.uk/government/uploads/system/uploads/attachment_ data/file/674046/understanding-costs-of-cyber-crime-horr96.pdf (accessed 8 August 2019).

Homer-Dixon, T. (2002) 'The rise of complex terrorism', *Foreign Policy*, January/February (128), 52–62.

Hook, D. (2005) 'Genealogy, discourse, "effective history": Foucault and the work of critique', *Qualitative Research in Psychology*, 2(1), 3–31.

Hopf, T. (1998) 'The promise of constructivism in international relations theory', *International Security*, 23(1), 171–200.

House of Commons (2012) 'Internet-based media companies', speech by Fiona Mactaggart MP, 31 October 2012, vol. 552. House of Commons. Available at https://hansard.parliament.uk/Commons/2012–10–31/debates/12103153000001/Internet-BasedMediaCompanies?highlight=mcafee#contribution-12103153000004 (accessed 2 April 2019).

House of Commons (2013) *Written Evidence from McAfee*, Commons Select Committee on Defence, 8 January 2013. House of Commons. Available at https://publications.parliament.uk/pa/cm201213/cmselect/cmdfence/106/106vw09.htm (accessed 2 April 2019).

House of Lords (2010) *Cyberattacks: EU Committee Report*, 14 October, vol. 721. House of Lords. Available at https://hansard.parliament.uk/Lords/2010–10–14/debates/10101424000811/CyberattacksEUCommitteeReport?highlight=sophos#contribution-10101424000487 (accessed 5 April 2019).

House of Representatives (2000) *The Love Bug Virus: Protecting Lovesick Computer from Malicious Attack,* hearings before the Committee of Science, 106th Congress, 10 May, 2000. House of Representatives. Available at www.congress.gov/congressional-report/106th-congress/house-report/1052/1?q=%7B%22search%22%3A%5B%22mcafee%22%5D%7D&r=18 (accessed 2 April 2019).

House of Representatives (2004) *Locking Your Cyber Front Door – The Challenges Facing Home Users and Small Businesses*, hearings before the Committee on Government Reform, 108th Congress, 16 June 2004. House of Representatives. Available at www.congress.gov/congressional-report/108th-congress/house-report/815/1?q=%7B%22search%22%3A%5B%22symantec%22%5D%7D&r=12 (accessed 2 April 2019).

House of Representatives (2007) 'Chinese cyber spies – an emergent threat', speech of Hon. Cliff Stearns, 110th Congress, 10 September 2007. House of Representatives. Available at www.congress.gov/crec/2007/09/10/CREC-2007-09-10-pt1-PgH10323-4.pdf (accessed 2 April 2019).

House of Representatives (2009) *Assessing Cybersecurity Activities at NIST and DHS*, hearings before the Subcommittee on Technology and Innovation, 111th Congress, 25 June 2009. House of Representatives. Available at www.congress.gov/congressional-report/111th-congress/house-report/698/1?q=%7B%22search%22%3A%5B%22symantec%22%5D%7D&r=31 (accessed 2 April 2019).

House of Representatives (2010) 'Cybersecurity Enhancement Act of 2009, Committee of the Whole', speech of Hon. Bart Gordon, 111th congress, 3 February 2010. House of Representatives. Available at www.congress.gov/congressional-record/2010/2/3/house-section/article/h495-2?q=%7B%22search%22%3A%5B%22symantec%22%5D%7D&r=26 (accessed 2 April 2019).

House of Representatives (2011a) *Cybersecurity: Protecting your Small Business*, hearings before the Subcommittee on Healthcare and Technology of the Committee on Small Business, 112th Congress, 1 December 2001, House of Representatives. Available at www.

congress.gov/congressional-report/112th-congress/house-report/339/1?q=%7B%22 search%22%3A%5B%22mcafee%22%5D%7D&r=65 (accessed 2 April 2019).

House of Representatives (2011b) *Cybersecurity: Threats to the Financial Sector*, hearings before the Subcommittee on Financial Institutions and Consumer Credit and Oversight and Investigations, 112th Congress, 14 September 2011. House of Representatives. Available at www.congress.gov/congressional-report/112th-congress/house-report/355/1?q=%7B %22search%22%3A%5B%22symantec%22%5D%7D&r=39 (accessed 2 April 2019).

House of Representatives (2011c) *Cybersecurity: Assessing the Immediate Threat to the United States*, hearings before the Subcommittee on National Security, Homeland Defense and foreign Operations, 112th Congress, 25 May 2011. House of Representatives. Available at www.congress.gov/congressional-report/112th-congress/house-report/128/1?q= %7B%22search%22%3A%5B%22symantec%22%5D%7D&r=34 (accessed 2 April 2019).

House of Representatives (2011d) 'Intelligence Authorization Act for Fiscal Year 2011 (extension of remarks)', speech of Hon. Peter Welch of Vermont, 12 May 2011. House of Representatives. Available at www.congress.gov/crec/2011/05/13/CREC-2011-05- 13-pt1-PgE905.pdf (accessed 2 April 2019).

House of Representatives (2013) 'Challenges and opportunities', speech of Hon. Vicky Hartzler, 14 October 2013. House of Representatives. Available at www. congress.gov/congressional-record/2013/10/14/house-section/article/h6580-4?q=% 7B%22search%22%3A%5B%22mcafee%22%5D%7D&r=85 (accessed 2 April 2019).

Howarth, D. (2000) *Discourse*. Maidenhead: Open University Press.

Howe, N. (1988) 'Metaphor in contemporary American political discourse', *Metaphor and Symbolic Activity*, 3(2), 87–104.

Howorth, J. (2004) 'Discourse, ideas and epistemic communities in European security and defence policy', *West European Politics*, 27(2), 211–34.

Hua, J. and Bapna, S. (2012) 'How can we deter cyber terrorism?', *Information Security Journal: A Global Perspective*, 21(2), 102–14.

Huey, L., Nhan, J. and Broll, R. (2012) '"Uppity civilians" and "cyber-vigilantes": the role of the general public in policing cyber-crime', *Criminology and Criminal Justice*, 13(1), 81–97.

Hughes, L. A. and DeLone, G. J. (2007) 'Viruses, worms, and Trojan horses: serious crimes, nuisance, or both?', *Social Science Computer Review*, 25(1), 78–98.

Hughes, R. (2010) 'A treaty for cyberspace', *International Affairs*, 86(2), 523–41.

Hult, F. and Sivanesan, G. (2013) 'What good cyber resilience looks like', *Journal of Business & Emergency Planning*, 7(2), 112–25.

Hunton, P. (2012) 'Managing the technical resource capability of cybercrime investigation: a UK law enforcement perspective', *Public Money & Management*, 32(3), 225–32.

Huysmans, J. (2006) *The Politics of Insecurity: Fear, Migrations and Asylum in the EU*. Abingdon: Routledge.

Huysmans, J. and Buonfino, A. (2008) 'Politics of exception and unease: immigration, asylum and terrorism in parliamentary debates in the UK', *Political Studies*, 56(4), 766–88.

Hyppönen, M. (2007) *There's Nothing to See Here, Please Move Along*. F-Secure. Available at www.f-secure.com/weblog/archives/00001315.html (accessed 30 August 2015).

Hyppönen, M. (2008) *Greetings from India!* F-Secure. Available at www.f-secure.com/weblog/ archives/00001559.html (accessed 30 August 2015).

Hyppönen, M. (2012a) *A Pandora's Box We Will Regret Opening*. F-Secure. Available at www.f-secure.com/weblog/archives/00002378.html (accessed 30 August 2015).

Hyppönen, M. (2012b) *Cyber Armament*. F-Secure. Available at www.f-secure.com/weblog/ archives/00002401.html (accessed 30 August 2015).

ICS-CERT (2015) *Cyber Threat Source Descriptions*. ICS-CERT. Available at https://ics-cert. us-cert.gov/content/cyber-threat-source-descriptions#gao (accessed 30 August 2015).

Ilie, M., Mutulescu, A., Artene, D. A., Bratu, S. and Făinişi, F. (2011) 'International cyber security through co-operation', *Economics, Management, and Financial Markets*, 6(2), 438–48.

Internet World Stats (2019) *Internet Usage Statistics*. Available at www.internetworldstats. com/stats.htm (accessed 6 August 2019).

Ionescu, L., Mirea, V. and Blajan, A. (2011) 'Fraud, corruption and cyber crime in a global digital network', *Economics, Management and Financial Markets*, 6(2), 373–80.

ITU (2018) *Global and Regional ICT Data*. ITU Statistics. Available at www.itu.int/en/ ITU-D/Statistics/Pages/stat/default.aspx (accessed 31 March 2019).

Jackson, R., Jarvis, L., Gunning, J. and Smyth, M. B. (2011) *Terrorism: A Critical Introduction*. Basingstoke: Palgrave Macmillan.

Jarvis, L. (2009) *Times of Terror: Discourse, Temporality and the War on Terror*. London: Basingstoke: Palgrave Macmillan.

Jarvis, L. and Holland, J. (2015) *Security: A Critical Introduction*. Basingstoke: Palgrave.

Jarvis, L. and Macdonald, S. (2014) 'Locating cyberterrorism: how terrorism researchers use and view the cyber lexicon', *Perspectives on Terrorism*, 8(2), 52–65.

Jarvis, L., Macdonald, S. and Nouri, L. (2014) 'The cyberterrorism threat: findings from a survey of researchers', *Studies in Conflict and Terrorism*, 37(1), 68–90.

Jarvis, L., Macdonald, S. and Whiting, A. (2015) 'Constructing cyberterrorism as a security threat: a study of international new media coverage', *Perspectives on Terrorism*, 9(1), 60–75.

Jarvis, L., Macdonald, S. and Whiting, A. (2016) 'Analogy and authority in cyberterrorism discourse: an analysis of global news media coverage', *Global Society*, 30(4), 605–23.

Jarvis, L., Nouri, L. and Whiting, A. (2014) 'Understanding, locating and constructing cyberterrorism', in T. Chen, L. Jarvis and S. Macdonald (eds) *Cyberterrorism: Understanding, Assessment and Response*. London: Springer, pp. 25–42.

Jefferson, J. (1997) 'Deleting cyber crooks', *ABA Journal*, 83(10), 68–75.

Jespersen, C. (2005) 'Analogies at war', *Historical Review*, 74(3), 411–26.

Jewkes, Y. (2011) *Media and Crime. 3rd Edition*. London: Sage.

Jones, B. R. (2007) 'Virtual neighbourhood watch: open source software and community policing against cybercrime', *The Journal of Criminal Law and Criminology*, 97(2), 601–30.

Judge, K. (2013a) *Free APT Assessment: Are You Under Attack?* Comodo. Available at https:// blogs.comodo.com/comodo_news/free-apt-assessment-are-you-under-attack/ (accessed 30 August 2015).

Judge, K. (2013b) *So You Want to Be a Cyber Warrior? Prospects are Good*. Comodo. Available at https://blogs.comodo.com/it-security/so-you-want-to-be-a-cyber-warrior-prospects-are-good/ (accessed 30 August 2015).

Kalnai, P. (2013) *Fallout from Nuclear Pack Exploit Kit Highly Toxic for Windows Machines*. Avast! Available at https://blog.avast.com/2013/11/20/fallout-from-nuclear-pack-exploit-kit-highly-toxic-for-windows-machines/ (accessed 30 August 2015).

Kamluk, V. (2008) *The Botnet Business*. Kaspersky Labs. Available at https://securelist.com/ analysis/publications/36209/the-botnet-business/ (accessed 30 August 2015).

Kapto, A. (2013) 'Cyberwarfare: genesis and doctrinal outlines', *Herald of the Russian Academy of Sciences*, 83(4), 357–64.

Kaspersky Labs (1999a) *Win32.FunLove: Rock Fans Create Computer Viruses Too*. Kaspersky Labs. Available at www.kaspersky.com/about/news/virus/1999/Win32_FunLove_Rock_Fans_Create_Computer_Viruses_Too [(accessed 30 August 2015).

Bibliography

Kaspersky Labs (1999b) *Anti-Virus Companies Help Spreading Virus Hysteria on Y2K Virus.* Kaspersky Labs. Available at www.kaspersky.com/about/news/virus/1999/Anti_Virus_Companies_Help_Spreading_Virus_Hysteria_on_Y2K_Virus (accessed 30 August 2015).

Kaspersky Labs (2001a) *Kaspersky Anti-Virus vs. Script Virus Generators.* Kaspersky Labs. Available at www.kaspersky.com/about/news/product/2001/Kaspersky_reg_Anti_Virus_vs_Script_Virus_Generators (accessed 1 September 2015).

Kaspersky Labs (2001b) *The Return of 'Magistr'.* Kaspersky Labs. Available at www.kaspersky.com/news?id=225 (accessed 30 August 2015).

Kaspersky Labs (2002a) *Kaspersky Goes East.* Kaspersky Labs. Available at www.kaspersky.com/news?id=963304 (accessed 30 August 2015).

Kaspersky Labs (2002b) *Kaspersky® Anti-Hacker – A New Weapon in the War against Hackers.* Kaspersky Labs. Available at www.kaspersky.com/news.html?id=964757 (accessed 30 August 2015).

Kaspersky Labs (2003a) *'Helkern' – The Beginning of End as Anti-Virus Experts Have Long Warned.* Kaspersky Labs. Available at www.kaspersky.com/about/news/virus/2003/_Helkern_The_Beginning_of_End_As_Anti_virus_Experts_Have_Long_Warned (accessed 30 August 2015).

Kaspersky Labs (2003b) *Kaspersky Guards the Zoo for BlackSpider.* Kaspersky Labs. Available at www.kaspersky.com/about/news/business/2003/Kaspersky_Guards_the_Zoo_for_BlackSpider (accessed 30 August 2015).

Kaspersky Labs (2004a) *Novarg: New Worm – New Epidemic.* Kaspersky Labs. Available at www.kaspersky.com/news.html?id=3629137 (accessed 30 August 2015).

Kaspersky Labs (2004b) *Recommendations for Deflecting Virus and Hacker Attacks.* Kaspersky Labs. Available at *Corporate news,* www.kaspersky.co.uk/news?id=151825151 (accessed 30 August 2015).

Kaspersky Labs (2009a) *Drive-By Downloads: The Web under Siege.* Kaspersky Labs. Available at www.kaspersky.co.uk/about/news/virus/2009/Drive_by_Downloads_The_Web_Under_Siege (accessed 30 August 2015).

Kaspersky Labs (2009b) *Kaspersky Lab Issues 2010 Cyberthreat Forecast.* Kaspersky Labs. Available at www.kaspersky.com/about/news/virus/2009/Kaspersky_Lab_issues_2010_cyberthreat_forecast (accessed 30 August 2015).

Kaspersky Labs (2009c) *Kaspersky Lab Publishes the Article 'Browsing Malicious Websites'.* Kaspersky Labs. Available at www.kaspersky.co.uk/news?id=207575960 (accessed 30 August 2015).

Kaspersky Labs (2010a) *Kaspersky Lab Provides Its Insights on Stuxnet Worm.* Kaspersky Labs. Available at www.kaspersky.com/about/news/virus/2010/Kaspersky_Lab_provides_its_insights_on_Stuxnet_worm (accessed 30 August 2015).

Kaspersky Labs (2010b) *Kaspersky Lab Calls on Businesses to Reconsider Their IT Security Strategies.* Kaspersky Labs. Available at www.kaspersky.com/about/news/virus/2010/Kaspersky_Lab_Calls_on_Businesses_to_Reconsider_Their_IT_Security_Strategies (accessed 29 September 2015).

Kaspersky Labs (2010c) *Kaspersky Lab Hosts the Kaspersky Security Symposium.* Kaspersky Labs. Available at www.kaspersky.com/about/news/events/2010/Kaspersky_Lab_Hosts_the_Kaspersky_Security_Symposium (accessed 29 September 2015).

Kaspersky Labs (2011a) *Threatpost DEF CON Panel to Weigh Conflict between Cyber Security, Civil Liberties.* Kaspersky Labs. Available at http://usa.kaspersky.com/about-us/press-center/press-releases/threatpost-def-con-panel-weigh-conflict-between-cyber-security- (accessed 30 August 2015).

Kaspersky Labs (2011b) *Kaspersky PURE Total Security for Homes and Families Now Available*. Kaspersky Labs. Available at https://usa.kaspersky.com/about/press-releases/2011_kaspersky-pure-total-security-for-homes-and-families-now-available (accessed 2 April 2019).

Kaspersky Labs (2012a) *CeBIT 2012: Eugene Kaspersky Calls for Creation of an International Cyber-Security Organization to Combat Cyber-Terrorism*. Kaspersky Labs. Available at www.kaspersky.com/about/news/events/2012/CeBIT_2012_Eugene_Kaspersky_calls_for_creation_of_an_International_Cyber_Security_Organization_to_combat_cyber_terrorism (accessed 28 January 2015).

Kaspersky Labs (2012b) *Eugene Kaspersky Pushes for a Military-Free Internet at Infosecurity Europe 2012*. Kaspersky Labs. Available at www.kaspersky.co.uk/about/news/events/2012/Eugene_Kaspersky_Pushes_for_a_Military_Free_Internet_at_Infosecurity_Europe_2012 (accessed 29 September 2015).

Kaspersky Labs (2012c) *Eugene Kaspersky to Deliver Exclusive Keynote at 3rd Annual Billington Cybersecurity Summit*. Kaspersky Labs. Available at www.kaspersky.co.uk/about/news/business/2012/Eugene_Kaspersky_to_Deliver_Exclusive_Keynote_at_3rd_Annual_Billington_Cybersecurity_Summit (accessed 29 September 2015).

Kaspersky Labs (2012d) *The Mystery of the Encrypted Gauss Payload*. Kaspersky Labs. Available at www.securelist.com/en/blog/208193781/The_Mystery_of_the_Encrypted_Gauss_Payload (accessed 30 August 2015).

Kaspersky Labs (2013a) *Eugene Kaspersky to Address INTERPOL General Assembly*. Kaspersky Labs. Available at www.kaspersky.com/about/news/business/2013/Eugene_Kaspersky_to_address_INTERPOL_General_Assembly (accessed 29 September 2015).

Kaspersky Labs (2013b) *Kaspersky Lab to Host First Annual Government Cybersecurity Forum in Washington D.C.* Kaspersky Labs. Available at http://usa.kaspersky.com/about-us/press-center/press-releases/kaspersky-lab-host-first-annual-government-cybersecurity-forum- (accessed 29 August 2015).

Kaspersky Labs (2013c) *MWC 2013: Kaspersky Lab Unveils Its Latest Corporate Solution Featuring Mobile Device Management Functionality – Kaspersky Security for Mobile*. Kaspersky Labs. Available at www.kaspersky.co.uk/about/press-releases/2013_mwc-2013-kaspersky-lab-unveils-its-latest-corporate-solution-featuring-mobile-device-management-functionality-kaspersky-security-for-mobile (accessed 2 April 2019).

Kaspersky Labs' Global Research & Analysis Team (2012a) *Gauss: Nation-state Cyber-Surveillance Meets Banking Trojan*. Kaspersky Labs. Available at http://securelist.com/blog/incidents/33854/gauss-nation-state-cyber-surveillance-meets-banking-trojan-54/ (accessed 30 August 2015).

Kaspersky Labs' Global Research & Analysis Team (2012b) *Securing Critical Information Infrastructure: Trusted Computing Base*. Kaspersky Labs. Available at http://securelist.com/analysis/36594/securing-critical-information-infrastructure-trusted-computing-base/ (accessed 30 August 2015).

Kaspersky Labs' Global Research & Analysis Team (2013) *The Icefog APT: A Tale of Cloak and Three Daggers*. Kaspersky Labs. Available at www.securelist.com/en/blog/208214064/The_Icefog_APT_A_Tale_of_Cloak_and_Three_Daggers (accessed 30 August 2015).

Kaspersky Labs' Global Research & Analysis Team (2014) *El Machete*. Kaspersky Labs. Available at https://securelist.com/blog/research/66108/el-machete/ (accessed 30 August 2015).

Katyal, N. K. (2001) 'Criminal law in cyberspace', *University of Pennsylvania Law Review*, 149(4), 1003–114.

Bibliography

Kello, L. (2017) *The Virtual Weapon and International Order*. London: Yale University Press.

Kelly, B. B. (2012) 'Investing in a centralised cybersecurity infrastructure: why "hacktivism" can and should influence cybersecurity reform', *Boston University Law Review*, 92(5), 1663–711.

Kelsey, J. T. G. (2008) 'Hacking into international humanitarian law: the principles of distinction and neutrality in the age of cyber warfare', *Michigan Law Review*, 106(7), 1427–52.

Kendall, G. and Wickham, G. (2003) *Using Foucault's Methods*. London: Sage.

Kettemann, M. C. (2017) 'Ensuring cybersecurity through international law', *Revista Espaiola de Derecho Internacional Seccion*, 69(2), 281–9.

Khan, F. U. (2011) 'States rather than criminals pose a greater threat to global cyber security: a critical analysis', *Strategic Studies*, 31(3), 91–108.

Kizza, J. M. (2014) *Computer Network Security and Cyber Ethics*. Jefferson, NC: McFarland & Company.

Kohlmann, E. F. (2006) 'The real online terrorist threat', *Foreign Affairs*, 85(5), 115–24.

Kostopoulos, G. (2008) 'Cyberterrorism: the next arena of confrontation', *Communications of the IBIMA*, 6(1), 165–9.

Kotenko, I. V. and Saenko, I. B. (2013) 'Creating new-generation cybersecurity monitoring and management systems', *Herald of the Russian Academy of Sciences*, 84(6), 424–31.

Kováč, P. (2011) *Hot on the Trail of Duqu with Microsoft's MAPP*. Avast! Available at https://blog.avast.com/2011/11/11/hot-on-the-trail-of-duqu-with-microsoft%E2%80%99s-mapp/ (accessed 30 August 2015).

Krahmann, E. (2003) 'Conceptualizing security governance', *Cooperation and Conflict: Journal of the Nordic International Studies Association*, 38(1), 5–26.

Kramer, S. and Bradfield, J. C. (2010) 'A general definition of malware', *Journal in Computer Virology*, 6(2), 105–14.

Krepinevich, A. (2011) 'Get ready for the democratization of destruction', *Foreign Policy*, September/October (188), 80–1.

Kshetri, N. (2016) 'Cybercrime and cybersecurity in India: causes, consequences and implications for the future', *Crime, Law and Social Change*, 66(3), 313–38.

Kumar, A. V., Pandey, K. K. and Punia, D. K. (2014) 'Cyber security threats in the power sector: need for domain specific regulatory framework in India', *Energy Policy*, 65(1), 126–33.

Lakoff, G. (2001) *Metaphors of Terror*. Chicago, IL: Chicago University Press. Available at www.press.uchicago.edu/sites/daysafter/911lakoff.html (accessed 30 August 2015).

Lakoff, G. and Johnson, M. (2003) *Metaphors We Live By*. Chicago, IL: University of Chicago Press.

Latour, B. (1987) *Science in Action: How to Follow Scientists and Engineers through Society*. Cambridge: Cambridge University Press.

Lawson, S. (2012) 'Putting the "war" in cyberwar: metaphor, analogy, and cybersecurity discourse in the United States', *First Monday*, 17(7). Available at https://journals.uic.edu/ojs/index.php/fm/article/view/3848/3270 (accessed 22 February 2019).

Lawson, S. (2013) 'Beyond cyber-doom: assessing the limits of hypothetical scenarios in the framing of cyber-threats', *Journal of Information Technology and Politics*, 10(1), 86–103.

Leander, A. (2005) 'The power to construct international security: on the significance of Private Military Companies', *Millennium*, 33(3), 803–26.

Leander, A. (2010) 'Commercial security practices', in P. Burgess (ed.) *The Routledge Handbook of New Security Studies*. Abingdon: Routledge, pp. 208–16.

Ledbetter, J. (2011) *Unwarranted Influence: Dwight D. Eisenhower and the Military Industrial Complex*. New Haven, CT: Yale University Press.

Lessig, L. (1999) *Code: And Other Laws of Cyberspace*. New York, NY: Basic Books.

Bibliography

Leuprecht, C., Skillicorn, D. B. and Tait, V. C. (2016) 'Beyond the Castle Model of cyber-risk and cyber-security', *Government Information Quarterly*, 33(2), 250–57.

Lewis, J. (2018) *Economic Cost of Cybercrime – No Slowing Down*. McAfee. Available at https://csis-prod.s3.amazonaws.com/s3fs-public/publication/economic-impact-cybercrime.pdf?kab1HywrewRzH17N9wuE24soo1IdhuHd&utm_source=Press&utm_campaign=bb9303ae70-EMAIL_CAMPAIGN_2018_02_21&utm_medium=email&utm_term=0_7623d157be-bb9303ae70-1940938 (accessed 5 April 2019).

Lewis, J. A. (2005a) 'Aux armes, citoyens: cyber security and regulation in the United States', *Telecommunications Policy*, 29(11), 821–30.

Lewis, J. A. (2005b) *The Internet and Terrorism*. CSIS. Available at http://csis.org/files/media/csis/pubs/050401_internetandterrorism.pdf (accessed 30 August 2015).

Li, L., He, W., Xu, L., Ash, I., Anwar, M. and Yuan, X. (2019) 'Investigating the impact of cybersecurity policy awareness on employees' cybersecurity behavior', *International Journal of Information Management*, 45, 13–24.

Liberatore, A. (2007) 'Balancing security and democracy, and the role of expertise: biometrics politics in the European Union', *European Journal of Criminal Policy and Research*, 13(1–2), 109–37.

Liff, A. P. (2012) 'Cyberwar: a new "absolute weapon"? The proliferation of cyberwarfare capabilities and interstate war', *Journal of Strategic Studies*, 35(3), 401–28.

Lin, H. (2010) 'Responding to sub-threshold cyber intrusions: a fertile topic for research and discussion', *Georgetown Journal of International Affairs*, 11(special issue), 127–35.

Lin, H. (2012) 'A virtual necessity: some modest steps toward greater cybersecurity', *Bulletin of the Atomic Scientists*, 68(5), 75–87.

Lindvall, J. (2009) 'The real but limited influence of expert ideas', *World Politics*, 61(4), 703–30.

Lippert, R. K., Walby, K. and Wilkinson, B. (2016) 'Spins, stalls and shutdowns: pitfalls of qualitative policing and security research', *Forum: Qualitative Social Research*, 17(1), n.p.

Lord Carlile (2007) *The Definition of Terrorism*. Norwich: The Stationary Office.

Lukes, S. (2005) *Power: A Radical View*. London: Palgrave Macmillan.

Lupovici, A. (2016) 'The "attribution problem" and the social construction of "violence": taking cyber deterrence literature a step forward', *International Studies Perspective*, 17(3), 322–42.

Macdonald, S., Jarvis, L. and Nouri, L. (2015) 'State cyberterrorism: a contradiction in terms?' *Contemporary Voices: St Andrews Journal of International Relations*, 6(3), 62–75.

McAfee (2009) *McAfee Inc. Provides Guidance to Improve Critical Infrastructure Security*. McAfee. Available at www.mcafee.com/mx/about/news/2009/q2/20090409-01.aspx (accessed 20 February 2014).

McAfee (2011a) *Is This SCADA Hacking Friday?* McAfee. Available at http://blogs.mcafee.com/mcafee-labs/is-this-scada-hacking-friday (accessed 30 August 2015).

McAfee (2011b) *McAfee Labs 2012 Threat Predictions Include High-Profile Industrial Attacks, Cyberwarfare Demonstrations and New Hacktivist Targets*. McAfee. Available at www.mcafee.com/uk/about/news/2011/q4/20111228-01.aspx (accessed 30 August 2015).

McAfee (2012) *McAfee All Access 2013 Enhances Cross-Device Protection for Consumers*. McAfee. Available at www.mcafee.com/uk/about/news/2012/q4/20121114-02.aspx (accessed 28 January 2015).

McAfee (2018) *Public–Private Partnerships*. McAfee. Available at www.mcafee.com/enterprise/en-us/about/public-policy/partnerships.html (accessed 2 April 2019).

McAleavey, K. (2011) *The Birth of the Antivirus Industry*. Available at www.infosecisland.com/blogview/15068-The-Birth-of-the-Antivirus-Industry.html (accessed 22 March 2019).

Bibliography

McCarthy, D. R. (2018) 'Privatizing political authority: cybersecurity, public–private partnerships, and the reproduction of liberal political order', *Politics and Governance*, 6(2),
5–12.

McCusker, R. (2006) 'Transnational organised cyber crime: distinguishing threat from reality', *Crime, Law and Social Change*, 46(4–5), 257–73.

McDermott, S. (2012) *The Future of Privacy Legislation, Part One.* AVG. Available at http://
blogs.avg.com/privacy/future-privacy-legislation-part/ (accessed 28 January 2015).

McGraw, G. (2013) 'Cyber war is inevitable (unless we build security in)', *Journal of Strategic
Studies*, 36(1), 109–19.

McGregor, S. L. T. and Murnane, J. A. (2010) 'Paradigm, methodology and method: intellectual integrity in consumer scholarship', *International Journal of Consumer Studies*, 34(4),
419–27.

McGuire, M. (2013) *Cyber Crime: A Review of the Evidence.* London: Home Office.

McLean, D. (2009) *Combatting Cyber-Terrorism Requires We Play Defense AND Offense.* Symantec.
Available at www.symantec.com/connect/blogs/combatting-cyber-terrorism-requires-
we-play-defense-and-offense (accessed 28 January 2015).

Malcolm, J. G. (2004) *Testimony of Deputy Assistant Attorney General John G. Malcolm on Cyberterrorism, before the Senate Judiciary Committee Subcommittee on Terrorism, Technology, and Homeland Security.* United States Senate Committee on the Judiciary. Available at www.judiciary.senate.
gov/imo/media/doc/malcolm_testimony_02_24_04.pdf (accessed 30 August 2015).

Mallinder, J. and Drabwell, P. (2013) 'Cyber security: a critical examination of information
sharing versus data sensitivity issues for organisations at risk of cyber attack', *Journal of
business Continuity & Emergency Planning*, 7(2), 103–11.

Margulies, P. (2017) 'Global cybersecurity, surveillance, and privacy: the Obama administration's conflicted legacy', *Indiana Journal of Global Legal Studies*, 24(2), 459–95.

Market Research Engine (2018) *Cybersecurity Market: Global Industry Analysis and Opportunity
Assessment 2017–2024.* Market Research Engine. Available at www.marketresearchengine.
com/reportdetails/cyber-security-market (accessed 2 April 2019).

Marland, A. (2003) 'Marketing political soap: a political marketing view of selling candi-
dates like soap, of electioneering as a ritual, and of electoral military analogies', *Journal
of Public Affairs*, 3(2), 103–15.

Marsh, D. (2009) 'Keeping ideas in their place: in praise of thin constructivism', *Australian
Journal of Political Science*, 44(4), 679–96.

Martinez, J. (2012) *Napolitano: US Financial Institutions 'Actively Under Attack' by Hackers.* The Hill.
Available at http://thehill.com/blogs/hillicon-valley/technology/265167-napolitano-
us-financial-institutions-qactively-under-attackq-by-hackers (accessed 28 January 2015).

Mashevsky, Y. (2010) *Crimeware: A New Round of Confrontation Begins…* Kaspersky Labs. Available at http://securelist.com/analysis/36298/crimeware-a-new-round-of-confrontation-
begins/ (accessed 30 August 2015).

Matrosov, A., Rodionov, E., Harley, D. and Malcho, J. (2010) *Stuxnet under the Microscope.*
Available at www.eset.com/us/resources/white-papers/Stuxnet_Under_the_Microscope.
pdf (accessed 30 August 2015).

Meadmore, D., Hatcher, C. and Mcwilliam, E. (2000) 'Getting tense about genealogy',
International Journal of Qualitative Studies in Education, 13(5), 463–76.

Mearsheimer J. (2014) *The Tragedy of Great Power Politics.* London: W.W. Norton & Company.

Messerchmidt, J. (2014) 'Hackback: permitting retaliatory hacking by non-state actors as
proportionate countermeasures to transboundary cyberharm', *Columbia Journal of
Transnational Law*, 52(1), 275–324.

Milliken, S. (1999) 'The study of discourse in international relations: a critique of research and methods', *European Journal of International Relations*, 5(2), 225–54.

Milone, M. (2003) 'Hacktivism: securing the national infrastructure', *Knowledge, Technology, & Policy*, 16(1), 75–103.

Mishler, E. G. (1990) 'Validation in inquiry-guided research: the role of exemplars in narrative studies', *Harvard Educational Review*, 60(4), 415–42.

Mody, S. (2011) *MalwAsia: In Operation since 1986 (Part 2)*. K7. Available at http://blog.k7computing.com/2011/12/malwasia-in-operation-since-1986-part-2/ (accessed 28 January 2015).

Moore, T., Clayton, R. and Anderson, R. (2009) 'The economics of online crime', *Journal of Economic Perspectives*, 23(3), 3–20.

Morgenthau, H. (1960) *Politics among Nations: The Struggle for Power and Peace*. New York: Knopf.

Motion, J. and Leitch, S. (2007) 'A toolbox for public relations: the oeuvre of Michel Foucault', *Public Relations Review*, 33(3), 263–68.

Mral, B. (2006) 'The rhetorical state of alert before the Iraq war 2003', *Nordicom Review*, 27(1), 45–62.

Mueller, J. (2005) 'Six rather unusual propositions about terrorism', *Terrorism and Political Violence*, 17(4), 487–505.

Mueller, J. (2006) *Overblown: How Politicians and the Terrorism Industry Inflate National Security Threats, and Why We Believe Them*. London: Free Press.

Mueller, M. (2017) 'Is cybersecurity eating internet governance? Causes and consequences of alternative framings', *Digital Policy, Regulation and Governance*, 19(6), 415–28.

Mulligan, D. K. and Schneider, F. B. (2011) 'Doctrine for cybersecurity', *Dædalus*, 140(4), 70–92.

Mustaca, S. (2010a) *The First Two Days of VB Conference 2010*. Avira. Available at https://aviratechblog.wordpress.com/2010/10/01/the-first-two-days-of-vb-conference-2010/ (accessed 28 January 2015).

Mustaca, S. (2010b) *The Third Day of the VB Conference 2010*. Avira. Available at http://techblog.avira.com/2010/10/02/third-day-of-the-vb-2010-conference/en/ (accessed 20 August 2014).

Mustaca, S. (2013) *Planned Cyberattack Attack against the USA Infrastructure (Updated)*. Avira. Available at http://techblog.avira.com/2013/05/06/planned-cyberattack-attack-against-the-usa-infrastructure/en/ (accessed 13 August 2014).

Mutimer, D. (1997) 'Reimagining security: the metaphors of proliferation', in K. Krause and M. C. Williams (eds) *Critical Security Studies: Concepts and Cases*. London: UCL Press, pp. 187–222.

Mythen, G. and Walklate, S. (2006) 'Criminology and terrorism: which thesis? Risk society or governmentality', *British Journal of Criminology*, 46(3), pp. 379–398.

Mythen, G. and Walklate, S. (2008) 'Terrorism, risk and international security: the perils of asking "what if?"', *Security Dialogue*, 39(2–3), 221–42.

Namestnikov, Y. (2010a) *IT Threat Evolution for Q3–2010*. Kaspersky Labs. Available at www.securelist.com/en/analysis/204792153/IT_Threat_Evolution_for_Q3_2010 (accessed 28 January 2015).

Namestnikov, Y. (2010b) *Information Security Threats in the First Quarter of 2010*. Kaspersky Labs. Available at www.securelist.com/en/analysis/204792120/Information_Security_Threats_in_the_First_Quarter_of_2010 (accessed 28 January 2015).

Naraine, R. (2009) *Drive-By Downloads. The Web under Siege*. Kaspersky Labs. Available at https://securelist.com/analysis/publications/36245/drive-by-downloads-the-web-under-siege/ (accessed 28 January 2015).

Bibliography

NASDAQ (2018) *Stock Charts*. NASDAQ. Available at www.nasdaq.com/quotes/stock-charts.aspx (accessed 2 April 2019).

National Research Council (1991) *Computers at Risk*. Washington, DC: National Academy Press.

Nelson, B., Choi, R., Iacobucci, M., Mitchell, M. and Gagnon, G. (1999) *Cyberterror: Prospects and Implications*. Monterey, CA: Centre for the Study of Terrorism and Irregular Warfare. Available at: www.nps.edu/academics/centers/ctiw/files/Cyberterror%20Prospects%20and%20Implications.pdf (accessed 29 August 2015).

Nelson, S. D. and Simek, J. W. (2005) 'Spyware: exorcising the demons', *GPSOLO*, 22(8), pp. 18–21.

Nguyen, R. (2013) 'Navigating jus ad bellum in the age of cyber warfare', *California Law Review*, 101(4), 1079–129.

Nicolaidis, K. and Shafer (2005) 'Transnational mutual recognition regimes: governance without global government', *Law and Contemporary Problems*, 68(3), 263–318.

Nietzsche, F. (1989) *On the Genealogy of Morals and Ecce Homo*. W. Faufmann (ed.). Translated from German by W. Kaufmann and R. J. Hollingdale. New York, NY: Vintage Books.

Nigerian Computer Emergency Response Team (2014) *National Cyber Security Strategy*. Nigeria.gov. Available at https://cert.gov.ng/images/uploads/NATIONAL_CYBESECURITY_STRATEGY.pdf (accessed 6 September 2017).

Nissenbaum, H. (2005) 'Where computer security meets national security', *Ethics and Information Technology*, 7(2), 61–73.

Nye, J. Jr., (2011) 'Nuclear lessons for cyber security', *Strategic Studies Quarterly*, 5(4), 18–38.

Nye, J. S. (2013) 'From bombs to bytes: can our nuclear history inform our cyber future?', *Bulletin of the Atomic Scientists*, 69(5), 8–14.

Nyman, J. (2013) 'Securitization theory', in L. J. Shepherd (ed.) *Critical Approaches to Security: An Introduction to Theories and Methods*. Abingdon: Routledge, pp. 51–62.

O'Brien, K. (2010) 'Information age, terrorism and warfare', *Small Wars & Insurgencies*, 14(1), 183–206.

O'Reilly, C. (2010) 'The transnational security consultancy industry: a case of state-corporate symbiosis', *Theoretical Criminology*, 14(2), 183–210.

Olson, K. K. (2005) 'Cyberspace as place and the limits of metaphor', *Convergence*, 11(1), 10–18.

Onuf, N. G. (1989) *World of Our Making: Rules and Rule in Social Theory and International Relations*. Abingdon: Routledge.

Osenga, K. (2013) 'The internet is not a super highway: using metaphors to communication information and communications policy', *Journal of Information Policy*, 3(1), 30–54.

Ostache, A. (2013) *How to Hack an iPhone in 60 Seconds*. BullGuard. Available at www.bullguard.com/blog/2013/09/how-to-hack-an-iphone-in-60-seconds (accessed 2 April 2019).

Owen, D. (2002) 'Criticism and captivity: on genealogy and critical theory', *Continental Philosophy*, 10(2), 216–30.

Paget, F. (2012) *Cyberwarfare Inspires Analysts, Cover on YouTube, Twitter*. McAfee. Available at http://blogs.mcafee.com/mcafee-labs/cyberwarfare-inspires-analysts-coverage-on-youtube-twitter (accessed 30 August 2015).

Panda (2010) *The Brazilian Army and Panda Security Join Forces to Combat Cyber-Warfare*. Panda. Available at www.pandasecurity.com/mediacenter/press-releases/the-brazilian-army-and-panda-security-join-forces-to-combat-cyber-warfare/ (accessed 30 August 2015).

Bibliography

Panda (2011a) *Cyber-Activism and Cyber-War, Main Issues at the 3rd Security Blogger Summit*. Panda. Available at www.pandasecurity.com/mediacenter/press-releases/cyber-activism-and-cyber-war-main-issues-at-the-3rd-security-blogger-summit/ (accessed 28 January 2015).

Panda (2011b) *Privacy Violations Biggest Security Threat in 2012, Reports PandaLabs*. Panda. Available at www.pandasecurity.com/mediacenter/press-releases/privacy-violations-biggest-security-threat-in-2012-reports-pandalabs/ (accessed 1 September 2015).

Panda (2012) *Vulnerabilities Will Be the Main Target for Cybercriminals in 2013*. Panda. Available at www.pandasecurity.com/mediacenter/press-releases/vulnerabilities-will-be-the-main-target-for-cybercriminals-in-2013/ (accessed 1 September 2015).

Panda (2018) *Support for Innovation*. Panda. Available at www.pandasecurity.com/inno-support/ (accessed 2 April 2019).

Parameswaran, R. (2006) 'Military metaphors, masculine modes, and critical commentary', *Journal of Communication Inquiry*, 30(1), 42–64.

Paredes, J. (2007) *When Terrorists Come Out to Play*. Trend Micro. Available at http://blog.trendmicro.com/trendlabs-security-intelligence/when-terrorists-come-out-to-play/ (accessed 1 September 2015).

Paris, R. (2002) 'Kosovo and the metaphor war', *Political Science Quarterly*, 117(3), 423–50.

Parker, D. B. (1976) *Crime by Computer*. New York, NY: Scribner.

Parker, M. (2011a) *Beyond Stuxnet and Duqu: Security Implications to Our Infrastructure*. Symantec. Available at www.symantec.com/connect/blogs/beyond-stuxnet-and-duqu-security-implications-our-infrastructure (accessed 31 August 2015).

Parker, M. (2011b) *Cyber Security: A State of Digital Denial*. Symantec. Available at www.symantec.com/connect/blogs/we-should-be-more-concerned-about-cyber-attack (accessed 31 August 2015).

Parks, C. (2003) 'Cyber terrorism: hype or reality?', *The Journal of Corporate Accounting and Finance*, 14(5), 9–11.

Peng, L., Wijesekera, D., Wingfield, T. C. and Michael, J. B. (2006) 'An ontology-based distributed whiteboard to determine legal responses to online cyber attacks', *Internet Research*, 16(5), 475–90.

Penn, J. (2012) *US Government, Stuxnet, and Cyber-Attacks: Caveat Coder*. Avast! Available at https://blog.avast.com/2012/06/04/us-government-stuxnet-and-cyber-attacks-caveat-coder/ (accessed 1 September 2015).

Pew Research Centre (2016) *Smartphone Ownership and Internet Usage Continues to Climb in Emerging Economies*. Pew Research Centre. Available at www.pewglobal.org/2016/02/22/smartphone-ownership-and-internet-usage-continues-to-climb-in-emerging-economies/ (accessed 2 April 2019).

Pew Research Centre (2018) *Mobile Fact Sheet*. Pew Research Centre. Available at www.pewinternet.org/fact-sheet/mobile/ (accessed 2 April 2019).

Pickett, B. L. (1996) 'Foucault and the politics of resistance', *Polity*, 28(4), 445–66.

Platt, V. (2012) 'Still the fire proof house?', *International Journal*, 67(1), 155–67.

Podesta, J. and Goyle, R. (2005) 'Lost in cyberspace? Finding American liberties in a dangerous digital world', *Yale Law and Policy Review*, 23(2), 509–27.

Popp, N. (2010) *Google Hacked or Why the Cyber World Could Get M.A.D***. Symantec. Available at www.symantec.com/connect/blogs/google-hacked-or-why-cyber-world-could-get-mad (accessed 30 August 2015).

Post, J. M., Ruby, K. G. and Shaw, E. D. (2000) 'From car bombs to logic bombs: the growing threat from information terrorism', *Terrorism and Political Violence*, 12(2), 97–122.

Bibliography

Pradillo, J. C. O. (2011) 'Fighting cybercrime in Europe: the admissibility of remote searches in Spain', *European Journal of Crime, Criminal Law and Criminal Justice*, 19(4), 368–81.

Preist, D. and Arkin, W. M. (2010) *National Security Inc, The Washington Post*, 20 July. Global Policy Forum. Available at www.globalpolicy.org/pmscs/50502-top-secret-america-national-security-inc.html (accessed 5 April 2019).

President's Commission on Critical Infrastructure Protection (1997) *Critical Foundations: Protecting America's Infrastructure*. Available at https://fas.org/sgp/library/pccip.pdf (accessed 19 March 2019).

Price, R. (2017) *UK Home Secretary Amber Rudd Says 'Real People' Don't Need End-to-End Encryption*. Business Insider UK. Available at http://uk.businessinsider.com/home-secretary-amber-rudd-real-people-dont-need-end-to-end-encryption-terrorists-2017-8 (accessed 27 October 2017).

Purser, S. (2011) 'The European cooperative approach to securing critical information infrastructure', *Journal of Business Continuity & Emergency Planning*, 5(3), 237–45.

Quigley, K. and Roy, J. (2012) 'Cyber-security and risk management in an interoperable world: an examination of governmental action in North America', *Social Science Computer Review*, 30(1), 83–94.

Quigley, K., Burns C. and Stallard, K. (2015) 'Cyber gurus: a rhetorical analysis of the language of cybersecurity specialists and the implications for security policy and critical infrastructure protection', *Government Information Quarterly*, 32(2), 108–17.

Rabinow, P. and Rose, N. (2003) 'Foucault today', in P. Rabinow and N. Rose (eds) *The Essential Foucault: Selections from the Essential Works of Foucault, 1954–1984*. New York: New Press, pp. vii–xxxv.

Radaelli, C. (1999) The public policy of the European Union: whither politics of expertise? *Journal of Eu-ropean Public Policy*, 6(1), 757–74.

Raffnsøe, S., Gudmand-Høyer, M. and Thaning, M. S. (2014) 'Foucault's dispositive: the per-spicacity of dispositive analytics in organizational research', *Organization*, 23(2), 272–98.

Raiu, C. (2009) *Browsing Malicious Websites*. Kaspersky Labs. Available at http://securelist.com/analysis/publications/36273/browsing-malicious-websites/ (accessed 30 August 2015).

RAND (2015) *Cyber Warfare*. RAND. Available at www.rand.org/topics/cyber-warfare.html (accessed 30 August 2015).

Redfield, W. (2012) *The Current State of Mobile Malware*. Symantec. Available at www.symantec.com/connect/blogs/current-state-mobile-malware (accessed 30 August 2015).

Reisfield, G. M. and Wilson, G. R. (2004) 'Use of metaphor in the discourse on cancer', *American Society of Clinical Oncology*, 22(19), 4024–7.

Renn, O. (2008) *Risk Governance: Coping with Uncertainty in a Complex World*. Abingdon: Earthscan.

Reuters (2012) *'End of the World as We Know It': Kaspersky Warns of Cyber-Terror Apocalypse*. Reuters. Available from http://rt.com/news/kaspersky-fears-cyber-pandemic-170/ (accessed 29 August 2015).

Reynolds, G. (2011) *Ethics in Information Technology*. Boston, MA: Course Technology Cengage Learning.

Rid, T. (2011) 'Cyber war will not take place', *Journal of Strategic Studies*, 35(1), 5–32.

Rid, T. (2012) *Cyberwar Will Not Take Place*. London: C. Hurst & Co. Publishers Ltd.

Rid, T. (2013) 'More attacks, less violence', *Journal of Strategic Studies*, 36(1), 139–42.

Rid, T. (2018) *1 November*. Twitter. Available at https://twitter.com/RidT/status/1058030036580753408 (accessed 13 February 2019).

Rishikof, H. and Lunday, K. (2011) 'Corporate responsibility in cybersecurity: building international global standards', *Georgetown Journal of International Affairs*, 12(1), 17–24.

Robinson, N. T. (2014) 'Have you won the war on terror? Military videogames and the state of American exceptionalism', *Millennium – Journal of International Studies*, 43(2), 450–70.

Rollins, J. and Wilson, C. (2005) *Terrorist Capabilities for Cyberattack: Overview and Policy Issues*. Congressional research service. Available at www.fas.org/sgp/crs/terror/RL33123.pdf (accessed 1 September 2015).

Rothkopf, D. (2002) 'Business versus terror', *Foreign Policy*, 130 (May/June), 56–64.

Rothkopf, D. (2014) *We Are Losing the War on Terror*. Foreign Policy. Available at www.foreignpolicy.com/articles/2014/06/10/we_are_losing_the_war_on_terror_mosul_karachi_9_11 (accessed 1 September 2015).

RSM (2018) *Department for Digital, Culture, Media and Sport UK Cyber Security Sectoral Analysis and Deep-Dive Review*. HM Government. Available at https://assets.publishing.service.gov.uk/government/uploads/system/uploads/attachment_data/file/751406/UK_Cyber_Sector_Report_-__June_2018.pdf (accessed 2 January 2019).

Rudd, A. (2017) *We Don't Want to Ban Encryption, but Our Inability to See What Terrorists Are Plotting Undermines Our Security*, *The Telegraph*. Available at www.telegraph.co.uk/news/2017/07/31/dont-want-ban-encryption-inability-see-terrorists-plotting-online/ (accessed 1 February 2018).

Rumsfeld, D. (2002) *Press Conference*. NATO HQ Brussels, 6 June. Nato Speeches. Available at www.nato.int/docu/speech/2002/s020606g.htm (accessed 5 April 2019).

Ruohonen, J., Hyrynsalmi, S. and Leppanen, V. (2016) 'An outlook on the institutional evolution of the European Union security apparatus', *Government Information Quarterly*, 33(4), 746–56.

Rychnovska, D., Pasgaard, M. and Berling, T. V. (2017) 'Science and security expertise: authority, knowledge, subjectivity', *Geoforum*, 84, 327–31.

Sales, N. A. (2013) 'Regulating cyber-security', *Northwestern University Law Review*, 107(4), 1504–67.

Salmi, D. (2011) *Top 5 Cyberthreats for 2012 (and How to Avoid Them)*. Avast! Available at https://blog.avast.com/2011/12/27/top-5-cyberthreats-for-2012-and-how-to-avoid-them/ (accessed 1 September 2015).

Salter, M. B. (2008) 'Securitization and desecuritisation: a dramaturgical analysis of the Candasian Air Transport Security authority', *Journal of International Relations and Development*, 11(4), 321–49.

Sandro, G. (2012) *Das Wettrüsten hat längst begonnen: Vom digitalen Angriff zum realen Ausnahmezustand*. Munich: Goldmann.

Sanger, D. E. and Shanker, T. (2013) *Broad Powers Seen for Obama in Cyberstrikes*, *The New York Times*. Available at www.nytimes.com/2013/02/04/us/broad-powers-seen-for-obama-in-cyberstrikes.html?pagewanted=all&_r=0 (accessed 11 June 2015).

Scheuer, G. (2012) *Why So Many Anti Virus Products Fail and Comodo Antivirus Does Not*. Comodo. Available at https://blogs.comodo.com/uncategorized/why-so-many-anti-virus-products-fail-and-comodo-antivirus-does-not/ (accessed 1 September 2015).

Schudson, M. (2006) 'The trouble with experts – and why democracies need them', *Theory and Society*, 35(5/6), 491–506.

Seabian, J. A. (2000) *Cyber Threats and the US Economy: Statement for the Record before the Joint Economic Committee on Cyber Threats and the US Economy*. CIA. Available at www.cia.gov/news-information/speeches-testimony/2000/cyberthreats_022300.html (accessed 1 September 2015).

Bibliography

Seabrooke, L. (2014) 'Epistemic arbitrage: transnational professional knowledge in action', *Journal of Professions and Organizations*, 1(1), 49–64.

Sebenius, J. K. (1992) 'Challenging conventional explanations of international cooperation: negotiation analysis and the case of epistemic communities', *International Organization*, 46(1), 323–65.

Securelist (2019) *Securelist Homepage*. Kaspersky Labs. Available at www.securelist.com (accessed 31 March 2019).

Sejtko, J. (2010) *Ads Poisoning – JS:Prontexi*. Avast! Available at https://blog.avast.com/2010/02/18/ads-poisoning-%E2%80%93-jsprontexi/ (accessed 1 September 2015).

Senate (2010) *Protecting Cyberspace as a National Asset Act of 2010*, report of the Committee on Homeland Security and Governmental Affairs, 15 December 2010. Senate. Available at www.congress.gov/111/crpt/srpt368/CRPT-111srpt368.pdf (accessed 2 April 2019).

Senate (2012) 'Cybersecurity Act of 2012 – motion to proceed', speech of Hon. Dianne Feinstein, 26 July 2012. Senate. Available at www.congress.gov/crec/2012/07/26/CREC-2012-07-26-pt1-PgS5450-2.pdf (accessed 2 April 2019).

Senate (2013) *Electronic Communications Privacy Act Amendments Act 2013*, report of the committee on the Judiciary, 16 May 2013. Senate. Available at www.congress.gov/congressional-report/113th-congress/senate-report/34/1?q=%7B%22search%22%3A%5B%22symantec%22%5D%7D&r=56 (accessed 2 April 2019).

Shackelford, S. J. and Craig, A. N. (2014) 'Beyond the new "digital divide": analysing the evolving role of national governments in the internet governance and enhancing cybersecurity', *Stanford Journal of International Law*, 50(1), 119–84.

Shanahan, T. (2010) 'Betraying a certain corruption of mind: how (and how not) to define 'terrorism', *Critical Studies on Terrorism*, 3(2), 173–90.

Shiner, L. (1982) 'Reading Foucault: anti-method and the genealogy of power-knowledge', *History and Theory*, 21(3), 382–98.

Shires, J. (2018) 'Enacting expertise: ritual and risk in cybersecurity', *Politics and Governance*, 6(2), 31–40.

Silva-Castañeda, L. and Trussart, N. (2016) 'Sustainability standards and certification: looking through the lens of Foucault's dispositif', *Global Networks*, 16(4), 490–510.

Skilling, P. (2014) 'Everyday emergency: crisis, unease and strategy in contemporary political discourse', *Critical Policy Studies*, 8(1), 61–77.

Skoudis, E. and Zeltset, L. (2004) *Malware: Fighting Malicious Code*. Upper Saddle River, NJ: Pearson Education.

Solansky, S. T. and Beck, T. E. (2009) 'Enhancing community safety and security through understanding interagency collaboration in cyber-terrorism exercises', *Administration & Society*, 40(8), 852–72.

Speer, D. L. (2000) 'Redefining borders: the challenge of cybercrime', *Crime, Law and Social Change*, 34(3), 259–73.

Spieker, J. (2011) 'Foucault and Hobbes on politics, security and war', *Alternatives: Global, Local, Political*, 36(3), 187–99.

Stackpole, B. (2018) *Future of Public–Private Security Partnerships Still in Doubt*. Symantec. Available at www.symantec.com/blogs/feature-stories/future-public-private-security-partnerships-still-doubt (accessed 3 September 2018).

Steuter, E. and Wills, D. (2009) *At War with Metaphor: Media, Propaganda, and Racism in the War on Terror*. Plymouth: Lexington Books.

Stevens, T. (2016) *Cyber Security and the Politics of Time*. Cambridge: Cambridge University Press.

Bibliography

Stevens, T. (2018) 'Global cybersecurity: new directions in theory and methods', *Politics and Governance*, 6(2), 1–4.

Stohl, M. (2006) 'Cyber terrorism: a clear and present danger, the sum of all fears, breaking point or patriot games?', *Crime, Law and Social Change*, 46(4–5), 223–38.

Sullivan, S. (2010) *Stuxnet Redux: Questions and Answers*. F-Secure. Available at www.fsecure.com/weblog/archives/00002066.html (accessed 30 September 2015).

Symantec (1997) *Symantec Announces Bloodhound Technology, an Advanced System for Detecting New and Unknown Viruses on the World Wide Web*. Symantec. Available at www.symantec.com/about/news/release/article.jsp?prid=19970203_02 (accessed 30 September 2015).

Symantec (2000) *Symantec Executive Named as Delegate to G-8 Paris Conference*. Symantec. Available at www.symantec.com/about/news/release/article.jsp?prid=20000515_01 (accessed 29 August 2015).

Symantec (2002) *Symantec Security Check Serves More than 30 Million Users*. Symantec. Available at www.symantec.com/about/news/release/article.jsp?prid=20021217_01 (accessed 29 August 2015).

Symantec (2006) *Malaysian Government Appoints Symantec's John W. Thompson to the International Advisory Board of Impact*. Symantec. Available at www.symantec.com/about/news/release/article.jsp?prid=20060627_02 (accessed 30 September 2015).

Symantec (2009a) *IT Embracing Managed Security to Meet Security Challenges*. Symantec. Available at www.symantec.com/about/news/release/article.jsp?prid=20090323_01 (accessed 30 September 2015).

Symantec (2009b) *Symantec's Newest Norton Ghost Packs Powerful Detection and Threat Protection Punch*. Symantec. Available at www.symantec.com/about/news/release/article.jsp?prid=20080225_01 (accessed 1 September 2015).

Symantec (2010) *Statistical-Based Intrusion Detection*. Symantec. Available at www.symantec.com/connect/articles/statistical-based-intrusion-detection (accessed 30 August 2015).

Symantec (2011a) *Cyber Attack Toolkits Dominate the Internet Threat Landscape*. Symantec. Available at www.symantec.com/about/news/release/article.jsp?prid=20110117_04 (accessed 30 August 2015).

Symantec (2011b) *Cybersecurity Focus Increasing as Organizations Adopt New Computing Models Press Release*. Symantec. Available at www.symantec.com/about/news/release/article.jsp?prid=20110831_01 (accessed 30 August 2015).

Symantec (2011c) *Symantec Endpoint Protection 12 Delivers Unrivaled Security with Fastest Performance*. Symantec. Available at www.symantec.com/about/news/release/article.jsp?prid=20110215_01 (accessed 30 August 2015).

Symantec (2015) *Zero-Day Vulnerabilities*. Symantec. Available at http://securityresponse.symantec.com/threatreport/topic.jsp?id=vulnerability_trends&aid=zero_day_vulnerabilities (accessed 30 August 2015).

Symantec (2018) *Government Symposium – Program*. Symantec. Available at https://symantecgovsymposium.com/program/ (accessed 2 April 2019).

Symantec (2019) 'Product A–Z'. Available at https://support.symantec.com/en_US/product-a-z.html (accessed 31 March 2019).

Tarnoff, B. (2016) *The Internet Should Be a Public Good*. Jacobin. Available at www.jacobinmag.com/2016/08/internet-public-dns-privatization-icann-netflix (accessed 31 July 2019).

Taupiac-Nouvel, G. (2012) 'The principle of mutual recognition in criminal matters: a new model of judicial cooperation within the European Union', *European Criminal Law Review*, 2(3), 236–51.

Bibliography

Tehrani, P. M., Manap, N. A. and Taji, H. (2013) 'Cyber terrorism challenges: the need for a global response to a multi-jurisdictional crime', *Computer Law & Security Review*, 29(3), 207–15.

The White House (2002) *Appointments to National Infrastructure Advisory Committee*. The White House. Available at https://georgewbush-whitehouse.archives.gov/news/releases/2002/09/20020918-12.html (accessed 4 February 2019).

The White House (2003) *The National Strategy to Secure Cyberspace*. The White House. Available at www.us-cert.gov/sites/default/files/publications/cyberspace_strategy.pdf (accessed 1 September 2015).

The White House (2011a) *President Obama Announces More Key Administration Posts*. The White House. Available at https://obamawhitehouse.archives.gov/the-press-office/2011/05/26/president-obama-announces-more-key-administration-posts (accessed 2 April 2019).

The White House (2011b) *President's Management Advisory Board*. The White House. Available at https://obamawhitehouse.archives.gov/administration/advisory-boards/pmab/members/enrique-salem%20 (accessed 14 January 2019).

The White House (2013) *President Obama Announces More Key Administration Posts*. The White House. Available at https://obamawhitehouse.archives.gov/the-press-office/2013/06/04/president-obama-announces-more-key-administration-posts (accessed 2 February 2019).

TheSecDev Group (2009) *Tracking GhostNet: Investigating a Cyber Espionage Network*. University of Toronto: Munk Centre For International Studies. Available at www.scribd.com/doc/13731776/Tracking-GhostNet-Investigating-a-Cyber-Espionage-Network#scribd (accessed 1 September 2015).

Theys, S. (2017) 'Constructivism', in S. McGlinchey, R. Walters and C. Scheinpflug (eds) *International Relations Theory*. Bristol: E-International Relations Publishing, pp. 36–41.

Thimbleby, H., Anderson, S. and Cairns, P. (1998) 'A framework for modelling Trojans and computer virus infection', *The Computer Journal*, 41(7), 444–58.

Thomas, N. (2009) 'Cyber security in East Asia: governing anarchy', *Asian Security*, 5(1), 3–23.

Thompson, R. (2009) *I Think I Know What the DDoS Was About*. AVG. Available at http://blogs.avg.com/news-threats/i-think-i-know-what-the-ddos-was-about/ (accessed 13 August 2014).

Thompson, R. (2010) *iPhone-Based Cyber Attack?* AVG. Available at http://blogs.avg.com/news-threats/iphonebased-cyber-attack/ (accessed 28 August 2014).

Thornborrow, J. (1993) 'Metaphors of security: a comparison of representation in defence discourse in post-Cold War France and Britain', *Discourse & Society*, 4(1), 99–119.

Thornburg, E. G. (1995) 'Metaphors matter: how images of battle, sports and sex shape the adversary system', *Wisconsin Women's Law Journal*, 10(2), 225–83.

Tierney, K. (2005) 'The 9/11 Commission and disaster management: little depth, less context, not much guidance', *Contemporary Sociology*, 34(2), 115–20.

Trend Micro (2011a) *European Officials Making Moves to Thwart Cybercrime*. Trend Micro. Available at http://blog.trendmicro.com/european-officials-making-moves-to-thwart-cybercrime/ (accessed 1 September 2015).

Trend Micro (2011b) *Western Countries Concerned about Cyber Retaliation for Osama Killing*. Trend Micro. Available at http://blog.trendmicro.com/western-countries-concerned-about-cyber-retaliation-for-osama-killing/ (accessed 1 September 2015).

Trend Micro (2012) *Report Identifies Vulnerabilities in US Government IT Supply Chain.* Trend Micro. Available at http://blog.trendmicro.com/report-identifies-vulnerabilities-in-us-government-it-supply-chain/ (accessed 1 September 2015).

Trend Micro (2013) *Latin American and Caribbean Cybersecurity Trends and Government Responses.* Trend Micro. Available at www.trendmicro.co.uk/media/wp/latin-american-and-caribbean-cybersecurity-trends-and-government-responses-whitepaper-en.pdf (accessed 1 September 2015).

Turner, F. J. (1940) *The Frontier in American History.* New York, NY: Henry Holt and Company.

Urquhart, L. (2012) *Cyberwar: Hype or Reality?* Sophos. Available at http://nakedsecurity.sophos.com/2012/03/20/CYBER-WAR-HYPE-OR-REALITY/ (accessed 1 September 2015).

Valdes, A. R. (2015) 'The mutual recognition principle in criminal matters: a review', *ERA Forum*, 16(3), 291–303.

Valeriano, B. and Maness, R. C. (2014) 'The dynamics of cyber conflict between rival antagonists, 2001–11', *Journal of Peace Research*, 51(3), 347–60.

Van Eeten, M. (2017) 'Patching security governance: an empirical view of emergent governance mechanisms for cybersecurity', *Digital Policy, Regulation and Governance*, 19(6), 429–48.

Vande Putte, D. and Verhelst, M. (2013) 'Cyber crime: can a standard risk analysis help in the challenges facing business continuity managers?', *Journal of Business Continuity & Emergency Planning*, 7(2), 126–37.

Vass, L. (2012) *Is Digital Pearl Harbor the Most Tasteless Term in IT Security?* Sophos. Available at http://nakedsecurity.sophos.com/2012/02/09/digital-pearl-harbor/ (accessed 1 September 2015).

Vatis, M. (2006) 'The next battlefield', *Harvard International Review*, 28(3), 56–61.

Vegh, S. (2002) 'Hacktivists or cyberterrorists? The changing media discourse on hacking', *First Monday*, 7(10), n.p.

Virilio, P. (2006) *The Original Accident.* Translated from French by J. Rose. Cambridge: Polity Press.

von Clausewitz, C. (1989) *On War.* Translated from German by M. Howard and P. Paret. Princeton, NJ: Princeton University Press.

Vorenberg, J. (1972) *The War on Crime: The First Five Years.* The Atlantic Online. Available at www.theatlantic.com/past/politics/crime/crimewar.htm (accessed 1 September 2015).

Vucetic, S. (2011) 'Genealogy as a research tool in international relations', *Review of International Studies*, 37(3), 1295–312.

Wakefield, J. (2015) *Can the Government Ban Encryption?* London: BBC. Available at www.bbc.co.uk/news/technology-30794953 (accessed 1 September 2015).

Wall, D. S. (1998) 'Catching cybercriminals: policing the internet', *Computers & Technology*, 12(2), 201–18.

Wall, D. S. (2001a) *Crime and the Internet: Cybercrime and Cyberfears.* New York, NY: Routledge.

Wall, D. S. (2001b) 'Cybercrimes and the internet', in D. Wall (ed.) *Crime and the Internet: Cybercrime and Cyberfears.* New York, NY: Routledge, pp. 1–17.

Wallis, P. and Nerlich, B. (2005) 'Disease metaphors in new epidemics: the UK media framing of the 2003 SARS epidemic', *Social Science and Medicine*, 60(11), 2629–39.

Walt, S. M. (1991) 'The renaissance of security studies', *International Studies Quarterly*, 35(2), 211–39.

Walter, J. (2010) *Making Sense of McAfee Risk Advisor.* McAfee. Available at http://blogs.mcafee.com/business/security-connected/making-sense-of-mcafee-risk-advisor (accessed 1 September 2015).

Bibliography

Waltz, K. N. (1979) *Theory of International Politics*. Reading: Addison-Wesley.

Wanglai, G. (2018) 'BRICS cybersecurity cooperation: achievements and deepening paths', *China International Studies*, 68, 124–39.

Watt, N., Mason, R. and Traynor, I. (2015) *David Cameron Pledges Anti-Terror Law for Internet after Paris Attacks, The Guardian*. Available at www.theguardian.com/uk-news/2015/jan/12/david-cameron-pledges-anti-terror-law-internet-paris-attacks-nick-clegg (accessed 28 January 2015).

Waugh, R. (2013a) *Cybersecurity Is 'As Important' as Nuclear Deterrent, Says Top U.S. Admiral*. Available at www.welivesecurity.com/2013/05/13/cybersecurity-is-as-important-as-nuclear-deterrent-says-top-u-s-admiral/ (accessed 1 September 2015).

Waugh, R. (2013b) *Cyber-Warriors, Your Country Needs You: Governments Hit By 'Shortage' of Experts*. Available at www.welivesecurity.com/2013/10/14/cyber-warriors-your-country-needs-you-governments-hit-by-shortage-of-trained-defenders/ (accessed 1 September 2015).

Waugh, R. (2013c) *Obama Uses TV Interview to Raise Cyber Awareness*. Available at www.welivesecurity.com/2013/03/13/obama-uses-tv-interview-to-raise-cyber-awareness/ (accessed 1 September 2015).

Waugh, R. (2013d) *Pentagon to Boost Cyber Security Force to Combat Increased Global Threat*. Available at www.welivesecurity.com/2013/01/28/pentagon-to-boost-cyber-security-force-to-combat-increased-global-threat/ (accessed 1 September 2015).

Waugh, R. (2013e) *Phantom Menace? A Guide to APTs – and Why Most of Us Have Little to Fear from These 'Cyberweapons'*. Available at www.welivesecurity.com/2013/12/09/phantom-menace-a-guide-to-apts-and-why-most-of-us-have-little-to-fear-from-these-cyberweapons/ (accessed 1 September 2015).

Waugh, R. (2013f) *UK and India to Co-Operate on Cyber Security*. Available at www.welivesecurity.com/2013/02/19/uk-and-india-to-co-operate-on-cyber-security/ (accessed 1 September 2015).

Weimann, G. (2005) 'Cyberterrorism: the sum of all fears?', *Studies in Conflict and Terrorism*, 28(2), 129–49.

Weimann, G. (2006) *Terror on the Internet: The New Arena the New Challenges*. Washington, DC: United Institute of Peace Press.

Weinberg, L., Pedahzur, A. and Hirsch-Hoefler, S. (2004) 'The challenges of conceptualizing terrorism', *Terrorism and Political Violence*, 16(4), 777–94.

Wendt, A. (1992) 'Anarchy is what sates make of it: the social construction of power politics' *International Organisation*, 46(2), 391–425.

Wendt, A. (1999) *Social Theory of International Politics*. Cambridge: Cambridge University Press.

Wible, B. (2003) 'A site where hackers are welcome: using hack-in contests to shape preferences and deter computer crime', *The Yale Law Journal*, 112(6), 1577–623.

Wichum, R. (2013) 'Security as a dispositif: Michel Foucault in the field of security', *Foucault Studies*, 15, 164–71.

Wilhoit, K. and Balduzzi, M. (2013) *Vulnerabilities Discovered in Global Vessel Tracking System*. Trend Micro. Available at http://blog.trendmicro.com/trendlabs-security-intelligence/vulnerabilities-discovered-in-global-vessel-tracking-systems/ (accessed 1 September 2015).

Williams, G. (1999) *French Discourse Analysis: The Method of Post-Structuralism*. London: Routledge.

Williams, M. and McDonald, M. (2018) *Security Studies: An Introduction*. Abingdon: Routledge.

Williams, P., Shimeall, T. and Dunlevy, C. (2010) 'Intelligence analysis for internet security', *Contemporary Security Policy*, 23(2), 1–38.

Bibliography

Williamson, C. W. (2008) *Carpet Bombing in Cyberspace*, Armed Forces Journal. Available at www.armedforcesjournal.com/carpet-bombing-in-cyberspace/ (accessed 1 September 2015).

Wolff, J. (2014) 'Cybersecurity as metaphor: policy and defense implications of computer security metaphors' (March 31, 2014). TPRC Conference Paper. Available at https://papers.ssrn.com/sol3/papers.cfm?abstract_id=2418638 (accessed 22 February 2019).

Wulf, W. A. and Jones, A. K. (2009) 'Reflections on cybersecurity', *Science*, 326(5955) 934–44.

Yadron, D., Ackerman, S. and Thielman, S. (2016) *Inside the FBI's Encryption Battle with Apple*, *The Guardian*. Available at www.theguardian.com/technology/2016/feb/17/inside-the-fbis-encryption-battle-with-apple (accessed 27 October 2017).

Yang, D. W. and Hoffstadt, N. M. (2006) 'Countering the cyber-crime threat', *American Criminal Law Review*, 43(2), 201–15.

Yen, F. (2002) 'Western frontier or feudal society? Metaphors and perceptions of cyberspace', *Berkeley Technology Law Journal*, 17(4), 1207–63.

Yost, D. S. (2010) 'NATO's evolving purpose and the next strategic concept', *International Affairs*, 86(2), 489–522.

Zarefsky, D. (1986) *President Johnson's War on Poverty: Rhetoric and History*. Tuscaloosa, AB: University of Alabama Press.

Zetter, K. (2011) *Researchers Uncover RSA Phishing Attack, Hiding in Plain Sight*. Wired. Available at www.wired.com/2011/08/how-rsa-got-hacked/ (accessed 1 September 2015).

Zhang, Y., Xiao, Y., Ghaboosi, K., Zhang, J. and Deng, H. (2012) 'A survey of cyber crimes', *Security and Communication Networks*, 5(4), 422–37.

Zolkipli, M. F. and Jantan, A. (2011) 'A framework for defining malware behaviour using run time analysis and resource monitoring', in J. M. Zain, W. M. Wan Mohd and E. El-Qawasmeh (eds) *Software Engineering and Computer Systems, Second International Conference ICSECS 2011*, Kuantan, Pahang, Malaysia, 27–29 June. London: Springer Heidelberg Dordrecht, pp. 199–209.

ZoneAlarm (2013) *Zero-Days: Exploits that Take Advantage of the Unknown*. ZoneAlarm. Available at www.zonealarm.com/blog/2013/11/zero-days-exploits-that-take-advantage-of-the-unknown/ (accessed 1 September 2015).

Zulaika, J. and Douglass, W. A. (1996) *Terror and Taboo: The Follies, Fables, and Faces of Terrorism*. London: Routledge.

Index

Note: The letter 'n' following locators refers to notes.

9/11 attacks 36, 37, 78, 87, 88, 89, 90, 95, 105, 121, 159n, 160n
Adler, Emanuel 58
Advanced Persistent Threat (APT) 75, 85, 89, 111
Al-Qaeda 82, 159n
analogy *see* metaphor
Anderson, Ben 95
anti-malware 109, 135
anti-virus 9, 28, 76, 82, 83, 101, 102, 103, 110, 134, 152, 157n
Aradau, Claudia 43, 53, 95
arms control 104
arms race 101, 103–4, 107
ARPANET 32
attribution 26, 29

best practice 28, 30, 34
Bigo, Dider
   on communities of mutual recognition 138
   on fear, unease and anxiety 53, 60, 126, 132
   on Foucault and security 51–2
   on governmentality and liberalism 52
   on security professionals 59, 60–1, 131
biopolitics 50, 160n
Black, Cofer 87, 159n
Budapest Convention *see* European Convention on Cyber Crime
bugs 28, 71
Bush, George W. 82, 127, 143

Cameron, David 147
China 33, 37, 86, 121, 154
   cyber capability 22, 116, 119, 142
   Golden Shield 149
   national cybersecurity strategy 2
   and Nimda 90
   and SARS 121
   and Stuxnet 89
Clausewitz, Karl Von 16, 103
Clinton, Bill 127
Cohn, Carol 96–7, 124–5
Cold War 29, 39, 55, 101, 104
   between industry and political professionals 131, 138–9, 144, 146
   communities of mutual recognition 60, 137–44
computerisation 1, 2, 78, 92
computer networks 1, 2, 3, 11, 15, 16, 18, 24, 28, 30, 33, 34, 35, 41, 70, 85, 110, 122, 151, 158n
   vulnerability of, 3, 21, 71–3, 118
conditions of possibility 4, 52, 147, 155
constructivism 39
   and cybersecurity 5, 7
   and cyber-threats 7, 151
   deconstruction 41, 42
   and knowledge 6, 10, 126
cooperation 1, 30–3, 116, 138, 158n
Cooperative Cyber Defence Centre of Excellence 32
counterfactual *see* hypothetical
counter-terrorism 4, 26, 159n

Index

Critical Foundations: Protecting Americans Infrastructure 127, 128
critical infrastructure 18, 34, 38, 119, 122, 148
  effect of attack 38, 72, 78, 87, 88, 140
  ownership of 28, 33
  as referent 22, 97
  vulnerability of 21, 72, 73, 74, 117
critical national infrastructure *see* critical infrastructure
cyber-attack 16, 34, 38, 71, 73, 87, 88, 97, 99, 105, 106, 107, 108, 114, 115, 118, 119, 123, 136
  and anonymity 26
  as complex and simple 112–13
  definitions of 15–16
  destructiveness of 15
  ease of 25–6
  effect of 78, 85, 121, 140, 141
  extent of 2, 79
  inevitability of 93
  response to 30
cyber-crime 20, 21, 24, 28, 30, 75, 99, 122, 132, 141, 142, 158n
  definitions of 19–21
  ease of 25
  extent of 23, 80 102
  havens 26, 31
  response to 30
  statistics on 23
cyber-criminals 23–6, 31, 72, 77, 84, 86, 90, 91, 92, 101, 102, 103, 114, 131, 135
cyber-espionage 16, 86, 91, 101, 103, 107, 108, 113, 115, 116, 118, 122, 123, 158n
cyber-sabotage 24, 78, 91, 101, 115, 117, 118, 122, 123
cybersecurity 3, 5
  ambiguity of 3, 4
  as analogous with national security 3, 4, 11, 40, 55, 144, 146, 152
  definition of 3, 14
  as double-edged sword 2, 4
  as new security challenge 2, 4
  as part of security imaginary 4
  as technified field 5, 62, 108, 124–5, 152

cybersecurity discourse
  analysis of metaphor usage 128
  dissident 35
  dominant 11, 94, 129
  heterogeneity of 14
  as natural 64
  US 127
  see also cybersecurity knowledge
Cybersecurity Enhancement Act 142
cybersecurity imaginary 4, 151
cybersecurity knowledge 6, 8, 9, 13, 25, 45, 67, 68, 137, 150
  as analogous of national security 10, 14, 35, 40, 42, 43, 121, 144
  constitutive effect of 14, 42
  construction of 11, 14, 149, 155
  as contingent 4, 7, 43, 133
  counter-hegemonic 13
  as 'critical'/constructivist 10, 14, 39, 40, 41
  dissident 14, 35, 39, 155
  dominant 4, 8, 13, 14, 42, 70, 116, 130, 147, 148
  heterogeneity of 10, 14,
  homogeneity of 10, 13, 42, 130, 140
  orthodox 54, 55, 121
  as political 146
  as politically neutral 43
  as 'problem solving'/objectivist 10, 35, 40, 131, 151
  as product of power 54
  rapid emergence of 13, 14
  scepticism/sceptical realism 14, 35–9, 40, 43, 74
  sedimentation of 9, 11, 125, 151
  as truth 149
cybersecurity research 5, 6, 14, 151
  critical/constructivist agenda 6, 8, 10, 11, 14, 36, 39–42, 43, 44, 46, 69, 128, 151, 155
  current limitations of 5, 10, 14, 45, 151
  heterogeneity of 6, 37
  homogeneity of 6
  objectivist/realist agenda 6, 36, 40, 151
cyberspace 70
  as battlefield 22, 101, 116, 128
  constructions of 41–2
  emergence of 2

Index

and internet 70
as milieu 73
ownership of 32
securitisation of 4, 122
transformative effect of 2
vulnerability of 11, 42, 71–84, 79
as unknown 42
as warzone 85
as wilderness 83–4
cyber-terrorism 11, 20, 21, 24, 25, 37, 38,
    75, 78, 90, 92, 117, 122, 123, 124,
    127, 143
    definitions of 16–19
    ease of 112
    reality of 119
    scepticism around 37–8, 106
    threat to US 99
    'true' and 'pure' 18, 19, 27
cyber-terrorists 24–5, 77, 111, 113, 118
cyber-threat
    anonymity of 131
    apprehension around 136
    complexity of 4, 108–10, 111, 114, 120,
        124, 125
    construction of 40, 41, 44, 90, 106,
        124, 151
    credibility of 11, 21, 35, 36, 86, 87, 91,
        94, 100, 114–20, 129, 132, 136
    danger of 2, 36, 37, 94, 100
    definition of 14–15
    destructiveness of 88, 99–108
    evolution of 141
    extent of 2, 4, 21, 22, 77, 78, 79, 99
    location of 22–7
    novelty of 25, 26, 97
    responses to 27–34
    simplicity of 25, 89, 100, 112–14, 120
    as stealthy 85, 86, 91
cyber-warfare 11, 22, 37, 38, 75, 78, 89,
    92, 100, 101, 103, 107, 108, 116, 122,
    123, 127, 129, 160n
    comparison with war 25
    definitions of 15, 16
    destructiveness of 104
    inevitability of 26
    revolution 115
    scepticism around 38, 106
    and violence 16

cyber-warriors 102, 103, 116
cyber-weapons 26, 77, 100–3, 106, 107, 127

data
    accumulation of 148, 149
    big 2
    reliance on 2
    security of 2, 75
    theft of 3, 85, 92, 99
    vulnerability of 3, 23, 75
DDOS (distributed denial of service) 19,
    20, 21, 22, 24, 36, 112, 113
Debrix, Franciois
    on language of cyber-terrorism 124
defence 27, 30, 34, 35, 79, 83, 102, 110,
    111, 127, 132
    of CNI 34
    national 28
    pre-emptive 29, 34
Deleuze, Gilles
    creativity and sedimentation 130, 145
    lines of power 51
Department of Homeland Security (DHS)
    88, 139, 141
dependence 3, 4, 70, 78, 79, 91
deterrence 29, 41, 42, 104
digital signatures 75–6
Dillon, Michael 96
discourse analysis 11, 46, 64, 67
dispositif 8, 45, 50–1, 61, 132–3, 147,
    149, 151
    of cybersecurity 42
    definition of 50
    functioning of 53
    lines of creativity and sedimentation 51,
        130, 151, 152
    of pre-cautionary risk 53
    of security 8, 51–3, 95, 97, 124, 127,
        131, 145, 155
    sources within 51, 54, 130, 137
dominant threat frame 12, 126, 127, 129,
    130, 144, 152, 154
Douglass, William 94
drive-by download *see* drive-by malware
drive-by malware 83, 84, 159n
Dunn Cavelty, Myriam 43, 128, 158n
    Cyber-Security and Threat Politics 40
    on dominant threat frame 126, 127

on historical analogies 117
on link between cybersecurity and
    national security 40, 55
Duqu 102, 116, 117

Electronic Communications Privacy
    Act 142
encryption 27, 147
epistemic communities 10, 53, 57–9, 61
    definition of 58
Estonia
    2007 cyber-attack 22, 38
European Convention on Cyber Crime 31
European Union (EU) 31, 35
expert knowledge *see* expertise
expertise 55–63
    constitutive effect of 7, 8, 11, 45, 55, 57,
        60, 61, 62, 68, 144
    effect in securitisation 56
    epistemic authority of 68
    and exclusionary language 124–5
    expert discourse/knowledge 5, 12,
        57, 63
    as 'extra valid'/scientific 5, 56, 57
    as politically neutral and objective 5–6
    private 12, 143–4
    proliferation of 5
    within the *dispositif* 14, 61

Flame 92, 103, 105, 108, 116, 117
Foucault, Michel, 8, 10
    and anti-method 64
    authorities of delimitation 55
    on discourse 97
    on *dispositif* 50–2 130
    enunciative modalities 56
    genealogy 64
    on governmentality, 48–9 149
    grids of specification 55
    History of Sexuality 65
    on method 64–5
    on milieu 49, 70
    on power 46–50, 54
    on role of intellectual 66, 150
    Security, Territory, Population 51
    Society Must Be Defended 51
    surfaces of emergence 55
    toolbox 47, 64, 150

future
    as foreboding 31, 37, 87–91, 93, 95,
        115, 117, 129

Gauss 103
GCHQ 148
Georgia
    2008 cyber-attack 22
GhostNet 86, 159n
governmentality 8, 10, 42, 45, 46–50, 53,
    69, 145, 146, 147, 149, 151, 152
    circulation 49, 50, 51, 52, 53, 73, 95, 98,
        146, 147, 148, 149, 153, 156
    function of security *dispositif* 51, 52,
        54, 145
    management 42, 48, 49, 50, 73, 148
    pre-emptive 53, 71, 94
    unit of affection 48

Haas, Peter
    definition of epistemic community 58
    on epistemic communities 57–9
    functioning of epistemic communities 58
hacking 17, 19, 34, 83, 91, 102, 112
    hackers 16, 22, 23, 72, 76, 78, 79, 82,
        84, 85, 88, 89, 99, 103, 105, 108, 113,
        142, 158n, 160n
    hacktivism 24, 25, 30, 123
    hacktivists 23, 24, 112
Hagmann, Jonas 56, 117, 158n
Hansen, Lene
    on hypersecuritisation 124
    on technification of cybersecurity 62, 108
    on 'techno-utopia' 93
hardware 3, 28, 91
Harvey, David,
    on neoliberalism 49
Helen, Nissenbaum
    on technification of cybersecurity 62, 108
    on hypersecuritisation 124
    on 'techno-utopia' 93
Helkern 92, 117–18
Hiroshima 37
home user
    as audience 74–5, 134, 140
    as vulnerability 76–7
Hurricane Irene 119
Hurricane Sandy 87, 88, 120

industry expert discourse 4, 5, 8, 66
  and constructing cybersecurity 5, 6, 84,
    95, 126, 150
  and constructing cyberspace 70, 84, 90,
    101, 128
  and constructing cyber-threats 5, 11, 63,
    86, 87, 90–1, 95, 97, 114, 104–5
  counter-hegemonic 11
  heterogeneity/scepticism within 73–4,
    88–90, 105–7, 111–12, 129–30, 155
  homogeneity within 90, 123, 126, 128,
    129, 130, 144, 145, 155
  and intertextuality 80, 82
  speculation within 86, 87, 90
  technical language within 108–11, 125
  see also internet security industry
industry expert knowledge *see* industry
  expert discourse
information warfare 15, 20, 143
(in)security 2, 7, 11, 41, 54, 55, 61, 71,
  94, 97, 98 125, 131, 146, 148 149,
  153, 156
insider 22, 24, 27
intelligence 25, 29, 75, 95, 102, 115, 132,
  139, 148
interconnectivity 1, 3, 30, 55, 70, 76, 148
international relations 10, 13, 33, 39, 57,
  158n, 160n
internet security companies *see* internet
  security industry
internet security industry 5, 11, 54, 69, 76,
  81, 157n
  alignment with state 144, 146, 153
  and constructing security 5, 120
  emergence of 5
  epistemic authority of 5, 68, 94, 126,
    130, 144
  and expertise 5, 53, 151
  financial incentive of 63, 132–7, 144
  as regime of truth 8, 132
  as security professionals 126, 130, 132
  as source within security *dispositif* 70, 144
  statistics around value of 136
internet 1, 11, 25, 31, 38, 93, 118, 127
  and cyberspace 70
  dependence upon 78
  and neoliberalism 146
  statistics on usage 1, 32

  of things 78, 91, 159n
intertextuality 7, 80, 115, 130, 153
Iran
  cyber capability of 22, 119
  and Stuxnet 101
Iraq
  cyber capability of 22
Israel
  and Stuxnet 89

Jackson, Richard
  on effect of word terrorism 122
Jantan, Aman
  definition of malware 100

Kello, Lucas
  on sovereignty gap 145–6
Koobface 109

Leander, Anna 145
Lessig, Lawrence 145
Love Bug 140
Lukes, Steven 46

Madi 113
Maginot Line 27, 29
malware 19, 21, 23, 37, 62, 71, 74, 76,
  81, 82, 84, 86, 88, 89, 101, 103, 115,
  117, 159n
  2.0 92
  complexity of 113
  definitions of 100–1
  destructive 73, 99, 108, 113
  evolution of 81, 110, 117
  extent of 79, 80
  industrialisation 92
  infection 93, 109, 112
  mobile 79
  spread 75
  statistics on 79, 81
  as stealthy 84
  as toxic/poisonous 80–1
metaphor
  analysis in cybersecurity research 41,
    42, 128
  biological/medical 80–2
  effect of 80, 96–7
  military historical 104–6

as tactics of power 80
war and militarism 100–7, 120–2, 128
wilderness 82–4
methodology and method 9–10, 63–7
definitions of, 63
milieu 11, 49, 50, 70–1, 73, 98, 128, 145
military–industrial complex 107, 138
Millennium Bug 129
Moonlight Maze 22, 158n
Mral, Brigitte 82
Mueller, John 118
mutual recognition 138
Mythen, Gabe 114

Nagasaki 37
national security 3, 4, 13, 131
national security strategies 2–3, 136
neoliberalism 49, 146
as strategy of governance 4, 12, 44, 69,
127, 131, 146, 152, 155
news media 7, 37, 62, 111, 112, 121, 122,
123, 124
constructing cybersecurity knowledge
47, 60, 130
hyperbole of 37, 89
and reproduction of expert knowledge
62–3
Nietzsche, Friedrich 67
nightmare scenario 24, 36, 41, 87, 88, 90,
100, 129
Nimda 89–90
North Korea 103, 116
Nuclear Pack exploit kit 81
nuclear weapons 22, 37, 104, 114, 124
compared to cyber-attack 21
compared to cyber-crime 99

Obama, Barack 115, 143
Obamacare 142

password
security 28, 76
theft of 20, 23
Pearl Harbor 106
cyber/digital 21, 105, 107
phishing 23, 75, 110, 159n
plausible deniability 26, 27, 29
PLC (programmable logic controller) 71,
72, 103

post-structuralism 36, 39
power 10, 45, 46–50, 64, 145, 151
capillary functioning of 8, 47, 51
disciplinary 47–8, 53, 145
lines of 51
as machine 47, 53, 54
microphysics of 69
as productive 11, 47, 54, 65, 94
relationship with expertise 57
sovereign 47, 48, 53, 145
theorisation of 46
power/knowledge 8, 10, 47, 51, 53, 54,
58, 61, 66, 94, 97, 133, 138, 150,
151, 153
Prism 148, 149
professionals of politics 5, 8, 11, 60,
122, 123, 127, 131, 137, 138,
141, 142, 144, 146, 147, 152,
153, 155
professionals of security 6, 9, 10, 45, 53,
59–63, 79, 95, 100, 122, 126, 130,
132, 136
as authorities of delimitation 60
and communities of mutual recognition
8, 44, 137, 143, 146
connections between other sources 137,
138, 144, 152
and construction of security 62, 144
epistemic authority of 59, 60, 94,
121, 130
as producers and managers of unease
95, 98
scientific/technical capital of 130
as source within security *dispositif*
132, 133
and threat assessment 59, 60, 62

ransomware 83
realism 4, 14, 39
referent object 5, 21, 23, 74, 82, 97, 125,
127, 131
regimes of truth 60
reliance
on computers 2, 62
on technical expertise 62, 139, 143
resilience 27, 28, 30
Rid, Thomas
on cyber-war 16, 38
risk knowledge 11, 53, 70, 126, 131

Index

Russia 33, 154
    cyber capability of 22
    and Nimda 90
    SORM 149

Saudi Aramco attack 72
SCADA (supervisory control and data
        acquisition)
    effect of attack 85
    threats to 36, 86, 105
    vulnerability of 71, 72, 77
securitisation 41, 56, 93, 120, 122, 131,
        133, 146
    desecuritisation 41
    hypersecuritisation 62, 124
security professionals *see* professionals of
        security
security 10
    commercialisation/privatisation of 5, 133
    conceptualisations of 2
    theorisation of 46
Slammer 81
smartphones
    statistics on usage 134
    threats to 99, 135
    users (as audience) 133, 134
social construction *see* constructivism
social engineering 21, 23, 76, 84
software 3, 28, 72, 75, 76, 91, 101,
        143, 151
sovereignty gap 12, 127, 145, 146
spam 19, 75, 83, 102, 111, 160n
spyware 23, 92
    2.0 92
state 2, 3, 12, 16, 18, 25, 26, 29, 38, 60,
        101, 102, 103, 113, 143, 145, 147
    cooperation with private sector 33
    as guarantor of security 43, 106, 146,
        147, 153
    not neutral 146, 153
    as referent 2, 74
    rogue 111
    sponsoring attacks 102, 123
    and surveillance 147–9
    as threat 3, 16, 22–3, 86, 112, 114,
        116, 131
    vulnerability of 78, 84, 117
Steuter, Erin
    At War with Metaphor 96

Stevens, Tim 4, 39
    Cybersecurity and the Politics of Time 129
    on 'cybersecurity imaginary' 129
    definition of cybersecurity 3
Stuxnet 22, 26, 73, 81, 101, 103, 104,
        116–17, 123, 141
    hype surrounding 73–4, 89, 123, 129
    surveillance 2, 29, 48, 52, 132, 148–9

technification
    of cybersecurity 5, 62, 108, 124–5, 152
Tempora 148, 149
terrorism 16–17, 24, 43, 59, 79, 99, 107,
        114, 118, 122–3, 124, 158n, 160n
terrorists 16, 18, 22, 24, 25, 26, 38, 72, 78,
        84, 86, 89, 99, 101, 112, 113, 114,
        117, 119, 131, 147, 158n
threat assessment 13, 21–7, 37, 38, 41, 73,
        86, 87, 90, 91, 95, 98, 114, 115, 125,
        129, 135, 142, 151, 155
    and hypotheticals 24, 35–9, 41, 87, 96,
        100, 114, 115, 118, 119
Trojan Horse 23, 102, 108
Turner, Fredrick Jackson
    frontier thesis 83

uncertainty 49, 53, 58, 61, 70, 77, 84–94,
        97, 123, 124, 129, 131, 136
    of cybersecurity 59, 68, 90, 132, 143
    of cyberspace 73, 131
    of cyber-threats 111, 127, 131
    of malware 118
UK 2, 23, 24, 74, 79, 99, 104, 121, 136,
        141, 147, 148, 158n
unknown 11, 84, 86, 87, 89, 90, 95, 97,
        129, 144
US 2, 21, 22, 31, 35, 36, 82, 87, 89,
        99, 101, 105, 112, 115, 116,
        139, 141
    National Strategy to Secure Cyberspace 93

violence 20
    and cyber-attack 15
    and cyber-terrorism 17–18
    and cyber-war 16, 38
Virilio, Paul 132
virus 23, 37, 81, 82, 85, 89, 90, 102, 108,
        109, 112, 113, 140, 160n
    as metaphor 80

203

Index

vulnerability 2, 3 24, 42, 71–80, 84, 94, 96, 99,120, 127, 159n
   human 28, 77, 111
   as inherent features 3, 11, 41, 82
   vulnerabilities 3, 4, 24, 28, 30, 85, 86, 117

Walklate, Sandra 114
Wannacry 22, 73, 136
Weber, Max 12, 127, 145
wilderness 82–4, 128
   predators and prey 80, 82, 84, 128
   'the wild' 74, 80, 82, 83, 85, 110, 159n
   Wild West/Old West 82, 83

Wills, Deborah
   At War with Metaphor 96
World Wide Web 1, 82, 83
worms 23, 102, 103, 108, 109
worst-case scenarios *see* nightmare scenarios

Yen, Alfred 83

zero-day vulnerability 76, 85, 159n
Zeus 113
Zolkipil, Mohamad Fadil
   definition of malware 100
Zulaika, Joseba 94

Lightning Source UK Ltd.
Milton Keynes UK
UKHW020156100721
386947UK00002B/32